The Triple Bottom Line:
Does it All Add Up?

Assessing the Sustainability of Business and CSR

Edited by
Adrian Henriques and Julie Richardson

London • Sterling, VA

First published by Earthscan in the UK and USA in 2004
Reprinted 2005

ISBN: 1-84407-015-8 paperback
      1-84407-016-6 hardback

Typesetting by MapSet Ltd, Gateshead, UK
Printed and bound in the UK by Creative Print and Design (Wales), Ebbw Vale
Cover design by Ruth Bateson

For a full list of publications please contact:

Earthscan
8–12 Camden High Street
London, NW1 0JH
Tel: +44 (0)20 7387 8558
Fax: +44 (0)20 7387 8998
Email: earthinfo@earthscan.co.uk
Web: **www.earthscan.co.uk**

22883 Quicksilver Drive, Sterling, VA 20166-2012, USA

Earthscan is an imprint of James and James (Science Publishers) Ltd and publishes in
association with the International Institute for Environment and Development

A catalogue record for this book is available from the British Library

Library of Congress Cataloging-in-Publication Data

The triple bottom line, does it all add up? : assessing the sustainability of business and
CSR / editors Adrian Henriques, Julie Richardson.
        p. cm.
Includes bibliographical references.
    ISBN 1-84407-016-6 (alk. paper) – ISBN 1-84407-015-8 (pbk. : alk paper)
    1. Social responsibility of business. 2. Industrial management–Environmental
aspects. I. Henriques, Adrian, 1954- II. Richardson, Julie.

HD60.T735 2004
658.4'083–dc22

                                                                    2003022772

Contents

List of Figures, Tables and Boxes

Figures

Tables

Boxes

List of Contributors

John Elkington (Chapter 1)

John Elkington is a co-founder and chair of SustainAbility, the world's most long-established sustainable business consultancy, based in London, Washington, DC, and Zurich. He is a leading authority on sustainable development and triple bottom line business strategy. His latest book is *The Chrysalis Economy: How Citizens, CEOs and Corporations Can Fuse Values and Value Creation* (2001). He is also chair of the Environment Foundation; chair of the Environmental and Social Committee of the Association of Chartered Certified Accountants (ACCA); a member of the Board Sustainability Committee of Anglian Water; a member of the board of trustees of the Business and Human Rights Resource Centre; a member of the advisory board of an ING sustainability investment fund; and a member of the advisory council of the UK Export Credit Guarantees Department. In 1989 he was elected to the UN Global 500 Roll of Honour for his 'outstanding environmental achievements'.

Carol Adams (Chapter 2)

Professor Carol Adams is director of the Monash Ethics in Stakeholder Relations Research Unit and an associate director of the Centre for Social and Environmental Accounting Research. She is a judge for the Association of Chartered Certified Accountants (ACCA) Australia Sustainability Reporting Awards and was previously a judge for the UK ACCA/AccountAbility Social Reporting Awards. Professor Adams has served as a director and council member of the Institute of Social and Ethical AccountAbility (ISEA). Her current research concentrates on social, community and environmental management, accounting and reporting, and has been published in numerous academic journals of international standing, in professional and business journals, and in books and edited volumes.

Geoff Frost (Chapter 2)

Geoff Frost is senior lecturer in accounting at the School of Business, University of Sydney. His current research concentrates on social and environmental accounting and reporting and has been published in numerous academic and professional journals and edited volumes.

Wendy Webber (Chapter 2)

Wendy Webber is a lecturer in management in the Faculty of Business and Economics, Monash University, Gippsland Campus. Her interests are in organizational aspects of triple bottom line activities, worker participation, equal employment opportunity, strategic human resource management, and new employment relationships.

Adrian Henriques (Chapter 3)

Adrian Henriques is director of JustAssurance, a social enterprise dedicated to sustainability report assurance and also an independent consultant on corporate responsibility and social accountability. Adrian is a council member of AccountAbility and a member of the Association of Chartered Certified Accountants' (ACCA's) Social and Environmental Committee. He was, until the formation of the Global Reporting Initiative (GRI) as an independent entity, a member of their steering committee. Adrian Henriques is professor of accountability and corporate social responsibility at Middlesex University Business School.

Julie Richardson (Chapter 4)

Julie Richardson is a writer, educator and policy analyst in the broad area of sustainable development. She is currently undertaking postgraduate study and research at Schumacher College, UK. Her interests include the application of chaos and complexity theory to environmental change and organizational behaviour. Previously she worked with Forum for the Future as principal sustainability adviser, where she developed and applied sustainability accounting within the corporate sector. She has also acted as a strategy adviser to the UK government in the area of international environmental policy and institutional reform and as an academic and consultant in the area of ecological and development economics. She has published widely in the fields of sustainability, international development and organizational change. Julie Richardson can be contacted by email at julie.richardson@blueyonder.co.uk.

Nancy Bennet (Chapter 5)

Nancy Bennet is based at the Global Reporting Initiative (GRI) Secretariat in Amsterdam seconded by the United Nations Environment Programme's (UNEP's) Division of Technology, Industry and Economics (DTIE). From 1992 to 1999, Nancy Bennet was based in Paris with the UNEP DTIE where she coordinated the Industry Outreach Programme. She represented UNEP on the GRI Steering Committee from late 1997 and facilitated the support to GRI from the United Nations Foundation, led UNEP's train-the-trainer activities in environmental management systems, and managed UNEP's input to the joint UNEP–Sustainability Engaging Stakeholders programme on corporate environmental and sustainability reporting. Before joining UNEP, Nancy Bennet was based in Bangkok at the Chulabhorn Research Institute. While still based in her home country of Canada, she was one of the core team who put together the well-known GLOBE Business and the Environment conferences during 1990 and 1992, which took place in Vancouver, Canada. Nancy is a graduate of the University of British Columbia Faculty of Science.

Cornis van der Lugt (Chapter 5)

Cornis van der Lugt has been based at the United Nations Environment Programme's (UNEP's) Division of Technology, Industry and Economics (DTIE) in Paris since January 2000. He is responsible for industry outreach, the Global Compact of the UN Secretary-General and the Global Reporting Initiative (GRI). He is also coordinator of the annual UNEP consultative meeting with trade and industry associations. Over the last three years he has represented UNEP at various international conferences on corporate citizenship and coordinated the launch of the UNEP/International Telecommunications Union (ITU) Global e-Sustainability Initiative (GeSI) with information and communication technology companies. He studied and taught political science and philosophy at the University of Stellenbosch (South Africa), at the Albert-Ludwigs Universität Freiburg (Germany) and at the Rijksuniversiteit Leiden (The Netherlands), where his extensive research focused on the environment. During the 1990s, he also gained professional experience of international environmental diplomacy (on climate change, depletion of the ozone layer, and trade and the environment) as a multilateral diplomat in the South African Foreign Ministry. In 1998 he received his PhD in International Relations, focusing on European Union (EU) environment policy, which was subsequently published in Germany (van der Lugt, 2000).

Jonathon Porritt (Chapter 6)

Jonathon Porritt, co-founder and programme director of Forum for the Future (www.forumforthefuture.org.uk) and chairman of the UK Sustainable Development Commission (www.sd-commission.gov.uk), is a leading writer, broadcaster and commentator on sustainable development. Partly as a result of the kind of approach that he has been pursuing through the Forum, Jonathon was appointed by the UK prime minister as chairman of the new UK Sustainable Development Commission in July 2000. This is the government's principal source of independent advice across the whole sustainable development agenda. In addition, he has been a member of the board of the South-West Regional Development Agency since December 1999, and is co-director of The Prince of Wales's Business and Environment Programme, which runs senior executives' seminars in Cambridge, Salzburg and the US. Jonathon is a trustee of the UK World Wide Fund For Nature (WWF-UK) and vice-president of the Socialist Environment Resources Association (SERA).

He was formerly director of Friends of the Earth (1984–1990); co-chair of the Green Party (1980–1983), of which he is still a member; chairman of the United Nations Environment Programme-UK (UNEP-UK) (1993–1996); and chairman of Sustainability South-West, the South-West Round Table for Sustainable Development (1999–2001). His most recent book is *Playing Safe: Science and the Environment* (2000). In January 2000, Jonathon Porritt received a CBE for services to environmental protection.

Rob Gray (Chapter 7)

Robert Gray is professor of accounting and director of the Centre for Social and Environmental Accounting Research at the University of Glasgow. He is a qualified chartered accountant, editor of *Social and Environmental Accounting Journal* and joint editor of the *BAR Research Register*. He is the author or co-author of over 200 books, monographs, chapters and articles, primarily on social and environmental accounting, sustainability, social responsibility and education.

Markus Milne (Chapter 7)

Markus J Milne holds the position of associate professor of accounting at the University of Otago, New Zealand. Markus has published extensively in international accounting and business journals on many aspects of social and environmental accounting and reporting. He currently serves on the editorial boards of six international accounting and business journals. Markus is currently involved in a three-year research programme on New Zealand business and sustainability supported by the Royal Society of New Zealand. Markus' research interests also closely align with many other interests he has in the outdoors, including rock climbing, mountaineering, and search and rescue.

Deborah Doane (Chapter 8)

Deborah Doane is head of corporate accountability at the New Economics Foundation. As chair of the Corporate Responsibility Coalition (CORE), she is a leading advocate for mandatory social and environmental reporting, and is a member of the independent Operating and Financial Review Working Group, making recommendations on reporting for forthcoming revisions to company law. She is a frequent writer, lecturer and media commentator on corporate accountability, ethical business and sustainable development issues. Previously, Deborah Doane was director of the Humanitarian Ombudsman Project, which established an International Ombudsman for Humanitarian Aid, now based in Geneva. Originally from Canada, she has an MSc in development studies from the London School of Economics and a BA (Hons) from Carleton University, Ottawa, Canada.

Rupesh Shah (Chapter 9)

Rupesh Shah is an action researcher with the New Academy of Business. He conducts research and education to support people acting for more sustainable patterns of human development. He works through a family of learning methodologies that are people-centred, including engagement in personal enquiry, developing collaborative sense-making and action-oriented methods. His work draws attention to 'ways of thinking', languages and systemic issues of power. He has a particular interest in exploring methods of personal and organizational change for creating ecological and people-centred societies. He also has fun in a community-energized organic garden near where he lives in Bath.

Rupert Howes (Chapter 10)

Rupert Howes is director of Forum for the Future's Sustainable Economy Programme. He is a qualified chartered accountant and has an MSc in environmental technology from Imperial College (1992) and a first degree in economics from Sussex University (1985). Rupert Howes was a research fellow at the Science Policy Research Unit (SPRU) at Sussex University during 1995–1996 and researcher at the International Institute for Environment and Development (IIED) during 1992–1995. He also has freelance and consultancy experience with several other environment and development non-governmental organizations (NGOs), including the World Wide Fund For Nature (WWF-International) and the Institute for European Environmental Policy (IEEP). He joined Forum for the Future in January 1997. His current projects include work on capital markets and the environment, the transformation of the UK energy sector, material and resource management, and local and regional economic development. His own major research areas include corporate environmental and sustainability accounting and reporting, sustainable agriculture and integrated land-use management, ecological tax reform and environmental taxation, and climate change.

Tom Baxter (Chapter 11)

Tom Baxter is a chemical engineer with 30 years' experience. He has worked for BP and other major operators. He is currently the technical director of Genesis Oil and Gas Consultants in Aberdeen, Scotland.

Jan Bebbington (Chapter 11)

Jan Bebbington is a professor of accountancy at the University of Aberdeen, Scotland. Her research focuses on how business conceptualizes sustainable development and seeks to incorporate the principles of sustainable development into their business processes.

David Cutteridge (Chapter 11)

David Cutteridge is a self-employed consultant at Inchferry Consulting in Aberdeen, Scotland, having worked for 25 years for BP where he was, among other roles, their sustainable development coordinator in Scotland.

Alex MacGillivray (Chapter 12)

Alex MacGillivray is a senior associate of the New Economics Foundation, a leading UK think tank. Over the past 15 years he has worked on, and written widely about, business strategy and sustainable development. He lives in France and can be contacted by email at alex.macgillivray@neweconomics.org.

Ros Oakley (Chapter 13)

Ros Oakley is project director of Project SIGMA. The SIGMA (sustainability integrated guidelines for management) project is developing an integrated approach for organizations to manage sustainability issues in order to improve their social, economic and environmental performance. It is a partnership of AccountAbility, the British Standards Institute and Forum for the Future, and is backed by the UK government's Department of Trade and Industry (DTI). The project works directly with a number of leading companies.

Ros Oakley has a track record of working for social change – first, working for public policy changes and, increasingly, looking at the contributions that business and other organizations can make. She has more than a decade's experience working for NGOs, particularly in the disability field.

Ian Buckland (Chapter 13)

Ian Buckland has over ten years' experience of strategic environmental and sustainability consultancy with major UK organizations. As well as his diverse client portfolio, his research on governance has been published by the Centre for Tomorrow's Company and his pieces on socially responsible investment, stakeholder engagement and sustainable marketing, among other issues, have appeared in several practitioner journals. Ian Buckland is a senior adviser for Sd3 Ltd. Sd3 are client managers on Project SIGMA.

Paul Monaghan (Chapter 14)

Paul Monaghan joined the Co-operative Bank in 1994 and established the bank's Ecology Unit. The unit's activities cover three areas: operational performance, business development and corporate affairs. In 1997, Paul established a Partnership Development Team, tasked with assessing the degree to which the Co-operative Bank delivers value to a range of partners (for example, staff, customers and local community) and whether value is delivered in an ecologically sound and socially responsible manner. In April 1998, the team produced a ground-breaking first partnership report; this was commended as the best social and stakeholder report in both the UK and Europe. In 2003 he became the head of sustainable development of the newly formed Cooperative of Financial Services (CFS). Paul Monaghan is an elected member of the Council of the Institute of Social and Ethical AccountAbility. He is also a member of the World Wide Fund For Nature's (WWF-UK's) Programme Committee (where he advises on strategy and work programme); a member of the British Bankers' Association's Environmental Issues Advisory Panel; a director of Sustainability North-West; and a member of the Social Performance Indicators for the Finance Industry (SPI-Finance) Reporting Committee (which is due to announce a supplement to the pending Global Reporting Initiative for the financial services sector).

Vernon Jennings (Chapter 15)

Vernon Jennings is an independent sustainable development consultant. He has also been vice president of stakeholder relations for Novo Nordisk A/S and director of Sustainability, the sustainable business consultancy. Vernon Jennings can be contacted by email at vernon@vernonjennings.com.

List of Acronyms and Abbreviations

ABI	Association of British Insurers
ACCA	Association of Chartered Certified Accountants
AICPA	American Institute of Certified Public Accountants
APP	Asia Pulp and Paper
BA	British Airways
BAE	British Aerospace
BIE	Business in the Environment
BP	British Petroleum
BSI	British Standards Institution
BT	British Telecom
CCD	Convention to Combat Desertification
CCX	Chicago Climate Exchange
CEO	chief executive officer
CERES	Coalition for Environmentally Responsible Economies
CEROI	Cities Environment Reports on the Internet programme
CFO	chief financial officer
CFS	Co-operative Financial Services
CGG	Commission on Global Governance
CH_4	methane
CIA	Chemical Industry Association
CIS	Co-operative Insurance Society
CITES	Convention on the International Trade in Endangered Species
CO_2	carbon dioxide
CORE	Corporate Responsibility Coalition
CRTs	continuously regenerating traps
CSD	Commission on Sustainable Development
CSEAR	Centre for Social and Environmental Accounting Research
CSR	corporate social responsibility
DFSR	driving force, state and response
DJSI	Dow Jones Sustainability Index
DNA	deoxyribose nucleic acid
DTI	Department of Trade and Industry
DTIE	Division of Technology, Industry and Economics (UNEP)
EC	European Commission

EDM	early day motion
EFQM	European Foundation for Quality Management
EFS	environmental financial statement
EHS	environment, health and safety
EMA	environment-related management accounting
EMAS	Environmental Management and Auditing System
ETR	ecological tax reform
EU	European Union
FAO	Food and Agriculture Organization (UN)
FCA	full-cost accounting
G8	Group of 8 (industrialized countries, including the Russian Federation)
GCOS	Global Climate Observing System (UN)
GDP	gross domestic product
GEO	Global Environment Outlook
GeSI	Global e-Sustainability Initiative
GFT250	top 250 companies of the Global Fortune 500
GIS	geographical information system
GOOS	Global Ocean Observing System (UN)
GRI	Global Reporting Initiative
GRID	Global Resource Information Database
GTOS	Global Terrestrial Observing System (UN)
HC	hydrocarbon
HFC	hydrofluorocarbon
HR	human resources
IEEP	Institute for European Environmental Policy
IIED	International Institute for Environment and Development
ILO	International Labour Organization
IMF	International Monetary Fund
IOC	Inter-governmental Oceanographic Commission
IPCC	Inter-governmental Panel on Climate Change
ISEA	Institute of Social and Ethical AccountAbility
ISEW	Index of Sustainable Economic Welfare
ISO	International Organization for Standardization
IT	information technology
ITU	International Telecommunications Union
KPI	key performance indicators
kwh	kilowatt hour
M&S	Marks and Spencer
MEA	multilateral environmental agreement
MP	member of parliament
N_2O	nitrous oxide

NDWC	Niger Delta Wetlands Centre
NEF	New Economics Foundation
NGO	non-governmental organization
NI	national insurance
NO$_x$	nitrogen oxide
OECD	Organisation for Economic Co-operation and Development
3Ps	people, planet and profits
PFP	perfluoro chemical
PM	particulate matter
POP	persistent organic pollutant
PR	public relations
R&D	research and development
SAB	South African Breweries
SAM	Sustainability Assessment Model
SAM*i*	Sustainability Assessment Model indicator
SARS	severe acute respiratory syndrome
SD	sustainable development
SERA	Socialist Environment Resources Association
SF	sulphur hexaflouride
SI	sustainable investment
SIGMA	sustainability integrated guidelines for management
SMART	specific, measurable, achievable, realistic and timely
SO$_2$	sulphur dioxide
SPI-Finance	Social Performance Indicators for the Finance Industry
SPRU	Science Policy Research Unit (Sussex University)
SRI	socially responsible investment
SVA	shareholder value added
TBL	triple bottom line
TQM	total quality management
UK	United Kingdom
UN	United Nations
UNCTAD	United Nations Conference on Trade and Development
UNDP	United Nations Development Programme
UNEP	United Nations Environment Programme
UNESCO	United Nations Educational, Scientific and Cultural Organization
UNFCCC	United Nations Framework Convention on Climate Change
UNICEF	United Nations Children's Fund
UNSTAT	United Nations Statistical Office
US	United States
WBCSD	World Business Council for Sustainable Development
WCMC	World Conservation Monitoring Centre
WHO	World Health Organization

WMO   World Meteorological Organization
WRI   World Resources Institute
WSSD   World Summit on Sustainable Development
WTA   willingness to accept
WTO   World Trade Organization
WTP   willingness to pay
WWF   World Wide Fund For Nature

Introduction: Triple Bottom Line – Does it All Add Up?

Adrian Henriques and Julie Richardson

There are two main kinds of approach to sustainability – 'top down' and 'inside out'. Top-down approaches emphasize management, measurement and control. On this path, while you may know what you have done, it may not be enough – and it may not be possible to do enough within the structures and systems within which you are operating. Perfectly implemented environmental management systems that deliver poor environmental performance with the utmost care fall into this category. Working within the structures of the current paradigm can lead to lowest common denominator approaches and anomalies that reward process without regard to performance and vice versa.

Inside-out approaches stress the importance of change and innovation. It may not be entirely possible to predict what you will do, but you can bet the process will be exciting! Innovation allows new systems and methods to be tried and may facilitate a quantum leap towards a higher, and more sustainable, level of operation. This is about working outside and beyond the structures of the current paradigm. Going inside out is about relationships and 'connectedness'. Being connected and responsive to shareholders, suppliers, communities and customers is the foundation of sustainability. But going inside out can also be uncomfortable. Any creative process embraces risk and uncertainty and the emergence of unexpected outcomes; but it also has its shadow or destructive side as we move beyond the comfort of the known and old ways of doing things. Yet, it is only when stakeholders can see your vulnerability that you can be trusted.

The subject of this book is a metaphor that is drawn from the top-down world of accounting: the 'triple bottom line' or 'TBL'. This book is, therefore, about the powers and limits of that metaphor – from both a top-down and an inside-out perspective. To describe these limits, we must describe what is within the power of the metaphor or paradigm and what is beyond it. For example, if the metaphor were 'as good as gold', we would point out that gold is good for making electrical connections, that it sort of works as a medium of exchange; but, in the end, you cannot eat it – it will not sustain us.

The triple bottom line has become one of the main rallying cries for businesses trying to address sustainability. The task of this book is to assess it in several ways including:

- Does it provide a coherent framework?
- How far does it work in practice?

To do this we are presenting the views of a number of the key practitioners and academics in the field. The book is organized into a number of chapters that cover the history, background and theoretical issues; a critique of how the metaphor is being used, including an account of some tools based upon it; and, finally, some examples of how it is being used to good effect in practice.

History and theory

Chapter 1, 'Enter the Triple Bottom Line', has been written by John Elkington. He invented the TBL term and had a large part to play in its astonishing uptake. What is interesting in his chapter is how he emphasizes the inside-out aspect of sustainability. Much of his work has been about how change can take place, and John Elkington describes some of its necessary characteristics in his inimitable metaphorical style. He sees the TBL concept as a catalyst for moving beyond the existing paradigm towards a more pluralistic world – in which different types of corporates (from 'locusts' to 'honeybees') require different responses from government and civil society.

In Chapter 2, Carol Adams, Geoff Frost and Wendy Webber provide a useful resource in reviewing the multitude of texts written on the topic. This is divided into literature that deals with management and literature that deals with reporting. The authors highlight the important role of the accountancy profession in developing sustainability metrics and the need for standardized approaches. Like many authors in this volume, they remark on how the increase in the quantity of TBL reporting is not matched by the quality in accountability discharged.

In Chapter 3, Adrian Henriques explores some of the conceptual issues in using the TBL concept to deal with sustainability. Two issues, in particular, are identified that are not naturally covered by the TBL metaphor: accountability and diversity. Each of these has a critical place in a sustainable world.

In Chapter 4, Julie Richardson looks at how far accounting formulations can be taken in unfolding the TBL concept. The pressure to account in a single unit, and especially in financial terms, leads to pressures to compromise with sustainability, whether by trading off one sort of capital for another or by ignoring whole-system qualities and relationships that are a key part of sustainability.

Governing and governance

Implementing sustainability in a top-down fashion leads to a central focus on government in managing and regulating for corporate sustainability. Inside-out approaches focus on the looser notion of 'governance' as self-organizing alliances between government and non-government stakeholders.

In Chapter 5, Nancy Bennet and Cornis van der Lugt describe different forms of environmental governance that are emerging in a 'globalizing' world. They look at the range of voluntary and inter-governmental instruments and institutions (from the Global Reporting Initiative to multilateral environmental agreements) that are emerging to fill the governance gap at the global level. Their chapter assesses the effectiveness of these instruments and institutions, and reviews the practical and methodological problems that must be faced. One of the key issues that emerges is how to define boundaries of responsibility for individual organizations – across economic, legal and ecological systems.

In Chapter 6, Jonathon Porritt explores the role that the financial system and government will have to play in order to achieve sustainability. In addition to any monitoring or regulation that may be necessary, he points out that 'government' is also an organization in its own right. As such, it must also report on and manage its own impacts.

Moving on from the role of government, Chapters 7 to 9 reflect upon how effective corporate social and environmental responsibility has been as a model for corporate self-governance. All three chapters are critical of current practice and identify specific steps for improvement.

Rob Gray and Markus Milne, in Chapter 7, are very far from convinced that much of the current sustainability reports are anywhere near the level of development that they need to attain. They conclude, with a point that a number of contributors make, that sustainability is a systems concept and therefore cannot be captured at the individual organizational level alone. Again, Deborah Doane, in Chapter 8, describes the disillusionment of many in the non-governmental organization (NGO) community at what the bright new hope of 'social auditing' seems to have become. For her, it seems more like a broken promise – and one that cannot be mended without legislation. Finally, Rupesh Shah in Chapter 9 offers a personal reflection on involvement in the corporate social responsibility (CSR) industry. He observes the rise in the CSR profession but is pessimistic about whether the technocratic solutions that it offers are really able to change mind-sets or transform entrenched structures of power and inequality.

Metaphorical practice

Chapters 10 to 13 are based on tools, approaches or methods that have been applied in practice in various ways. Each of these draws on the top-down approach to sustainability. Rupert Howes, in Chapter 10, provides a clear account of a tool that shows the way in which key environmental impacts have been accounted for in financial terms for a number of companies. Tom Baxter, Jan Bebbington and David Cutteridge, in Chapter 11, describe a full-cost accounting method for modelling the economic, social and environmental impacts of an oil project for British Petroleum (BP). This concentrates on impacts that can be expressed financially. They specifically ask the question of whether it makes sense to add up the three components of sustainability across the triple bottom line.

Much less work has been done on accounting for the capital side of sustainability. Although Rupert Howes identifies the need for this, progress in accounting for natural capital or social capital has been slow. Alex MacGillivray, in Chapter 12, reviews a number of attempts to define and understand social capital and brings them together in a new framework for measuring this somewhat elusive concept.

The wealth of interest in the area of sustainability has led to a plethora of sustainability tools and standards. Ros Oakley and Ian Buckland, in Chapter 13, describe the SIGMA (sustainability integrated guidelines for management) project that attempts to bring together tools and standards to build a coherent approach to implementing sustainability. They address the oft-asked question: what are the arguments for and against moving towards harmonization of sustainability tools and standards?

Good practice

Although earlier chapters describe the work done with or by companies in implementing TBL concepts, Chapters 14 and 15 take a broad view of how large organizations see the task. Paul Monaghan writes about the Co-operative Bank in Chapter 14, describing the '*whys* and *hows* of producing a leading edge sustainability report'.

Vernon Jennings, in Chapter 15, describes not only how Novo Nordisk approaches the task of implementation, but specifically concentrates on how to approach 'economic foot-printing'. This is an area that, outside financial performance, has barely been addressed by the corporate world.

Chapter 1

Enter the Triple Bottom Line

John Elkington

In 1994, the author coined the term *triple bottom line*. He reflects on what got him to that point, what has happened since – and where the agenda may now be headed.

The late 1990s saw the term 'triple bottom line' take off. Based on the results of a survey of international experts in corporate social responsibility (CSR) and sustainable development (SD), Figure 1.1 spotlights the growth trend over the two years from 1999 to 2001. As originator of the term, I have often been asked how it was conceived and born. As far as I can remember – and memory is a notoriously fallible thing – there was no single *eureka!* moment. Instead, in 1994 we had been looking for new language to express what we saw as an inevitable expansion of the environmental agenda that SustainAbility (founded in 1987) had mainly focused upon to that point.

We felt that the social and economic dimensions of the agenda – which had already been flagged in 1987's Brundtland Report (UNWCED, 1987) – would have to be addressed in a more integrated way if real environmental progress was to be made. Because SustainAbility mainly works, by choice, with business, we felt that the language would have to resonate with business brains. By way of background, I had already coined several other terms that had gone into the language, including 'environmental excellence' (1984) and 'green consumer' (1986). The first was targeted at business professionals in the wake of 1982's best-selling management book *In Search of Excellence* (Peters and Waterman, 1982), which failed to mention the environment even once. The aim of the second was to help mobilize consumers to put pressure on business about environmental issues. This cause was aided enormously by the runaway success of our book *The Green Consumer Guide*, which sold nearly 1 million copies in its various editions (Elkington and Hailes, 1988).

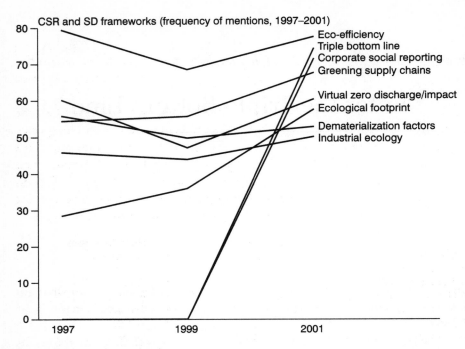

CSR and SD frameworks (frequency of mentions, 1997–2001)

Eco-efficiency
Triple bottom line
Corporate social reporting
Greening supply chains

Virtual zero discharge/impact
Ecological footprint

Dematerialization factors
Industrial ecology

Source: Environics International

Figure 1.1 *The triple bottom line takes off*

But back to the triple bottom line (often abbreviated to TBL). Like Paul McCartney waking up with *Yesterday* playing in his brain and initially believing that he was humming someone else's tune, when the three words finally came to me I was totally convinced that someone must have used them before. But an extensive search suggested otherwise. The next step was whether we should take steps to trademark or otherwise protect the language, as most mainstream consultancies would have done. Counter-intuitively, perhaps, we decided to do exactly the reverse, ensuring that no one could protect it. We began using the term in public, with early launch platforms, including an article in the *California Management Review* on 'win–win–win' business strategies (Elkington, 1994), SustainAbility's 1996 report *Engaging Stakeholders* and my 1997 book *Cannibals with Forks: The Triple Bottom Line of 21st Century Business* (Elkington, 1997). In 1995, we also developed the 3P formulation, 'people, planet and profits', later adopted by Shell for its first *Shell Report* and now widely used in The Netherlands as the 3Ps.

In the following sections we will look at the drivers of the TBL agenda, at the waves and downwaves in societal pressures on business, at the characteristics of a number of different business models, and at the emerging roles of governments.

Seven drivers

In the simplest terms, the TBL agenda focuses corporations not just on the economic value that they add, but also on the environmental and social value that they add – or destroy.

With its dependence on seven closely linked revolutions (see Figure 1.2), the sustainable capitalism transition will be one of the most complex our species has ever had to negotiate (Elkington, 1997). As we move into the third millennium, we are embarking on a global cultural revolution. Business, much more than governments or non-governmental organizations (NGOs), will be in the driving seat. Paradoxically, this will not make the transition any easier for business people. For many it will prove gruelling, if not impossible.

	Old Paradigm	→	**New Paradigm**
1 Markets	Compliance	→	Competition
2 Values	Hard	→	Soft
3 Transparency	Closed	→	Open
4 Life-cycle technology	Product	→	Function
5 Partnerships	Subversion	→	Symbiosis
6 Time	Wider	→	Longer
7 Corporate governance	Exclusive	→	Inclusive

Figure 1.2 *Seven sustainability revolutions*

Markets

Revolution 1 will be driven by competition, largely through markets. For the foreseeable future, business will operate in markets that are more open to competition, both domestic and international, than at any other time in living memory. The resulting economic earthquakes will transform our world.

When an earthquake hits a city built on sandy or wet soils, the ground can become 'thixotropic': in effect, it turns to jelly. Entire buildings can disappear into the resulting quicksands. In the emerging world order, entire markets will also go thixotropic, swallowing entire companies, even industries. Learning to spot the market conditions and factors that can trigger this process will be a key to future business survival, let alone success.

In this extraordinary environment, growing numbers of companies are already finding themselves challenged by customers and the financial markets about aspects of their TBL commitments and performance. Furthermore, although we will undoubtedly see continuing cycles based on wider economic, social and political trends, this pressure can only grow over the long term. As a result, business will shift to a new approach, using TBL thinking and accounting to build the business case for action and investment.

Values

Revolution 2 is driven by the worldwide shift in human and societal values. Most business people, indeed most people, take values as a given, if they think about them at all. Yet, our values are the product of the most powerful programming that each of us has ever been exposed to. When they change, as they seem to do with every succeeding generation, entire societies can go thixotropic. Companies that have felt themselves standing on solid ground for decades suddenly find that the world as they knew it is being turned upside down and inside out.

Remember Mrs Aquino's peaceful revolution in the Philippines? Or the extraordinary changes in Eastern Europe in 1989? Recall the experiences of Shell during the Brent Spar and Nigerian controversies, with the giant oil company later announcing that it would, in future, consult NGOs on such issues as environment and human rights before deciding on development options? Think, too, of Texaco. The US oil company paid US$176 million in an out-of-court settlement in the hope that it would bury the controversy about its poor record in integrating ethnic minorities. Now, with the dawn of the 21st century, we have a new roll-call of companies that have crashed and burned because of values-based crises, among them Enron and Arthur Andersen.

Transparency

Revolution 3 is well under way, is being fuelled by growing international transparency and will accelerate. As a result, business will find its thinking, priorities, commitments and activities under increasingly intense scrutiny worldwide. Some forms of disclosure will be voluntary, but others will evolve with little direct involvement from most companies. In many respects, the transparency revolution is now 'out of control'. Even China is being forced to open up by such factors as the global SARS epidemic that it helped to spawn.

This opening up process is itself being driven by the coming together of new value systems and radically different information technologies, from satellite television to the internet. The collapse of many forms of traditional authority also means that a wide range of different stakeholders increasingly demand information on what business is going and planning to do. Increasingly, too, they are using that information to compare, benchmark and rank the performance of competing companies. The 2001 inauguration of the Global Reporting Initiative (GRI), built on TBL foundations, is one of the most powerful symbols of this trend.

Life-cycle technology

Revolution 4 is driven by and – in turn – is driving the transparency revolution. Companies are being challenged about the TBL implications either of industrial or agricultural activities far back down the supply chain or about the implications of their products in transit, in use and – increasingly – after their useful life has ended. Here we are seeing a shift from companies focusing on the acceptability of their products at the point of sale to a new emphasis on their performance from cradle to grave – that is, from the extraction of raw materials right through to recycling or disposal. Managing the life cycles of technologies and products as different as batteries, jumbo jets and offshore oil rigs will be a key emerging focus of 21st-century business. Nike has been the 'poster child' for campaigners in this area; but we will see many other companies fall victim as the spotlight plays back and forth along their supply chains.

Partners

Revolution 5 will dramatically accelerate the rate at which new forms of partnership spring up between companies, and between companies and other organizations – including some leading campaigning groups. Organizations that once saw themselves as sworn enemies will increasingly flirt with and propose new forms of relationship to opponents who are seen to hold some of the keys to success in the new order. As even groups such as Greenpeace have geared up for this new approach, we have seen a further acceleration of the trends that drive the third and fourth sustainability revolutions. None of this means that we will see an end to friction and, on occasion, outright conflict. Instead, campaigning groups will need to work out ways of simultaneously challenging and working with the same industry – or even the same company.

Time

Time is short, we are told. Time is money. But, driven by the sustainability agenda, Revolution 6 will promote a profound shift in the way that we understand and manage time. As the latest news erupts through CNN and other channels within seconds of the relevant events happening on the other side of the world, and as more than US$1 trillion sluices around the world every working day, so business finds that current time is becoming ever 'wider'. This involves the opening out of the time dimension, with more and more happening every minute of every day. Quarterly – and even online – reporting requirements are key drivers towards this wide-time world.

By contrast, the sustainability agenda is pushing us in the other direction – towards 'long' time. Given that most politicians and business leaders find it hard to think even two or three years ahead, the scale of the challenge is indicated by the fact that the emerging agenda requires thinking across decades, generations and, in some instances, centuries. As time-based competition, building on the platform created by techniques such as 'just in time', continues to accelerate the pace of competition, the need to build in a stronger 'long time' dimension to business thinking and planning will become ever-more pressing. The use of scenarios, or alternative visions of the future, is one way in which we can expand our time horizons and spur our creativity.

Corporate governance

Ultimately, whatever the drivers, the business end of the TBL agenda is the responsibility of the corporate board. Revolution 7 is driven by each of the other revolutions and is also resulting in a totally new spin being put on the already energetic corporate governance debate. Now, instead of just focusing on issues such as the pay packets of 'fat cat' directors, new questions are being asked. For example, what is business for? Who should have a say in how companies are run? What is the appropriate balance between shareholders and other stakeholders? And what balance should be struck at the level of the triple bottom line?

The better the system of corporate governance, the greater the chance that we can build towards genuinely sustainable capitalism. To date, however, most TBL campaigners have not focused their activities at boards; nor, in most cases, do they have a detailed understanding of how boards and corporate governance systems work. This, nonetheless, constitutes a key jousting ground of tomorrow. The Coalition for Environmentally Responsible Economies (CERES) joint venture with Innovest on the corporate governance aspects of the risks associated with climate change is an early example of the trend.

It is clear that a growing proportion of corporate sustainability issues revolve not just around process and product design, but also around the design of corporations and their value chains, of 'business ecosystems' and, ultimately, of markets. Experience suggests that the best way to ensure that a given corporation fully addresses the TBL agenda is to build the relevant requirements into its corporate DNA from the very outset – and into the parameters of the markets that it seeks to serve. An early example here would be the Chicago Climate Exchange (CCX), which is experimenting with the trading of greenhouse emissions.

Clearly, we are still a long way from reaching this objective; but considerable progress has been made in recent decades. The centre of gravity of the sustainable business debate is in the process of shifting from public relations to competitive advantage and corporate governance – and, in the process, from the factory fence to the boardroom (see Table 1.1). A series of political pressure waves has been driving these shifts.

Table 1.1 *TBL agenda moves from factory fence to boardroom*

1970s	1970s–1980s	Late 1980s	Late 1990s
• PR managers • Lawyers	• Environment managers • Planners • Project managers • Process designers	• Marketers • Product designers • New product development specialists	• Chief executive officers • Board members • Chief financial officers • Investor relations specialists • Strategists

Three pressure waves

From 1960 to the present, three great waves of public pressure have shaped the environmental agenda. The roles and responsibilities of governments and the public sector have mutated in response to each of these three waves – and will continue to do so. Although each wave of activism has been followed by a downwave of falling public concern, each successive wave has significantly expanded the agendas of politics and business:

- *Wave 1* brought an understanding that environmental impacts and natural resource demands have to be limited, resulting in an initial outpouring of environmental legislation. The business response was defensive, focusing on compliance, at best.
- *Wave 2* brought a wider realization that new kinds of production technologies and new kinds of products are needed, culminating in the insight that development processes have to become sustainable – and a sense that business would often have to take the lead. The business response began to be more competitive.
- *Wave 3* focuses on the growing recognition that sustainable development will require profound changes in the governance of corporations and in the whole process of globalization, putting a renewed focus on government and on civil society. Now, in addition to the compliance and competitive dimensions, the business response will need to focus on market creation.

The environmental protection role that governments assumed after wave 1 turns out to be inadequate for supporting the larger economic metamorphosis that now needs to occur. Indeed, the whole concept of 'environmental protection' may be limiting our thinking in terms of the necessary scale of change required for sustainable development. Policies and regulations designed to force companies to comply with minimum environmental standards are inadequate

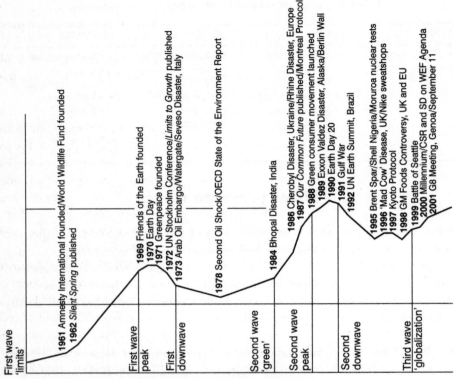

CSR and SD frameworks (frequency of mentions, 1961–2001)

Source: SustainAbility and UNEP (2002b)

Figure 1.3 *Pressure waves, 1961–2001*

for encouraging the creative, socially responsible entrepreneurship needed to evolve new and more sustainable forms of wealth creation – in what we call the 'chrysalis economy'.

To understand how the roles and responsibilities of government must change, we need to consider how the corporations and value chains whose activities governments regulate are themselves evolving through different stages in response to the three waves of public pressure (see Figure 1.3).

The first pressure wave – 'Limits' – was built from the early 1960s. The wave intensified at the end of the decade, peaking from 1969 to 1973. Throughout the mid 1970s, a wave of environmental legislation swept across the Organisation for Economic Co-operation and Development (OECD) region, and industry went into compliance mode. The first downwave followed, running from the mid 1970s to 1987. Acid rain had a major impact on European

Union (EU) politics during the early 1980s; but this was, on the whole, a period of conservative politics, with energetic attempts to roll back environmental legislation. However, a major turning point was reached in 1987.

The second – 'Green' – pressure wave began in 1988 with the publication of *Our Common Future* by the Brundtland Commission (UNWCED, 1987), injecting the term 'sustainable development' into the political mainstream.

Issues such as ozone depletion and rainforest destruction helped to fuel a new movement: Green consumerism. The peak of the second wave ran from 1988 to 1991. The second downwave followed in 1991. The 1992 UN Earth Summit in Rio delayed the impending downwave, triggering 'spikes' in media coverage of issues such as climate change and biodiversity, but against a falling trend in public concern. The trends were not all down, however: there were further spikes, driven by controversies around companies such as Shell, Monsanto and Nike, and by public concerns – at least in Europe – about 'mad cow disease' and genetically modified foods.

The third pressure wave – 'Globalization' – began in 1999. Protests against the World Trade Organization (WTO), World Bank, International Monetary Fund (IMF), Group of 8 industrialized countries (G8), World Economic Forum and other institutions called attention to the critical role of public and international institutions in promoting – or hindering – sustainable development. The 2002 UN World Summit on Sustainable Development (WSSD) brought the issue of governance for sustainable development firmly on to the global agenda – although not on to the agenda of the government of the US. The US, which helped to trigger and lead the first two waves, has remained in something of a downwave in relation to issues such as climate change, running counter to public opinion and pressure in other OECD countries.

The third downwave began, we believe, late in 2002. Intuitively, we expect it to last somewhere between five and eight years. The focus this time will be on new definitions of security, new forms of governance (both global and corporate), the 'access' agenda (for example, access to clean water, affordable energy, drugs for HIV/AIDS, malaria and tuberculosis, and so on), the role of financial markets (for example, evolving forms of liability, with the problems that have hit the asbestos and tobacco industries spreading to such industries as fast food, fossil energy and auto manufacture) and the increasingly central role of social entrepreneurs.

Further afield, we expect fourth and fifth waves, very likely on shorter time frequencies and – possibly – with less dramatic fluctuations in public interest. As these subsequent waves and downwaves develop, what we call the chrysalis economy will emerge and evolve.

The chrysalis economy

If it emerges at all, a sustainable global economy will emerge through an era of intense technological, economic, social and political metamorphosis (Elkington, 2001). A key driver will be the unsustainability of current patterns of wealth creation and distribution. Today's economy is highly destructive of natural and social capital, and is characterized by large and growing gaps between rich and poor. The events of 11 September 2001 and – intentionally or not – the subsequent aftermath served notice on the rich world that both absolute and relative poverty will be major issues in the future.

Because current patterns of wealth creation will generate worsening environmental and social problems, pressures will continuously build on both corporations and governments to make a transition to sustainable development. Figure 1.4 distinguishes four main types of company, or 'value webs', along the evolutionary path to a chrysalis economy – namely, corporate 'locusts', 'caterpillars', 'butterflies' and 'honeybees'.

The key to developing environmental policies that facilitate the transition to sustainability is to understand that the roles of government need to be different in relation to the four different types of corporation. For example, corporate butterflies and honeybees need to be treated very differently from corporate caterpillars and locusts.

Corporate locusts

Some corporations operate as destructive locusts throughout their life cycles; others only display locust-like behaviours occasionally. There are corporate locusts everywhere destroying social and environmental value and undermining the foundations for future economic growth. Some parts of Africa, Asia, Latin America and regions once controlled by the old Soviet Union are literally crawling with them.

Among the key characteristics of a corporate locust are:

- the destruction of natural, human, social and economic capital;
- collectively, an unsustainable 'burn rate', potentially creating regional or even global impacts;
- a business model that is unsustainable over the long run;
- periods of invisibility, when it is hard to discern the impending threat;
- a tendency to swarm (think gold rushes), overwhelming the carrying capacity of social systems, ecosystems or economies; and
- an incapacity to foresee negative system effects, coupled with an unwillingness to heed early warnings and learn from mistakes.

	Low impact	High impact
Regenerative (increasing returns)	Butterflies	Honeybees
Degenerative (decreasing returns)	Caterpillars	Locusts

Figure 1.4 *Corporate characteristics*

When most companies were corporate locusts, government had to take the offensive. Key tasks were to stamp on the worst offenders and on locust-like behaviours in business as a whole. In a globalizing world, one key challenge for environmental protection agencies is to extend their regulatory and enforcement reach to problem companies operating outside of their formal jurisdiction.

Corporate caterpillars

Usually, caterpillars are harder to spot than locusts because their impacts are more localized. But if you live or work right next door to a corporate caterpillar, their degenerative impacts may make it hard to see that these corporations have a significant potential for metamorphosis. Corporate caterpillars tend to:

- generate relatively local impacts, most of the time;
- show single-minded dedication to the business task at hand;
- depend upon a high 'burn rate', although usually of forms of capital that are renewable over time;
- operate on a business model that is unsustainable when projected forward into a more equitable world of 8 to 10 billion people;
- have the potential for transformation into a more sustainable guise, often based upon a mutated business model; and
- operate in sectors where there is evidence that pioneering companies are already starting to metamorphose towards more sustainable forms of value creation.

Here the challenge for governments is to provide appropriate conditions for old businesses to evolve and new businesses to grow, but at the same time to use regulatory and financial incentives to ensure that these businesses develop in line with environmental and sustainable development objectives. Key roles here include:

- support for research and development (R&D) and technology demonstration programmes;
- public–private partnerships;
- green purchasing;
- elimination of perverse subsidies; and
- ecological tax reform.

Corporate butterflies

Corporate butterflies are easy to spot, even though most are comparatively small. By their very nature, they are often highly conspicuous and, in recent years, have been abundantly covered in the media (think Ben & Jerry's, the Body Shop and Patagonia). An economic system fit for corporate butterflies would almost certainly be a world well down the track towards sustainability.

Yet, as Paul Hawken has argued, even if every company in the world were to model itself on such companies, our economies would still not be sustainable. For that, we will need to develop and call upon the swarm and hive strengths of the corporate honeybee. Even so, corporate butterflies have a crucial role to play in evolving 'chrysalis capitalism'. Among other things, they model new forms of sustainable wealth creation for the honeybees to mimic and, most significantly, scale up. Some characteristics include:

- a sustainable business model, although this may become less sustainable as success drives growth, expansion and increasing reliance on financial markets and large corporate partners;
- a strong commitment to the corporate social responsibility (CSR) and sustainable development (SD) agendas;
- the tendency to define its position by reference to locusts and caterpillars;
- a wide network, although not among locusts or honeybees;
- increasingly, involvement in symbiotic relationships;
- persistent indirect links to degenerative activities;
- a potential capacity to trigger quite disproportionate changes in consumer priorities and, as a result, in the wider economic system; and
- high visibility and a disproportionately powerful voice for such economic lightweights.

Like their natural counterparts, corporate butterflies tend to occur in 'pulses'. After rain, for example, a desert can suddenly come alive with butterflies. In much the same way, pulses of corporate butterflies were a feature of the 1960s, with booms in alternative publishing, wholefood and renewable energy technology businesses, and again during the 1990s, when sectors such as eco-tourism, organic food, SD consulting and socially responsible investments

(SRIs) began to go mainstream. Government policies designed to help sound corporate caterpillars will generally also serve corporate butterflies well. Government can also encourage change by identifying, supporting and celebrating any companies that move from the caterpillar stage to the butterfly stage.

Corporate honeybees

This is the domain into which growing numbers of government agencies, innovators, entrepreneurs and investors will head in the coming decades. A sustainable global economy would hum with the activities of corporate honeybees and the economic versions of beehives. Although bees may periodically swarm like locusts, their impact is not only sustainable but also strongly regenerative. The key characteristics of the corporate honeybee include:

- a sustainable business model, albeit based on constant innovation;
- a clear – and appropriate – set of ethics-based business principles;
- strategic sustainable management of natural resources;
- a capacity for sustained heavy lifting;
- sociability and the evolution of powerful symbiotic partnerships;
- the sustainable production of natural, human, social, institutional and cultural capital; and
- a capacity to moderate the impacts of corporate caterpillars in its supply chain, to learn from the mistakes of corporate locusts and, in certain circumstances, to boost the efforts of corporate butterflies.

Some implications for governments

Given current demographic trends, the selective pressures that work in favour of sustainable development can only increase. As this occurs, we will see many patterns of change in corporate behaviours. Some companies that remain strongly degenerative will attempt to improve their images through clever mimicry of butterfly and honeybee traits. It will not be uncommon to find the same corporation displaying some mix of caterpillar, locust, butterfly and honeybee behaviours simultaneously. But no company is fated to remain trapped forever in locust form. With the right stimulus and leadership, any organization can start the transformative journey, although it is usually easier to go from caterpillar to butterfly than from locust to honeybee.

The roles of government here will be many and various. Aspects of traditional environmental protection approaches will still be necessary; but to build truly sustainable wealth-creation clusters, the public sector will need to

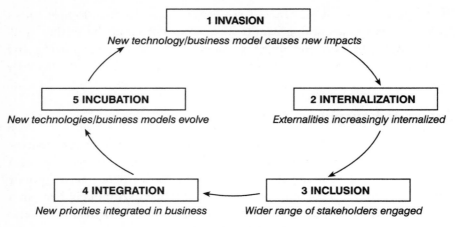

Figure 1.5 *The learning flywheel*

take a leaf out of the private sector's book and embark on major 'silo-busting' campaigns. Like corporations and value webs, governments and their agencies will need to move through the various stages shown in the learning flywheel (see Figure 1.5):

- The first stage focuses on *invasion* – the natural process by which an innovation, be it a new technology or a new business model, invades an opportunity space, creating economic, social or environmental impacts in the process. Here, government agencies play a key role in identifying new types of impact and pioneering assessment methods.
- In the second stage, we see the emphasis shift to the process of *internalization* – by which a company or value web absorbs some of the costs previously externalized to society or the environment. Government involvement is critical to ensure externalities are properly costed and internalized.
- As the burdens of internalization build, so management needs to know where the real priorities lie, and we see a new interest in *inclusion*. This is the process by which a wide range of internal and external stakeholders are progressively engaged, their priorities established and their legitimate needs met. The public sector has often lagged in this area; but its role will be increasingly significant in establishing key priorities for action and investment.
- Next comes the emerging challenge of *integration*. Every time business is required to address a new agenda, there is the problem of silos – as has successively been the case with environment, health and safety (EHS), total quality management (TQM), information technology (IT), shareholder value added (SVA) and corporate social responsibility (CSR). Even leading companies still have a great deal to do in terms of silo-busting and the

	Governance	Markets
Emerging	Boards	Business models
Existing	Balance sheets	Brands

Figure 1.6 *Integration challenges*

integration of triple bottom line thinking into corporate strategy and corporate governance. Governments, too, will find that silo-busting and integration are critical to success in their own operations.

In the process, the TBL language may sometimes be unhelpful, encouraging parallel activities rather than true integration. Early in 2003, as a result, we titled our fifth conference tour of Australia and New Zealand 'Beyond the Triple Bottom Line: Boards, Brands and Business Models'. The message was that the challenges of integration will increasingly play out in four key areas. As Figure 1.6 shows, these are the realms of balance sheets (transparency, accountability, reporting and assurance), boards (ultimate accountability, corporate governance and strategy), brands (engaging investors, customers and consumers directly in sustainability issues) and business models (moving beyond corporate hearts and minds to the very DNA of business).

- All of that said, even the best-run companies may not be sustainable if their business models or technologies are not sustainable in the long haul. In such cases, we need to focus on the prospects for *incubation*, considering how more sustainable technologies, business models and industries can be incubated in today's world. Even the most productive beehives have to start from a few brood-cells. And, apart from early projects around industrial ecology, we have hardly even begun to think how governments and other key actors can catalyse new clusters (geographical or virtual) of sustainable businesses (Rosenberg, 2002).

  In SustainAbility's own work, we will be focusing growing attention both on such clustering and on the role of social entrepreneurs in developing 'out-of-the-box', 'leapfrog' strategies, business models and technologies for tackling the unserved needs of the world's poorest communities.

In sum, the TBL agenda as most people would currently understand it is only the beginning. A much more comprehensive approach will be needed that involves a wide range of stakeholders and coordinates across many areas of government policy, including tax policy, technology policy, economic development policy, labour policy, security policy, corporate reporting policy and so on. Developing this comprehensive approach to sustainable development and environmental protection will be a central governance challenge – and, even more critically, a market challenge – in the 21st century.

Chapter 2

Triple Bottom Line: A Review of the Literature

Carol Adams, Geoff Frost and Wendy Webber

Introduction

John Elkington's *Cannibals with Forks: The Triple Bottom Line of 21st Century Business* (1997) offers an inspiring metaphor that challenges contemporary corporations to simultaneously deliver the triple bottom line (TBL) of economic prosperity, environmental quality and social equity. Why corporations? Hart (1997) argues that while the roots of the world's sustainability crisis are social and political, only corporations have the resources, global reach and motivation to achieve sustainability. Corporations now represent over half of the world's largest economies (Anderson and Cavanagh, 1996, quoted in Zadek, 2001) and sales of the top 200 corporations equate to one quarter of the world's economic activity (Wheeler and Sillanpää, 1997, quoted in Zadek, 2001). In this chapter, we review the literature considering the development of the TBL concept and the reasons for its increasing prominence on the business agenda. We consider the development of the TBL concept both as a management tool and a reporting tool.

Since the Brundtland Report (UNWCED, 1987) defined sustainability as 'development that meets the needs of the present world without compromising the ability of future generations to meet their own needs', the TBL concept appears to have had some success in articulating a philosophy of sustainability in a language accessible to corporations and their shareholders. The links between sustainability, corporate activity and accounting is explained in a 1995 report of the United Nations Conference on Trade and Development (UNCTAD, 1996). In brief, sustainability integrates achieving eco-efficiency (environmental) and eco-justice (inter- and intra-generational social equity) over the short and long term (UNCTAD, 1996). A sustainable economic system is one that protects the world's critical and renewable natural capital and addresses inequities between nations (UNCTAD, 1996). Sustainability seeks to change the measure of contemporary global activity that mostly values and accounts for economic capital at the expense of the world's natural and social capital. The world's natural and social capital is often considered free and therefore is often without economic value or a measure of its gain or loss (UNCTAD, 1996). Innovative accounting systems can embrace a corporation's *environmental* and *social values*, as well as traditional *economic values* (UNCTAD, 1996).

Elkington (1997) clearly and eloquently placed TBL on the global agenda. Both the timing and the terming were perfect. Deregulation of markets, privatization, compulsory pension investing, the Bhopal and the Exxon Valdez disasters, and extraordinary corporate profits and booming stock markets that affected many people and corporations resulted in a heightened global awareness. The 1990s saw new technology, particularly the internet, bring an explosion of information to environmental and social activists, corporations and investors alike. TBL provided a language that made sense of the sustainability concept to a population focused on the economic bottom line. It seems that the events of the 1990s legitimized the sustainability proposition, and the TBL concept articulated it.

Elkington's book reinforced the view that corporations were accountable for their impact on sustainability through TBL and that accountants had a substantial role in measuring, auditing, reporting, risk rating and benchmarking it (Elkington, 1997). Historically, most accounting activities had related mainly to the corporation's financial activities. Elkington (1997) acknowledged at the time that sustainability accounting, reporting and auditing for TBL was underdeveloped and imprecise. Zadek has since challenged the 'sustainable business' solution, suggesting that it 'creates more confusion than good. Social, environmental and economic gains and losses arising from a particular business process cannot simply be added up' (Zadek, 2001, p8).

Discussion of the quantification of social and environmental performance is not entirely new and predates Elkington's (1997) book. In 1972, David Rockefeller said that he 'can foresee the day when, in addition to the annual financial statements certified by independent accountants, corporations may be required to publish a social audit similarly certified' (cited in Gray, Owen, et al, 1987, pix). In 1992 the European Union Fifth Action Programme called for a redefinition of accounting concepts and methods to account for the full cost of environmental resources and product consumption for inclusion into product market prices (EU, 1992). In 1977, the American Institute of Certified Public Accountants published a book entitled *The Measurement of Corporate and Social Performance* (AICPA, 1977).

In the new millennium ethical, social and environmental reporting has gathered momentum. Initiatives include the release of South Africa's *King Report* in 2002 suggesting that every South African company report annually on its social, transformation, ethical, safety, health and environment policies and practices (Payne, 2002); the release of revised Global Reporting Initiative (GRI) guidelines (GRI, 2002); the Institute for Social and Ethical AccountAbility's proposed AA1000S standards for social auditing (AccountAbility, 2002); and MP Linda Perham's UK private member bill of June 2002 seeking to introduce mandatory corporate sustainability reports and to establish a new regulatory body for corporate social and environmental standards (Hayward, 2002).

Sustainable investment (SI) is also driving the increase in demand for TBL. There are several indices that attempt to quantify and rank the relative sustainability of competing companies. The Dow Jones Sustainability Index (DJSI, 2002a) is one of these. With a view that 'what gets measured gets done', the DJSI says that it offers investors corporate sustainability assessments creating long-term shareholder value based upon corporate sustainability criteria and weightings that assess opportunities and risks relating to sustainable factors (DJSI, 2002a). Its sources include an annual questionnaire completed by the companies, third-party documents, personal contacts with the companies and external verification by PricewaterhouseCoopers (DJSI, 2002a). Notable is that the assessment criteria used by the DJSI is unevenly weighted across the three TBL factors: economic is 30.1 plus specific industry criteria; environmental is 7.2 plus specific industry criteria; and social is 14.55 (DJSI, 2002b). The DJSI also 'bases 30 per cent of its entire sustainability criterion on external communications written by the companies about themselves' (Cerin, 2002a, p50).

Contributing to the interest in SI is the increasing evidence that good management and TBL accountability are positively related (Waddock and Graves, 1997). As Tippet and Leung (2001) point out, ethical investment is well defined in principle; but its practical implementation is less precise. The same is true for ethical accounting. It is estimated that more than US$1 trillion (SustainAbility and UNEP, 1999) and possibly as much as US$2 trillion were invested in 'ethical' investment funds in 1999 (Gilmour and Caplan, 2001). In 2002 a US$30 billion venture fund was formed to invest in the alternative energy fuel-cell industry, halving the time expected to bring this technology to market; it has the potential to return US$1.6 trillion per annum (Reid, 2002). Investors are also calling corporations to account. Following a 2002 Coalition for Environmentally Responsible Economies (CERES) report entitled *Value At Risk: Climate Change and the Future of Governance*, over 30 investment institutions wrote to the world's 500 largest companies 'to demand that they reveal how they are tackling ethical and environmental issues such as global warming' (Hayward, 2002, p14).

Legislation in the UK and Australia is forcing pension funds to look at TBL reporting. In Australia, the 2001 Financial Services Reform Act requires fund managers and pension trustees to disclose, within their product statements, 'the extent, if any, to which labour standards and environmental, social or ethical considerations are taken into account in the selection, retention or realization of the investments' (Newson, 2001, p1). According to Dale Hanson, chief executive officer (CEO) of the California Public Employees Retirement System from 1987 to 1994, the Investor Responsibility Research Center analysis of proxy voting records indicates 'shareholders in record numbers want companies to adopt global labour standards to ensure fair, decent working conditions for overseas employees' (Hanson, 2002, p1). Similarly, New York City's pension fund of US$26 billion is checking human rights and labour records of corporations in developing countries (Schwartz and Gibb, 1999).

Investment organizations also play a role in informing corporations of the benefits of the TBL of sustainability. For example, the DJSI sustainability website advises that 'Corporate sustainability leaders achieve long-term shareholder value by gearing their strategies and management to harness the market's potential for sustainability products and services, while at the same time successfully reducing and avoiding sustainability costs and risks' (DJSI, 2002c). It also advises corporations about sustainability and how it can add to their TBL. For example, DJSI advises: 'Pollution prevention strategies add value, whereas end-of-pipe waste treatment often destroys it; early sustainability improvements have the biggest financial impacts... good environmental management can reduce companies' exposure to industry-wide risks; good corporate governance, workforce relations, product safety and corporate transparency can all create value' (Pearce, 2002, p1).

TBL as a management tool

For TBL to be successful, it must integrate the physical and financial activities of corporations. The TBL challenge facing both business and the accounting profession is to create the metrics to gauge corporate sustainability and to find new forms of accounting and accountability (Elkington, 1999b). Elkington said that 'this is an extremely complex task, but one which will probably look much easier once we have worked our way through a decade or two of experimentation in sustainability accounting, auditing and reporting' (Elkington, 1997, p93). Although innovative TBL concepts such as monetization, externalization and tracking of non-financial data are emerging, there does not appear to be any widely accepted accounting standards or metrics to account for or measure the environmental accounting and social activities, or the broader economic impact, of corporations. In traditional accounting the indicators, procedures and rules are strictly regulated by external legislation and professional standards (Cerin, 2002b). This is not the case for social and environmental accounting, where indicators are often determined inside the corporation, leading to bad information quality and causing bad quality reports (Schaltegger cited in Cerin, 2002b).

Costs traditionally influence most internal corporate decisions, whether they relate to financial, social or environmental performance. During recent years, much of the focus has been on accounting for the environmental aspect of TBL. The TBL approach to environmental cost accounting is 'to identify where a company is in terms of its environmental impacts, to determine appropriate "sustainability" targets or standards to aim for, and to work out the most cost-effective way for the company to close that "sustainability gap"' (Howes, 2002a, p3). Bennett and James (1998) advise that 'almost all the work in the field of environment-related management accounting is that of providing decision-makers and others with a better representation of reality through more accurate knowledge of environmental costs' (Bennett and James, 1998, p20). For example, environment, health and safety (EHS) managers usually operate with a focus on cost savings from environmental improvements in organizational processes and business opportunities, as well as cost minimization on insurance and eco-taxes and charges (Sullivan and Wyndham, 2001). Parker (1999) found that the environmental accounting techniques such as cost recognition were in a far more elementary stage than the application of environmental policies, management, impact statements and audits.

Bennett and James's (1998) edited book *The Green Bottom Line* identifies six domains of firm-level environmental accounting: energy and materials accounting; environment-related financial management; life-cycle assessment; life-cycle cost assessment; environmental impact assessment; and environmental externalities assessment. Bennett and James outline the major challenges in accounting for the environmental aspect of TBL, including:

- classifying environmental costs into conventional, hidden, contingent, image and relationship costs;
- tracking environmental costs that get lost in overheads using activity-based accounting;
- identifying hidden environmental costs that are often considerable and, if unidentified, create a bias against pollution control, hiding its potential savings and favouring new products and services;
- allocating production environmental emission costs;
- option pricing for uncertainties in investment appraisal (see Schaltegger and Müller, 1998);
- screening projects to include life-cycle analysis and monetizing of external environmental costs (see Epstein and Roy, 1998);

- using financial information that may be less useful than non-financial information for day-to-day management but is more effective in communicating the need for intervention to senior management (see Shields, Beloff et al, 1998);
- tracking hidden waste costs and inaccurate overhead allocations through life-cycle costing (see Bierma, Waterstraat et al, 1998);
- organizational issues such as staff willingness to accept economic evaluation of environmental processes, staff interest in environmental costs of processes and finding the best issue to focus upon for action.

Bennett and James (1998) suggest that environment-related management accounting (EMA) has the potential to demonstrate impact on the income statement; identify cost reduction and other improvement opportunities; prioritize environmental action; guide product-pricing mix and development; enhance customer value; future proof investments; and support sustainable businesses.

The TBL concept suggests that full-cost accounting (FCA) would be required to embrace sustainable development. O'Dwyer (2001a) notes that by internalizing external costs, through tools such as eco-taxes, FCA enables prices to reflect their full environmental costs, which would then flow to the consumption and production chain, consequently reinforcing more sustainable patterns of behaviour.

Schaltegger (2000) argues that the importance of accounting information is not always recognized in the decision-making process, while Burritt (1998) points to the political nature of accounting information, suggesting that no information is objective and the purpose of management accounting is not accuracy but to influence managers. Bennett and James (1998) suggest that EMA is not a distinctive but a 'virtual' activity that will continue to contribute to business success and sustainability; however, it is likely to develop in a discontinuous way.

In contrast to environmental accounting, current research in accounting for social issues is relatively limited. Koehler (2001) provides an example of accounting for EHS at Baxter International. The motivation for the development of the accounting system was to provide data on the true cost of EHS issues for the firm, and to enable evaluation of the performance of various systems, using both physical and financial data. Accounting for social issues changed the focus in Baxter from outputs (workdays lost) to inputs (activities – for example, how many nurses are required). For Baxter it was a move from focusing on compliance and external reporting to developing performance measures to 'craft' corporate strategy.

As Elkington (1997) envisioned, incorporating sustainable value drivers within business decisions rewards far-sighted and strategic corporations. For example, DuPont reports that since measuring and reporting its environmental impact, it has reduced environmental costs from US$1 billion per annum in 1993 to US$560 million in 1999. Similarly, Interface, a floor-covering manufacturer, says that it has eliminated more than US$165 million in waste (Gilmour and Caplan, 2001). It seems that, increasingly, governments, investors and consumers are acclaiming the work of corporations that are moving towards sustainability and adding pressure to those corporations that have not yet taken up the TBL of sustainability.

TBL as a reporting tool

A common view on the general debate on corporate social and environmental responsibility is that 'society will become increasingly vociferous in its insistence that the business sector should contribute to social prosperity in the long term' (Cramer, 2002, p106). TBL or 'sustainability' reporting is seen as potentially improving the quality of information reported to society. Recent research suggests '60 per cent of the Global 100 (excluding financial services) produce a global environmental report' (O'Dwyer, 2001b, p18). The DJSI annual report on 2001 highlighted a 'strong increase in companies' interest and participation in their sustainability review' (Knoepfel, 2002, p2).

Although there are international accounting standards concerned with reporting financial performance, there are no agreed standards on environmental and social reporting (Papmehl, 2002). While there are some mandatory reporting requirements in countries such as Australia, Denmark, France, Norway, Sweden and The Netherlands, there is no comprehensive legislation concerned with accounting, reporting and auditing of TBL. However, there are recommended guidelines, such as those of the Global Reporting Initiatives (GRI, 2002), outlining standards for accounting and reporting corporate economic, social and environmental performance.

A lack of mandatory requirements for TBL accounting and reporting or even widely accepted standards must be problematical for a sustainability industry that suggests, recommends, advises, certifies and consults. Zadek suggests that it 'is too early to say which (of the many) standards, guidelines, systems, procedures and practices will turn out to make the most sense for any one company, let alone for the wider business community and society at large' (Zadek, 2001, p12). Of concern is that, while there is an increased volume of disclosure, there are no parallel gains in their quality or the level of accountability discharged (Adams, forthcoming; Frost, 2000; Synnestvedt, 2001), leading to calls for greater legislation (Adams, forthcoming). An Australian survey found that 'legal requirements were cited as the most important driving force for addressing environmental issues by 49 per cent of primary/secondary industry'

(Sullivan and Wyndham, 2001, p9). In the UK, a MORI survey found that 'almost 90 per cent think the government should act to protect the environment, employment conditions and health even when this conflicts with the interests of the multinational, all of which adds to the pressure for mandatory CSR [corporate social responsibility] reporting' (Hayward, 2002, p15). The European Commission (EC) currently rejects a regulatory approach to TBL reporting (Hayward, 2002). When the UK prime minister challenged the FTSE-350 to publish environmental reports by the end of 2001, only a quarter of them did so (Hayward, 2002). Currently, the UK Company Law Review is proposing an expanded mandatory operating and financial review for listed companies that will include comment on environmental policies and performance and 'community, social, ethical and reputational issues' (Gilmour and Caplan, 2001). Adams predicts that 'Mandatory reporting on ethical, environmental and social issues will become a reality within ten years' (cited in Hayward, 2002, p16).

Adams's research has found very little integration of all three TBL issues, with most reporting focusing on environmental issues (Adams, 1999; Adams and Kuasirikun, 2000). There was very little stakeholder involvement in the selection of key performance indicators (KPIs) (Adams, 2002a), and there was a lack of completeness of reporting, both in terms of issues not being reported at all and the omission of key negative impacts (see Adams, forthcoming). Overall, the level of accountability on impacts found to be material to key stakeholder groups was found to be poor. Particular areas where there was a perceived demand for greater accountability comprised community activities; information on product safety; equal opportunities; working conditions around the world; policies regarding foreign direct investment; and reporting on ethical business practices (Adams, forthcoming). Adding to the call for horizontal integration of reporting across the three prongs of TBL, Larsen (2000) suggests that stakeholder demands also require environmental reporting to become a 'strategic issue in order to ensure consistency and balance between the business strategy, the environmental strategy and the reporting activities' (Larsen, 2000, p276).

As a result, there appears to be tension between stakeholder engagement for TBL reporting and the comparability and consistency opportunities that come with standardization of reporting. Elkington (1997) recognized the inherent difficulty in TBL and in the comparison of TBL reports when he referred to the constant flux of the three bottom lines, and how they often move independently and over, under and against each other. One explanation for there being no 'standard' social report is 'because the nature of each depends upon the variety of issues it covers; the range of stakeholders for whom it is intended; and what the reporting organization is trying to achieve' (SustainAbility and UNEP, 1999, p7). Today there are 'many systems aimed at aligning core business strategies and processes with elements of social and environmental aims and outcomes [that] have emerged in the last ten years' (Zadek, 2001, p11). Research on voluntary corporate environmental reports indicate that they tend to be unique, generally stand alone, are unbalanced, and lack consistency and comparability from year to year (O'Dwyer, 2001b). Quality is also often poor in the reports, possibly with the exception of companies whose core activities have a publicly observable environmental impact (O'Dwyer, 2001b). Some organizations determine what is important for their strategy and reporting through stakeholder consultation and/or the balanced scorecard approaches (Atkinson and Epstein, 2000). Others use models designed by management accounting consultants such as Pricewaterhouse Coopers' ValueReporting framework (Gilmour and Caplan, 2001). Cerin's analysis of environmental reporting points to a large credibility gap for the majority of large companies who appear to be trying to seek legitimacy, without following any one particular agreed set of environmental accounting or reporting guidelines. He concludes that the 'environmental reporting of today therefore functions more as a marketing tool than an accounting innovation' (Cerin, 2002a, p62).

Conclusions

The UNCTAD report of 1995 concluded that 'companies cannot be sustainable in the present economic climate' (UNCTAD, 1996, p16), while Visser and Sunter argue that the essential features of sustainable business include engagement with the organization's stakeholders, transparency and accountability (Visser and Sunter, 2002). These are important components of the AA1000 framework (AccountAbility, 1999), the AA1000S auditing guidelines (AccountAbility, 2002) and the GRI guidelines (GRI, 2002). The World Business Council for Sustainable Development (WBCSD, 2001) presents business with the difficult challenge of establishing the Earth's worth, which would require accounting for its social and environmental costs. The key challenge in working towards accountability for sustainable development in business is to integrate financial, social, environmental and ethical accounting, reporting and auditing. In order to improve performance this information must be used in corporate decision-making.

Chapter 3

CSR, Sustainability and the Triple Bottom Line

Adrian Henriques

Introduction

The triple bottom line (TBL) is a brilliant and far-reaching metaphor. It has stimulated much corporate activity and has generated tools that can yield quantified expressions of triple bottom line performance. But does this cover the full ground of sustainability and corporate social responsibility (CSR)? This chapter addresses this question through analysis of the following issues:

- Do the three dimensions covered by the triple bottom line (the environmental, social and economic) exhaust the field of sustainability? In particular, how does the central element of CSR, a concern with stakeholders, fit with the model?
- The economic dimension of the triple bottom line is only partly understood. It has often been identified simply with financial performance and at other times with something broader. What is the most helpful interpretation?
- The triple bottom line metaphor suggests that sustainability can be analysed through consideration of the periodic impacts in the three dimensions. How can this be squared with the long-term implications within the very word 'sustainability'?
- As has been argued elsewhere in this book, sustainability is a whole-system property. This raises questions of how an individual organization relates to the system as a whole – such as what is the proper corporate boundary of responsibility, and what mechanisms should exist for responsibly managing sustainability at national and international levels? Other chapters in this book deal with aspects of these problems. However, the book also raises

the question about how whole-system characteristics are best addressed at the level of corporations. This issue, which is beyond the metaphor of the triple bottom line, is explored through an analysis of the concept of 'diversity' and the business logic in pursuing it.

Environmental, social, economic: is that it?

There have been several treatments of the relationship between the three dimensions of sustainability (see, for example, Henriques, 2001, and Zadek and Tuppen, 2000). In summary, it is not possible to prove the priority of one dimension over another. Or to put it the other way round, while it is possible to show that the economic is 'nothing but' the social, it is also possible to reduce any one of the dimensions to either of the others, and it has even been argued that a constant focus on the monetary returns from environmental and social performance is the best route to sustainability.

On the other hand, nothing in such analyses suggests that these three dimensions *must* exhaust the field of sustainability. And such confirmation is unlikely, given the ever-moving spirit of the concept of sustainability. Despite all of this, it is possible to gain some confidence about the triple bottom line approach by relating the stakeholder approach to CSR to the three dimensions of the triple bottom line.

A fully developed approach to stakeholders involves a mapping of the range of issues with which they are concerned in their role as stakeholders. Taking all of the issues identified by all stakeholders together, they can be analysed as to the content of concern. And it is at this level that stakeholder issues can be grouped as environmental, social or economic. So, for example, for a large multinational, it is very likely that the issues of concern to stakeholders will include global warming, human rights violations and dividend payments. But stated in this way, the issues are 'orphaned' – that is, they are presented without any link to the stakeholders to whom they may be of concern. Any issue will have a stakeholder (or several) who 'owns' it; and any stakeholder is likely to have a range of different issues of concern. However, the 'catch' is that in order to be sustainable, organizations will have to be accountable to their stakeholders.

In one sense of the term, 'accountability' is about the ability to give an account of something to somebody who has an interest in it. Historically, accountability has been concerned with the duty on a company to report to its shareholders. In this sense, traditional corporate reporting is an important part of corporate accountability. Accountability compensates for the 'agency problem' – the fact that the owners of a large company, who have a clear interest in it but are not usually directly involved in its management, need to understand how their company is being managed and how it is performing financially. This part of accountability has been much developed and regulated for many years, even though recent events demonstrate that even in its traditional heartland it needs to be taken further.

The idea of 'transparency' is often mentioned in connection with accountability. Transparency tends to have two related meanings. It can either be used synonymously with accountability, or it can refer to the ethical dimension of business dealings. In the latter sense, transparency implies an absence of bribery and corruption in business affairs.

In relation to sustainability, accountability takes on a broader, though related, meaning. The greater breadth comes from including all stakeholders, in addition to shareholders, as part of those to whom an account is due. The related element of meaning is that all such stakeholders should be regarded as entitled to some kind of account of company activities. Currently, there is very limited support in law for such a wider accountability in most national jurisdictions. Nevertheless, in an attempt to respond to some of the pressures set out earlier, an increasing number of companies are reporting to their stakeholders, in various ways, in order to be more accountable.

At first glance, accountability seems like a social phenomenon. It is clearly true that accountability is about the relationship of a company to its stakeholders – which is how part of the social element of corporate sustainability can be defined. But while some stakeholders (such as the local community) may be primarily concerned with social issues, others (such as pressure groups) may be concerned with environmental issues. Yet others (such as shareholders and government) will be interested in economic issues. It is therefore not appropriate to confine accountability to the social dimension of sustainability.

So, in relation to the nature of corporate activity, accountability is an integral part of the process of implementing all aspects of sustainability. It is also true that the way in which accountability may be discharged is similar, whatever the sphere of accountability. Despite this, accountability does seem to have a particularly social 'feel' to it! This is because not only does it concern the way in which an organization relates to its various stakeholders, but also because how and whether it does this is intrinsically of social concern. In other words, 'accountability' is itself a social value. A rather complex picture, therefore, emerges, in which accountability relates to all aspects of sustainability, but also has a privileged place in relation to the social dimension. This situation is pictured in Figure 3.1.

All of this suggests that for organizations to have the greatest confidence that no relevant sustainability issues have been overlooked, it is crucial for them to work with the full range of their stakeholders. However, what it is also possible to say at this stage is that the great majority of sustainability issues can fit reasonably well into the three dimensions of the triple bottom line.

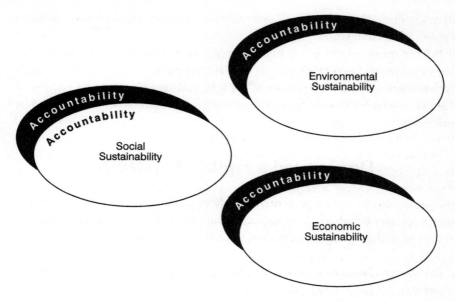

Figure 3.1 *Accountability and sustainability*

What about the *real* bottom line?

The real, or original, bottom line is about profit, such that increasing revenues without increasing costs improves the bottom line. But is that the same as the economic dimension of the triple bottom line? Recent work (Zadek, 2001), together with recent practice as exemplified in Chapter 15, suggests that it does not. Profitability, which is of central concern to shareholders, is one element of the economic dimension, but not all of it.

In practice, this means that the financial is but one component of economic impact and the economic performance of a company is wider than shareholder return. There are two particular consequences of this that need to be borne in mind.

Firstly, the issue of the scope of the economic dimension must be distinguished from the expression of environmental or social impacts in financial terms. Expressing environmental impact in terms of the cost of restoring or preventing damage is a way of measuring the environmental impact. This may or may not be a good way of doing so, but it is not in itself directly a measure of financial performance. It is just a way of using financial units (such as pounds or dollars) to capture environmental performance.

Secondly, it is sometimes argued that a sustainable market system would be one in which there were no economic externalities (where costs or benefits are not reflected in the price of goods or services). While no doubt true, it is extremely difficult to identify all externalities, and perhaps even more difficult to police their elimination.

So, the most helpful interpretation of the economic dimension is one that acknowledges and gives due weight to dividend payments, but also sets such payments in the context of economic impacts, such as effects on the viability of local economies or the net, rather than the gross, number of jobs created by some project.

Do we need a capitalist system?

A focus on profits is often presented as a short-term perspective and one that is either necessary or immoral, depending upon your point of view. However, the concept of 'enlightened capitalism' rests on the twin ideas that:

- Profits can be maximized if the best possible social and environmental performances are produced.
- Profit maximization over the longer term does not necessarily require (and may be undermined by) profit maximization over the short term.

In straightforward economic terms, the longer-term perspective is expressed as the need for investment, and it results in the accumulation of capital, which sustains higher profit levels than would otherwise be possible. Environmental and social sustainability is clearly immensely strengthened if this longer-term approach is combined with an appreciation of the interaction of social and environmental with economic performance (Sen, 2001; Stiglitz 2002).

But the triple bottom line analogy speaks only to the equivalent of short-term returns. It has encouraged systems of measurement that focus on the impact within a specific period. The impacts over a longer time frame – while possibly more difficult to capture – are, ultimately, the important ones. This would require the development of a system to measure and account for environmental and social capitals.

The significance of diversity

Edward Goldsmith (Goldsmith, 1998) among others has pointed out how natural systems are homeostatic or dynamically tend to equilibrium. In other words, they tend to remain in the same state, and also tend to return to that state if they do get disturbed. The first quality can be termed 'resistance' or 'robustness'; the second is 'resilience'. Although there is little reference to the word sustainability in Goldsmith's major work, it is obvious that without homeostasis, there can be no sustainability – by definition, there would be a slow drift or more cataclysmic disruption to the initial state.

What are the factors that make a system likely to be sustainable? At least one of them must be the diversity of its component elements. In the remainder of this chapter the general reasons for this will be set out; examples relevant to companies from each of the dimensions of the triple bottom line will then be described.

To cope with the widest possible range of challenges, a system needs to have many resources at its disposal. If, for example, an area is prone both to drought and floods, then it is advantageous to have a diverse mixture of seeds available for planting. In those years when it is wet, water-tolerant varieties can flourish; and the converse can occur when it is dry. Even a system with this minimal diversity will be more sustainable than a monoculture of similar size.

This suggests that beyond the quantitative characteristics of sustainable operations – the periodic impacts on the environment, the society and the economy – there are also qualitative characteristics necessary to achieve persistence through time. Foremost among these is diversity. How can organizations contribute to diversity? Some of the key ways include encouraging:

- environmental diversity;
- social diversity;
- economic diversity; and
- government policy.

Environmental diversity involves protecting and fostering the variety of species on the Earth. Companies, especially those which exert significant impacts on the Earth through mining, extracting or manufacturing, have a particular role to play. One of the reasons for taking biodiversity seriously is that it entails a serious and systematic review of site operations; this can contribute to efficiency. British Petroleum's (BP's) approach is captured by the following statement about biodiversity action plans:

> *Biodiversity action plans:*
> - *are applied at either regional, business unit or site level (as appropriate);*
> - *are developed in dialogue with stakeholders and partnerships with local groups/experts;*
> - *involve consideration of wide impacts, such as through the life cycle from supply chain to product and from construction to decommissioning;*
> - *involve a systematic review of biodiversity risks and impacts and the taking of action on those that are most significant;*

- *are an integrated part of business unit/site environmental management systems;*
- *are about taking action as part of a wider drive, demonstrating alignment with national processes and priorities;*
- *are to be externally verified to ensure quality and credibility* (BP website, January 2003, www.bp.com).

What about social diversity? While this can take many forms, one obvious manifestation is staff diversity, which entails ensuring that staffing is not dominated by gender, religion, age or any other single characteristic. This is the chief executive officer of BP Lord Browne's view of social diversity given in a keynote speech at the Women in Leadership Conference in Berlin on 19 June 2002:

> *If we want to recruit and retain the best women, we won't succeed if we tolerate what one commentator has described as 'a golf club culture' that can implicitly, if not explicitly, exclude women and sometimes minorities as well.*
>
> *If we want to be an employer of the most able people who happen to be gay or lesbian, we won't succeed unless we offer equal benefits for partners in same-sex relationships.*
>
> *If we want the best women to be part of the leadership team at every level, we won't succeed if we tolerate those old tired phrases: 'I'm not sure it would be in her own best interests to be promoted at the moment'; 'Wouldn't it be better to have someone we know'.*

Economic diversity often tends to be less obviously in the interests of the corporate sector. What it entails includes having a portfolio of products that may enjoy peak demand at different times. The classic investment advice to have a diverse range of shares follows this logic. However, it also suggests appealing to a multitude of markets, which can seem to fly in the face of the usual business logic. Why pursue markets other than the most profitable? The answer may range from simply being able to enjoy additional revenue to developing robustness against the time when market fashions change.

Finally, if your organization happens to be a government, diversity takes on a particular meaning. This is not only because any (democratic) government must cater for all of its citizens, but also for more profound reasons. To the extent that governments exhibit leadership, diversity can have a particularly prominent place in policy development. Governments have a responsibility to encourage those characteristics of their countries (which may be thought of as systems) that contribute to sustainability. Among these, one of the most prominent is diversity – in all of its forms.

Conclusions

This chapter has addressed the question of how far the triple bottom line metaphor captures sustainability. The concepts underlying the metaphor of the triple bottom line are absolutely necessary for sustainability; but on their own they cannot be sufficient.

In terms of the three dimensions, the answer appears to be that the triple bottom line approach is nearly sufficient, with two qualifications. Firstly, the economic dimension must be interpreted in a broad sense, not a narrow financial one; and, secondly, a further accounting, beyond the immediate tally of today's impacts, must take place that embraces the concept of capital and the time dimension of sustainability. However, as sustainability is essentially a system property, there are also critical qualitative characteristics that any sustainable system must embrace. Foremost among these is diversity.

Chapter 4

Accounting for Sustainability: Measuring Quantities or Enhancing Qualities?

Julie Richardson

Introduction

The triple bottom line (TBL) concept coined by John Elkington and now common currency recognizes that corporations not only add economic value (hopefully), but also impact on social and environmental value added. These concepts correspond to the three pillars of sustainable development, which have often been interpreted by economists as economic, social and environmental capitals.[1]

For the purposes of this chapter, I use the simplest three-capital model to explore how corporations might account for their contributions to value added across the triple bottom line. Contrary to popular belief, there is no 'how to do it' manual for triple bottom line or sustainability accounting. Neither is it a 21st-century quest – a short review of the accounting history books will reveal that developing methodologies to account for the social and environmental impacts of business was a popular pursuit during the 1970s. Indeed, the value-added statements that are developed in this chapter have their roots in this era. It is not entirely clear why these methodologies did not make it to common practice two or three decades earlier. Certainly, the Thatcherite era was not conducive to business taking a broader look at its social and environmental responsibilities. But perhaps the main constraint was that it has proved a minefield of ethical and methodological traps. Although some of the problems have now been resolved, others have not.

This chapter addresses two key themes. Firstly, it outlines what a sustainability accounting framework might look like in terms of the three components of the triple bottom line. Secondly, it explores some of the inherent difficulties surrounding sustainability accounting and, in particular, addresses the question of whether it is possible to add up across the triple bottom line. The chapter concludes that we need to move beyond our current focus of measuring sustainability in terms of quantities in separate silos (such as economic, environmental and social capitals) towards mapping the qualities of sustainable systems (such as diversity, learning, adaptation and self-organization).

Sustainability accounting: a short exploration

Hereafter, *sustainability accounting* is used to refer to a framework to account for the financial implications of sustainability across the triple bottom line for an individual organization or company. This is just one approach and others, such as the Sustainability Assessment Model (SAM), are presented in other chapters in this book. The sustainability accounting framework has evolved from the 'Green accounting' work developed and applied by Forum for the Future (see Chapter 10). Its development was supported by the sustainability integrated guidelines for management (SIGMA)[2] and different aspects have been piloted by a number of organizations.

The starting point for the sustainability accounting framework is the value (measured in financial terms) that organizations add to or subtract from society in terms of their contribution to economic, social and environmental well-being. The use of 'value-added statements' is rooted in the Global Reporting Initiative (GRI, 2002) and has been popularized by a number of companies in their social and environmental reports.[3]

At a high level, Figure 4.1 shows that there are two components to the sustainability accounting framework: a restatement of traditional financial accounts to highlight sustainability-related financial flows, and additional accounting to show the financial value of the economic, social and environmental impacts on external stakeholders.

Restatement of financial accounts: internal flows

Traditional accounting presents the internal financial flows of an organization in a summarized profit-and-loss account format that is of most interest to the shareholder. This financial information can be restated in a variety of different ways to draw out sustainability-related information that may be of interest to a wider group of stakeholders. For example, Table 4.1 illustrates how the financial accounts can be restated to show financial value added by stakeholder group using an example from South African Breweries.

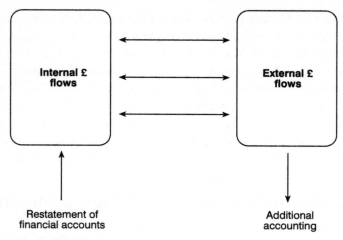

Figure 4.1 *Overview of the sustainability accounting framework*

Table 4.1 could be further disaggregated to show the cost-and-benefit flows that arise out of the organization's environmental or socially related programmes. South African Breweries did not carry out this task, but others have done so. See, for example, the environmental financial statement published by Baxter Healthcare.[4]

Additional accounting: external flows

The financial value-added statement only captures those financial flows that accrue to the individual organization. It takes no account of the external impacts (positive or negative) that accrue to third-party stakeholders. These external impacts or 'externalities' may be of an economic, environmental or social nature. For example, an economic externality may be the effect of an organization's operations on the economic regeneration of the local economy. A social externality may be the adverse health impacts of consuming the company's products (such as tobacco or alcohol). An environmental externality might include impacts on the local community from water pollution or air emissions.

Table 4.2 suggests a framework for the external account, which illustrates the types of costs and benefits of an economic, social or environmental nature that may accrue to third-party stakeholders as a result of company operations and products.

Calculating the triple bottom line in financial terms requires converting these externalities into monetary values. This is where much of the thinking is currently at, and a lot of effort has been devoted to methodological development and empirical estimates of these external impacts. The greatest

Table 4.1 *Financial value added by stakeholders*

	Stakeholder	Financial Value Added	South African Breweries (2002) US$ million
1	Customers	Cash received by company for supply of its products	3691
		Cash returns on investments	50
2	Suppliers	Cash payments outside the company for materials and services purchased	1622
3	Company value added	= 1 − 2	2119
4	Employees	Total remuneration to employees (including wages and benefits)	408
5	Community	Corporate social and environmental investment	7
6	Public sector	Regulatory charges and taxes paid	858
7	Investors	Interest payments on borrowings + Dividend payments	382
8	Balance	Monies retained in the business = (1 − 2) − (4 + 5 + 6 + 7)	464
9	Total	= 4 + 5 + 6 + 7 + 8	2119

Source: GRI (2002) www.globalreporting.org and South African Breweries plc (2002) Corporate Accountability Report 2002

strides have been made in environmental valuation; controversy still rages over the financial valuation of social impacts; and the valuation of economic externalities has received little attention until recently.

Suppose, for the sake of argument, that is was possible to identify and convert these 'externalities' into monetary values. Does it make sense to add these values up and is the remaining single figure an accurate indicator of 'sustainable profit'?

The triple bottom line: does it all add up?

There is tremendous temptation to derive the net financial value of external impacts and deduct this from financial profit to derive a new metric of sustainable profit. But what does such a metric mean from a sustainable development perspective? Such a figure should be interpreted with great caution and, in some cases, may even be meaningless from a sustainability perspective. Objections range for the technical to the ideological. In increasing order of severity they include the following.

Table 4.2 *Accounting for externalities*

| | Examples of External Costs and Benefits | | |
	Environment	Social	Economic
Customers	Environmental costs or benefits in the use and disposal of products	Ethical, social and health costs or benefits associated with the product	Consumer surplus over and above the market price
Suppliers	Environmental impacts associated with the production of purchased goods and services	Ethical, social and health costs or benefits associated with the production of purchased goods and services	Stimulation of economic growth through the supply chain
Employees	Environmental benefits or risks associated with the workplace	Workplace social costs (such as unpaid overtime) and benefits (such as training and development)	Employment creation through the economic multiplier effect
Community	Emissions, effluents and waste to land, air and water (local, regional, national and international)	Community health impacts; wider social impacts of redundancy and plant closure; nuisance and disturbance	Urban and rural regeneration; infrastructure (eg transport links and congestion)
Public sector	Environmental benefits from pubic-sector investment of corporate taxes in environmental protection	Social benefits from public-sector investment of corporate taxes in health, education and social programmes	Public-sector economic multiplier effects
Investors	Risks to investors from poor corporate environmental reputation	Risks to investors from poor corporate social and ethical reputation	Risks to investors from poor corporate economic reputation

Accounting for what you can count

There is a real danger that the sustainability accounts only include items that can easily be extracted or converted into monetary values. Many of the social and environmental costs and benefits are intangibles (such as reputation risks or impacts on biodiversity). Intangibles are notoriously difficult to capture and convert into monetary values, although significant progress has been made in doing so during recent years.

Whose boundaries?

Collecting data on sustainability impacts requires a clear definition of the boundary of responsibility. Financial accounting offers a set of principles and rules that define the operational boundaries within which financial data is collected and reported. This is not so with sustainability-related information.

Narrow or broad boundaries can be defined – and in actual sustainability reports we see both. Narrow boundaries mimic the operational boundaries defined by financial accounting systems. Other systems (such as the AA1000 Assurance Standard) recommend that boundaries are set according to a broader set of stakeholders – including all of those that can influence or are influenced by the organization. Others suggest a middle way, recommending that accounting boundaries are set according to the 'sphere of influence' of the organization.

Many of the chapters in this book wrestle with defining boundaries of responsibility for individual organizations. To date, there appears little consensus about whether organizational boundaries should be determined by economic activity, law or nature.

It is tempting to call for common boundaries, and, indeed, little progress will be made towards benchmarking organizational performance until this done. However, the establishment of boundaries of responsibility is not a mere technical problem that can easily be resolved. In practice, it is a highly political issue that, ultimately, can only be resolved through private negotiation (between affected stakeholders), changes in society's norms[5] or government regulation.

The divergence between the boundaries of corporate social and environmental responsibility enshrined in law and public perceptions of corporate responsibility is one of the key drivers behind corporate social responsibility (CSR) and TBL reporting. Ultimately, corporate concern about maintaining their 'licence to operate' and managing reputation risks is about responding to informal social norms, rather than the rights and responsibilities enshrined in statute. Social norms often appear slow to change; but they are by no means static and can be subject to dramatic shifts. Indeed, the worldwide shift in human and societal values is one of the key drivers behind triple bottom line reporting as identified by John Elkington in Chapter 1.

Money as the ultimate value?

Over the past decade a range of different methodologies has been developed to convert environmental resources and services into financial values.[6] Many are optimistic that the same reasoning can be applied to capture the value of social impacts in monetary terms. However, there is a common misconception that a unique monetary figure can be calculated to capture the value of environmental (and social) resources and services, and that the main difficulty of doing so is a technical or data issue. Unfortunately, the world is not so simple. A few of the complications are highlighted in this section; for a comprehensive review, see OECD (1995) and Dixon et al (1996).

Environmental valuation treats the environment as a commodity that can be broken down into different components and analysed just like any other commodity. For example, the economic value of a wetland ecosystem can be

Source: Madden (1991)

Figure 4.2 *Consumer preferences and ecosystem integrity*

broken down to show the value of different wetland products such as wild plants, fish and building materials. There are also important ecological functions (such as water filtration and climatic regulation) that also need to be factored into the accounting process. The next step is to estimate consumers' willingness to pay (WTP) for these products, services or functions or willingness to accept (WTA) compensation for their loss or degradation or the costs to restore, replace or prevent environmental damage. This mechanistic approach fails to capture the deep synergistic relationships between the different elements of the ecosystem, and is both optimistic about the role of the consumer in guiding sustainable resource allocations and our capacity to restore or replace ecosystem functions in the face of uncertainty or irreversible change.

The sovereign role of the consumer is at the heart of many environmental valuation approaches. Some reject this anthropocentric view of our relationship with nature out right, seeing it as part of the problem rather than the source of the solution. The cartoon in Figure 4.2 illustrates how our anthropocentric and consumer-based relationship with nature often conflicts with ecosystem integrity.

Others argue that the central role that existing market prices (either directly or implied) play in environmental valuation reinforce existing income inequalities and unsustainable consumption and production patterns. In addition, others cast doubt about whether citizen values can be adequately captured by reference to people's market behaviour (Sagoff, 1988).

Some of these problems are less severe when environmental valuation methods based on the costs of environmental prevention, replacement or restoration are used. These methods are popular with individual organizations that are primarily concerned with how much it will cost to reduce their environmental footprint. However, even these methods have their limitations. Not least, they still depend upon the use of existing market prices (which do not reflect those that would prevail in a more sustainable and equitable society) and are optimistic about substitution possibilities (between natural and human-made capital). Others caution about the sole use of such values in making resource decisions as they are only based on abatement costs and do not take into account the benefit side of the equation – that is, the impacts on social welfare (Atkinson et al, 1999). According to Hamilton (1996), environmental valuation based solely on abatement costs may grossly understate the impacts on human welfare.

Moves to standardize corporate environmental and sustainability accounting approaches will mean that the inherent problems of environmental valuation (and the extension of monetary valuation to the social sphere) will need to be addressed.

Adding up and across: is it possible and what does it mean?

Sustainability accounting and the conversion of social and environmental impacts into monetary values make it possible to add up the impacts and trade them off against each other. Within categories, this opens up the possibility of trading off an external environmental benefit for an external environmental cost – for example, offsetting cleaning up wastewater against increased production of carbon dioxide. In the social sphere, this may mean netting off a new investment in community provision against increases in workplace accidents. Even more controversial is the trade-off across categories – for example, trading off a reduction in transport emissions to cover for increasing health and safety risks of the product.

The power of converting environmental and social bottom lines into monetary values is that *prima facie* they can be added or subtracted to the financial bottom line. But by converting social and environmental impacts into monetary values, does it now mean that we can weigh up and trade off what were otherwise 'incommensurable' values? Michael Jacobs (1991, p202) suggests not:

> *One cannot say that, for example, a human life is worth more than the preservation of a scenic view, or that the lives of wild animals are more valuable than the maintenance of indigenous hunting cultures. These values are incommensurable: like apples and pears they cannot be added or subtracted from one another... To proponents of this objection, the incommensurable nature of*

> *environmental and other non-marketed values (such as human life, community, culture and so on) makes the whole process futile — if not actually dangerous.*

To what extent these types of trade-offs across the triple bottom line make sense from a sustainability perspective remains a crucial yet unresolved issue. Popular definitions of sustainability refer to the concept of inter-generational transfers of a portfolio of capital bequests (economic, social and environmental). In order to compensate the future for the damage that our activities today might cause means that this generation must ensure that it leaves the next generation a stock of capital no less than this generation has now. The distinction between *weak* and *strong* sustainability rests on whether what is required is the transfer of each capital stock intact, or whether transfer of an aggregate stock (economic plus environment plus social) of equal value meets the criteria for sustainability. The critical issue is whether a growth in human-made or economic capital can substitute for reductions or degradation in social and/or environmental capital.

Monetized triple bottom line accounting requires that a position be taken on this critical point. Reference to 'critical natural assets' sheds some light on this dilemma, at least in the environmental sphere. For example, Pearce et al (1996) argue that some classes of natural assets have no substitutes and therefore cannot be replaced or traded off. Baxter, Bebbington and Cutteridge in Chapter 11 suggest that the mainstream view allows substitution within a category (for example, for social capital it is permissible to trade off the creation of jobs in one location for the loss of jobs in another location) but not across economic, social or environmental categories. Others argue that sustainability requires us to move beyond measuring our economic, social and environmental systems in separate silos and searching for capital trade-offs. This critique is explored further in the following section.

Moving towards a systemic approach

A number of authors in this book have referred to the need for a paradigm shift in the way that we think about sustainable business. John Elkington in Chapter 1 envisages seven revolutions that are needed in our transition to sustainable capitalism. For Rupesh Shah in Chapter 9, sustainability requires a shift from a mechanistic to a systemic and participatory worldview. Similar conclusions are drawn by Gray and Milne in Chapter 7, who urge us to reorganize business around ecological systems.

Calls for more systemic and holistic thinking can be heard across the full political spectrum. This is not surprising as growing forces such as globalization mean that few can ignore our growing interdependence across all spheres of

Table 4.3 *Different approaches to sustainability accounting*

Mechanistic: top down	Systemic: inside out
System understood in terms of component parts	Emergent characteristics of the whole system are different from the characteristics of its component parts
Focus on capitals and money values	Focus on network patterns
Separate silos and trade-offs	Synergistic relationships, feedback loops and virtuous cycles
Measures static 'snapshots' in time	Measures patterns of change, adaptation and learning
Focus on measuring quantities relating to sustainability performance	Focus on enhancing qualities of sustainability
Reduces complex systems to a single denominator	Embraces diversity and complex patterns
Tools adapted from economics and accounting	Tools adapted from holistic science (physics, evolutionary biology and ecology)

our lives – economic, cultural and environmental. At the organizational level, boundaries are being challenged and renegotiated at the same time as greater openness and transparency are enforced through powerful communication networks and civil society alliances. This is a complex and uncertain world based on network patterns, synergistic relationships, feedback loops and non-linear dynamics. These are the forces that connect our economic, social and environmental systems both within individual organizations and beyond.

And yet, much of the language and many of the tools of sustainability have evolved from our mechanistic worldview. Breaking down our complex economic, social and environmental systems into separate silos to be traded off one against the other is symptomatic of this mind-set. Collapsing the economic, social and environmental footprint of an organization to a single value – money – effectively reduces a complex, diverse, dynamic and highly heterogeneous system to a single denominator. Again, this calls into question whether adding up the triple bottom line makes sense from a sustainability perspective.

The challenge is to develop a framework for sustainability accounting based on a genuine 'whole system' approach. It is hard to say what this might look like, but a good starting point would be to move beyond the three capitals approach of the triple bottom line towards the network as the main organizing principle. Advances in physics, ecology and other holistic systems recognize that the physical outcomes of any dynamic system that we observe actually manifest from a complex network of relationships, information flows and learning feedback loops between its component parts. In this context, sustainability is not about a series of TBL performance targets to be achieved but a self-organizing pattern to be understood. We need to take a step back and search for the 'qualitative' processes of a sustainable system, such as diversity, learning, adaptation and self-organization.

Viewed from this perspective, sustainability accounting could evolve into a tool for revealing organizational patterns and identifying virtuous feedback loops, rather than a system for setting targets and negotiating trade-offs across the triple bottom line. Guided more by advances in physics, ecology and evolutionary biology, the new tools would become learning feedback loops, organizational and stakeholder mapping, non-linear dynamics and pattern recognition. Table 4.3 offers some thoughts on the key differences between a mechanistic and systemic approach to sustainability accounting.

Notes

1   Others have further differentiated the capitals into four or five groups. For example, Baxter, Bebbington and Cutteridge in Chapter 11 refer to four capitals (economic, resource, environmental and social). Paul Ekins (1999) developed the five capital framework, making a distinction between social and human capital and separating out economic capital into manufacturing and financial components.
2   See SIGMA (2001).
3   See, for example, British Telecom's (www.btplc.com), South African Breweries' (www.sab.co.za) and Novo Nordisk's use of economic value statements in Chapter 15.
4   Baxter Healthcare (www.baxter.com)
5   Take, for example, the changing rights and responsibilities of smokers. The 'rights' of smokers have been gradually eroded over the years as public attitudes towards smoking in public places have shifted. This has been enshrined in law in some places (such as California); but in Europe it operates and is enforced through social norms rather than statute.
6   This includes the productivity approach, hedonic pricing, the replacement or restoration cost approach, preventive expenditure method, the travel cost method, and contingent valuation.

Chapter 5

Tracking Global Governance and Sustainability: Is the System Working?

Nancy Bennet and Cornis van der Lugt[1]

Introduction

This chapter examines global governance, the United Nations (UN) system and efforts within this governance system to develop processes of reporting with sustainability indicators that are globally applicable. In addition, it will be considered whether a global accounting of corporate triple bottom line (TBL) issues is feasible or desirable. Does it make sense to add it all up at the global level?

The development of environmental performance indicators at the global, regional, national, community and company levels has developed significantly over the past ten years. There is, however, less harmonization and agreement on common frameworks and indicators for sustainable development issues (economic, environmental and social). This chapter will outline the global governance system on environmental issues, as well as some initiatives that are being undertaken at different levels to develop a common framework for sustainability indicators.

The collection of data for the purpose of compiling a global assessment of the state of our planet and the well-being of its inhabitants takes place in a top-down and bottom-up manner. In its grandest scale, the top-down collection takes the form of global observing systems – for example, by satellite. At the micro-level scale, the bottom-up collection can take the form of small area estimations (for example, based on household unit interviews) and surveys of, or reports by, local authorities and individual companies. Between these macro- and micro-level methods of data collection, the processing and presentation of indicators of sustainability can take various forms, ranging from spatial (geographical information system or GIS) databases and indicator maps to state of the environment socio-economic reports and composite indices.

The Global Reporting Initiative (GRI) encourages sustainability reporting by organizations of all types, not only companies. Take, for example, environmental reporting by governments. These can take the form of state of the (national) environment reports and reporting on the environmental impact of the operations of government as an organization. While sustainability reporting at higher levels of aggregation becomes more complicated, state of the environment reports are being prepared today globally, regionally, nationally and locally. This process is being assisted by the *Cookbook for State of the Environment Reporting* developed by the United Nations Environment Programme (UNEP)/Global Resource Information Database (GRID)– Arendal, helping newcomers to make use of the improved cost-efficiency of reporting that internet publishing brings. The Cities Environment Reports on the Internet programme (CEROI) has engaged over 20 pilot cities in an effort to compile and share information along a common framework (see UNEP and GRID–Arendal, 2000).

State of the environment reports inevitably raise the question of impact resulting from public authority operations. Nothing prevents the local authority from reporting on its own operations. Examining environmental reporting by the governments of 12 Organisation for Economic Co-operation and Development (OECD) countries, Cash et al (2001) highlighted that most do not address the environmental impact of their operations, even though the size and scope of government activity – such as procurement and energy use – has wide-ranging environmental effects.

Environmental and sustainability reporting by large companies has increased steadily over recent years (see SustainAbility and UNEP, 2002a). A recent KPMG survey (see KPMG, 2002) of almost 2000 companies, including the top 250 companies of the Global Fortune 500 (GFT250) and the top 100 companies in 19 countries, showed that, in 2002, 45 per cent of the GFT250 and 28 per cent of the top 100 companies produced environmental, social or sustainability reports in addition to their annual financial reports. This compares to 35 per cent and 24 per cent respectively in 1999.

Each actor, whether public authority or civil society organization, plays a role in the broader context of global governance. Considering whether it makes sense to add it up at the global level requires a brief introduction to global governance.

Global governance: a multilevel of authorities and organization

We do not have a world government. We have global governance, a core part of which is the UN. We also have a world of some 200 sovereign states that find themselves in the company of, among others, some powerful organizations, including multinational enterprises. To start with, what is 'global governance'?

A pioneer in introducing the term global governance was James Rosenau (see Rosenau and Czempiel, 1992; Rosenau, 1990; Hewson and Sinclair, 1999), who noted a shift in the location of authority and both integration and fragmentation running parallel in the process of globalization. The notion of 'governance' signalled something looser than 'government'. It focused on global organization, implying 'organization' as verb rather than noun. Governance in this context also applied to public governance and the role of non-governmental stakeholders in the process. The post-Cold War world of the 1990s was full of expectation of global civil society becoming a source of revitalization for global organizations, the UN and its agencies included (see CGG, 1995).

As institutionalization in global governance becomes wider in scope, it becomes looser in structure. From the micro to the macro, this can be presented in the following order: national state < international organization (for example, the European Union) < international regime < international convention < international system. All of these represent multilevel governance of the 'multilevel international society' that Miall (1994, p6) spoke of when he described the international institutions, states and sub-national organizations that play important roles in 'managing cross-national transactions'.

Similar to these different levels of public governance, the private governance of multinational companies reflects equally complex structures and possible focal points for the collection and management of knowledge. How do these processes of public and private governance intersect? How can the collection and management of data, information and knowledge between these governance systems be linked (see Table 5.1)? Ditz and Ranganathan (1997, p6) argued that it would be useful to combine indicators, generated at the facility level or community level, into information that is meaningful at larger scales.

Table 5.1 *Linking public and private governance systems*

Public policy	Corporate management
Local community municipality	Facility/site
National authority	Business unit/company
Global/international organization/regime	Corporate group
Regional/international organization/regime	Sector association

This addresses the growing and still largely unrealized need to link company, sector, national and global reporting frameworks and targets in a meaningful way.

The boundary question: boundaries determined by economic activity, law or nature?

So, how does your company report feed into this global governance system and affect the global assessment and decision-making on the sustainable development agenda? The complexity of the matter can be best explained by making an analogy with that difficult question of *completeness* that you have to deal with when embarking on the compilation of your corporate environmental or sustainability report. Under the principle of completeness, the GRI guidelines (GRI, 2002) advise the user to address 'the boundary question' in terms of the operational boundary dimension, scope dimension and temporal dimension.[2] Based on this and considering different types of integration, one can expand these into four dimensions:

1 *Company operational boundaries*: these are the entities covered in the report – for example, the company group and/or subsidiaries, divisions and business units that may be based in different countries (internal vertical integration).
2 *Value chain boundaries*: this reflects the use of a life-cycle approach and involves questions that are organizational (are external partners, such as suppliers and waste treatment contractors, included?), questions concerning issues covered, and questions of relations with customers/consumers (life-cycle integration).
3 *Issue scope*: this comprises the inclusiveness of the report in terms of the range of issues that it addresses under the economic, environmental and social pillars of the triple bottom line (horizontal integration across issue areas).
4 *Temporal dimension*: the time period of the reported information needs to be made clear, helping to determine progress over time and to assess both short-term and long-term impacts (chrono-economics – that is, accounting that is not static; Dahl, 1995).

It is part of their mandate and in the public interest for public authorities to assess the state of the environment and development in their areas of jurisdiction. This implies that, in terms of the value chain, scope of issues and time frame involved, they need to be inclusive. Article 5.9 of the Aarhus Convention requires public authorities to establish pollution inventories or registers through standardized reporting. It is argued that the mere publication of quantities of pollutants released into the environment begins to involve the public in the related decision-making and that by reducing releases, the regulator and company can publicly demonstrate their commitment (Stec and Casey-Lefkowitz, 2000, p82).[3]

The key question from a global governance perspective is that related to *operational or organizational boundaries*. At what level does it make most sense to collect certain types of data; what level of aggregation is appropriate; and, accordingly, what is the appropriate level for analysis and policy action? The principle of subsidiarity would require that the collection of information, its analysis and policy action are required at the above-state level only in those instances where issues have transnational effects, and where action at the international or global level produces clear benefits by reason of scale or effects compared with action at the national or sub-national level.

For international action in support of the public good, traditional international law requires us to use the sovereign state as a main organizing unit. Keynesian macro-economics also left us with a tradition of using the national state as organizing principle (Milward, 1992, pp42–43). The national state is assumed to be the correct object and unit of measurement, as is reflected in the calculation of gross domestic product (GDP). National statistical services also use national GDP as their overall objective. Accordingly, 'adding it up' implies going from the level of company to national economy, to regional organization, to global institution. But is it that simple? Are we working with the same sustainability framework and similar indicators?

When deciding on what the 'key performance indicators' are for your company to report against, the main considerations are:

- relevance to you as the reporter;
- what is of interest to your stakeholders; and
- the sustainability context.

The latter consideration is the point of departure for a UN agency such as UNEP. This is where the micro level of organizational performance is linked with the macro level of global concerns. The GRI guidelines remind us that many aspects of 'sustainability reporting draw significant meaning from the larger context of how performance at the organizational level affects economic, environmental and social capital formation and depletion at a local, regional or global level' (GRI, 2002, p27).

If we then apply 'the boundary question' to consideration of the macro-level sustainability context and the appropriate level at which to collect, assess, interpret and act, we need to look at 'the boundaries of nature' and effects or impacts that go across 'the boundaries of the national state'. The transportation systems that dissipate unwanted materials, disperse them and spread locally acquired pollution transnationally are human trade, the food chain, air movements and water cycles (Rhode, 1992, pp208–213).

Studies of the vulnerability and assimilation capacity of natural environments and ecosystems in different regions help us to determine, for example, critical loads or levels that we should avoid bypassing. They help us to determine early warning signals. However, conducting these studies and strategic planning requires reporting of data on material inputs and outputs, emissions and determination of impacts. This is where the company sustainability report and national reporting by the public authority become crucial. Depending upon whether the approach in national legislation focuses upstream or downstream, the company and, ultimately, government as party to an international agreement need to meet and report on their performance against emission standards or quality standards.

Who is taking stock globally?

Global databases under the auspices of the UN on the global environment can be grouped under:

- global indexes;
- global observation systems; and
- multilateral environmental agreements (MEAs).

Since the 1990s, UNEP has supported the effort to develop comparable global or meta-databases through its collaborative centres such as GRID–Arendal in Norway and the World Conservation Monitoring Centre (WCMC) in the UK, while coordinating with the UN Statistical Office (UNSTAT). Today the UN System-Wide Earthwatch System provides a collection of UN-related databases on the state of the world environment and development (see Box 5.1).

The observing systems assist key MEAs and their scientific advisory bodies in developing information systems with necessary indicators. This is of growing importance as we seek ways of improving the monitoring and enforcement of international agreements. In addition to the convention secretariats, other user groups include the private sector. Companies from sectors such as energy, tourism and financial services with a special interest in the forecast of weather and climate are showing a growing interest in investing in these observing systems in return for more accurate data that is of direct relevance to their daily operations (Bernal, 2002, p7). This confirms that environmental information has become more economically valuable (Denisov and Christoffersen, 2000, p25). In some instances, the private sector is also directly involved in global observation. The assistance of commercial ships on

---

BOX 5.1 UN-RELATED DATABASES ON THE STATE OF THE WORLD ENVIRONMENT AND DEVELOPMENT

UN-related databases include the Global Environment Outlook (GEO) data portal of UNEP; the UN statistical databases with, for example, the UN's Millennium country profiles; the Commission on Sustainable Development's (CSD's) work programme on indicators; the World Bank online databases, with the World Bank's world development indicators; FAOSTAT of the Food and Agriculture Organization (FAO); EarthTrends of the World Resources Institute (WRI); and the Human Development Index of the UN Development Programme (UNDP). Earthwatch also provides access to the UN Global Observing Systems – namely, the Global Climate Observing System (GCOS), the Global Ocean Observing System (GOOS) and the Global Terrestrial Observing System (GTOS). These three observing systems are led by the World Meteorological Organization (WMO), the UN Educational, Scientific and Cultural Organization's (UNESCO's) Inter-governmental Oceanographic Commission (IOC) and the FAO.

---

the high seas, for example, continues to be used in the effort to collect data on the state of the ocean.

MEAs signify the existence of international environmental regimes in different issue areas. Of the over 500 international environmental agreements that exist today, the secretariats of most of the core global conventions and regional conventions of global significance are provided by six UN organizations, including UNEP.[4] In terms of substance, the core MEAs can be divided into five clusters: the biodiversity-related conventions; atmosphere conventions; land conventions; chemicals and hazardous wastes conventions; and the regional seas conventions (see UNEP, 2001).

MEAs provide for annual or biannual reporting by national governments that are parties. The Basel Convention requires an annual report on the 'amount of hazardous wastes and other wastes exported/imported, their category, characteristics, destination/origin, any transit country and disposal method(s)' (Article 13). On the production, use and import/export of ozone-depleting substances, the Montreal Protocol requires the reporting of annual statistical data, 'or the best possible estimates of such data where actual data are not available' (Article 7). The UN Framework Convention on Climate Change (UNFCCC) requires parties to develop and report their national inventories of anthropogenic emissions by sources and removals by sinks of greenhouse gases (Articles 4 and 12). Parties are also required to support international initiatives that involve, for example, related data collection and systemic observation (Article 5).

The performance of states in fulfilling reporting requirements under MEAs has often been disappointing. Yet, the experience of the Montreal Protocol has shown how parties and convention secretariats can make strenuous efforts to overcome this deficiency when accurate reporting is essential to the functioning of the regime (Chayes and Chayes, 1993, p200). The same is to be expected with the Kyoto Protocol, where accurate reporting is essential for the market mechanism to operate. Convention secretariats have also improved in formulating requests for data that are demand driven, easing submission by designing standardized reporting forms and demonstrating that information will be compiled (for example, in periodic country reviews) rather than simply filed away (Peterson, 1998, p425).

MEAs impose obligations on sovereign states and do not apply directly to companies. Their reporting requirements also tend to be very general. Still, an increasing number of MEAs identify specific substances that are controlled. These include the Montreal Protocol, UNFCCC, the Convention on the International Trade in Endangered Species (CITES), the Basel Convention, and the Persistent Organic Pollutants (POPs) Convention. There are a number of GRI environmental performance indicators that do relate directly to controlled substances and sites or areas listed under specific MEAs (some of which are now referred to in the 2002 GRI guidelines).

Mechanisms devised by the international community to institutionalize global responsibility in the environmental field can be categorized as liability or regulatory regimes (see Wapner, 1998, pp280–283). As international regulatory regimes display greater use of economic instruments (such as trade measures and emissions trading), the private sector is likely to show greater interest in helping to implement proactively. Once MEAs start listing specific substances and such listing forms the basis of an international market mechanism, transnational corporations pay special attention. This links with setting company targets and reporting against the related indicators.

The indicator question: a global effort to harmonize

Assessing progress toward sustainability and choosing relevant indicators is a challenging task for a number of reasons (see IISD and BFSD, 1999, p2):

- The concept of sustainability is one of both substance (expanded time horizon, broadened scale, more complex system) and process (enhanced transparency, collaborative, consensus seeking).
- The concept of sustainability is value based, with values that could vary between cultures and change over time.
- There are many different scales of analysis – from local to global – that are important, each of which should be used to inform the others.
- In tracking change we may be able to identify a trend, but we may not be able to identify if we are close to a critical breaking point.

A framework for organizing the selection and development of indicators and expressing the complexities and interrelationships encompassed by sustainable development (while it will always be imperfect) is essential and, ideally, should meet the needs and priorities of users. In a global effort, the UN CSD, with other UN agencies, and inter-governmental and non-governmental organizations, has developed a framework to guide the selection of sustainable development indicators at the national level. It proposes core indicators and methodology sheets for measuring and reporting on progress towards sustainable development.

What remains to be seen is whether this framework and indicators will be used by enough countries to become the *de facto* framework for assessing progress towards sustainability at the global level. In addition, most of the data collection will occur at a national level, and it is unclear how governments will encourage and use information generated through a bottom-up approach from business, local authorities and other stakeholders.

The initial framework proposed by the CSD was organized by the chapters of Agenda 21 under four dimensions of sustainable development: social, economic, environmental and institutions. Within these categories, the indicators were classified according to their 'driving force, state and response' (DFSR) characteristics, adopting a conceptual approach widely used for environmental indicator development, notably by the OECD, and also similar to the International Organization for Standardization's ISO14031 environmental performance indicators model used by companies worldwide.

This DFSR framework led to the development of 134 sustainable development indicators, which were tested at the national level by 22 countries from all regions of the world. Many countries concluded that the DFSR framework, although suitable in an environmental context, was not as appropriate for the social, economic and institutional dimensions of sustainable development (see CSD, 2002, p20).

Subsequently, a theme framework was developed, reflecting the goals of sustainable development. These goals echo basic human needs related to food, water, shelter, security, health, education, and good governance for which the international community has established more specific benchmarks or targets. In 2001, the final framework of 15 themes and 38 sub-themes was produced to guide national indicator development beyond the year 2001. Fifty-eight core indicators are proposed, compared to 134 initially, and methodology sheets for the core set have been published.

This CSD framework represents a common tool to assist governments in meeting international requirements for reporting, including national reporting to the CSD. The wide adoption and use of the core set would help to improve information consistency at the international level. The CSD recommends that each country establish a national coordinating mechanism to facilitate networking among interested partners. It could help to address the missing links between voluntary corporate initiatives, such as reporting, and public policy frameworks. This gap has been highlighted by UNEP in its overview of 22 industry-sector reports prepared for the World Summit on Sustainable Development (UNEP, 2002).

So, what does it all add up to?

For sustainable development indicators to be really effective a common set must emerge that are universally adopted and understood by all. In addition, there are many collection points in the global governance system and different scales of analysis, from local to global, that are important. Ideally, each should inform the others.

We have outlined an example of sustainable development indicators that have been developed at the global level under the auspices of the CSD for use by national government. National governments are advised to work with all stakeholders in their countries to gather data and test the indicators. This top-down approach has resulted in a concise set of meaningful indicators that are on the way to being understood and accepted worldwide, though it is too early to definitively judge their global relevance and ultimate effectiveness in measuring progress towards sustainable development.

The GRI guidelines, developed through a multi-stakeholder, inclusive, bottom-up approach, is also rapidly developing and making positive steps to become the globally accepted framework for sustainability reporting at the organizational level, in particular corporate sustainability reporting. The question, then, is whether these initiatives for reporting at the level of organization, state, sector and thematic or issue area are moving down the same track. Is there any possibility that we can 'add it all up'?

Between the macro and micro levels of reporting and the collection of data and information, international agreements such as MEAs in specific issue areas are likely to play an increasingly important role. As indicated, those that, in particular, include economic instruments and list specific substances are the ones that strengthen the link between reporting by public and private organizations. Take the example of climate change. The UN CSD emissions of greenhouse gases indicator is based on the national reporting requirements outlined by the Climate Change Convention. At the corporate level, the World Business Council for Sustainable Development (WBCSD)/WRI Greenhouse Gas Protocol and indicators for corporate accounting and reporting standard and calculation tools are consistent with those proposed by the Inter-governmental Panel on Climate Change for the compilation of inventories at the national level.

Table 5.2 allows for a comparison of selected indicators developed under the CSD and the GRI processes, with additional references to some MEAs in the environmental field. From this comparison, the following is evident:

- There is considerable similarity in the sustainable development themes addressed by the CSD and the categories examined in the GRI guidelines. The indicator detail varies, particularly in the economic and social issues, though this is to be expected given the different uses of the information being gathered and other key issues related to aggregation, weighting, units and scaling.
- CSD indicators on social issues, in particular, tend to focus on the empty part of the bottle, whereas company reporting tends to promote the full part of the bottle. Under, for example, poverty the CSD indicator refers to unemployment rate, while the company reports on number of jobs created.
- CSD indicators tend to focus on societal conditions (impacts), whereas company reporting tends to focus on management or technical processes. The one focuses on, for example, health, literacy rates and consumption patterns as matters of social concern, while the other highlights environment, health and safety (EHS), training and customers as management issues.
- The CSD framework uses different categories in some cases – for example, dealing with 'energy use' under economic indicators, while 'energy use' is categorized under environmental indicators in the GRI guidelines. While there is some consistency on the environment side, this is less apparent on the social and economic side.

Clearly, an important factor is how the reported information is used and to whom it will be communicated – whether you compile your report or database with the aim of the public good or with a profit motive. But these distinctions are becoming increasingly blurred as we integrate and realize the business case for sustainable development (see WBCSD, 2002). This is also reflected in the strategies we follow in global governance. In addition to the command-and-control approaches and economic-instruments approaches under regulatory regimes, a third possibility of growing significance is that of international voluntary initiatives.[5] These can be dubbed 'voluntary regimes'; some would say 'private governance'. Sceptics criticize these initiatives as being about window dressing. Mindful of this, UNEP has argued that company involvement in voluntary initiatives should be accompanied by sustainability reporting and independent verification. Again, the efficiency of international institutions and initiatives can be strengthened by making the link with sustainability reporting.

The task of judging how we are progressing towards sustainable development will always be a formidable one. There will always be a degree of

Table 5.2 *Comparison of CSD and GRI indicators*

CSD Theme Indicator Framework (total =)			GRI Framework (total core +)		
Theme indicator	*Sub-theme*	*Indicator*	*Theme*	*Issue area*	*Indicator*
Social			**Social**		
Equity	Gender equality (24)	Ratio of average female wage to male wage	Diversity and opportunity	Labour practices and decent work	LA11. Composition of senior management and corporate governance bodies (including the board of directors), including female/male ratio and other indicators of diversity as culturally appropriate
Environmental			**Environmental**		
Theme indicator	*Sub-theme*	*Indicator*	*Theme*	*Issue area*	*Indicator*
Atmosphere (9)	Climate change	Emissions of greenhouse gases	Emissions, effluents and waste	Gases listed in Annex A of the Kyoto Protocol of the UNFCCC Compare WRI–WBCSD Greenhouse Gas Protocol	EN8. Greenhouse gas emissions (CO_2, CH_4, N_2O, HFCs, PFCs, SF_6). Report separate sub-totals for each gas in tonnes and in tonnes of CO_2 equivalent for the following: • direct emissions from sources owned or controlled by the reporting entity; • indirect emissions from imported electricity, heat or steam

Table 5.2 (continued)

CSD Theme Indicator Framework (total =)		GRI Framework (total core +)	
Biodiversity (15)	Ecosystem	Protected area as a percentage of total area	Biodiversity	Sites listed under the World Heritage and Ramsar Conventions Arid ecosystems/ desertification under CCD Biodiversity areas identified and monitored under Article 7, Annex 1 of the Convention on Biological Diversity (CBD)	EN6. Location and size of land owned, leased or managed in biodiversity-rich habitats EN7. Description of the major impacts on biodiversity associated with activities and/or products and services in terrestrial, freshwater, and marine environments
Economic			**Environmental**		
Theme indicator	*Sub-theme*	*Indicator*	*Theme*	*Issue area*	*Indicator*
Consumption and production patterns (4)	Energy use	Annual energy consumption per capita	Energy		EN3. Direct energy use segmented by primary source. Report on all energy sources used by the reporting organization for its own operations, as well as for the production and delivery of energy products (eg electricity or heat) to other organizations. Report in joules

uncertainty and long debates over cause-and-effect relationships. In the midst of complexity, we will have to continue the international effort to refine and use integrated indicators that reflect both achievements in the form of leading practices, as well as integrated indicators that reflect *un*sustainable pressures that should be minimized in a precautionary approach to managing complex systems.

Notes

1   The views expressed are those of the authors and not necessarily those of the Global Reporting Initiative (GRI) or the United Nations Environment Programme (UNEP).
2   See www.globalreporting.org.
3   While some non-governmental organizations (NGOs) have noted limited private-sector participation in the creation of the Aarhus Convention (Hemmati, 2002, p124), it includes a number of requirements of direct relevance to business and industry – for example, Article 5.6, which requires the public dissemination of privately held information when the activities of operators (read companies) have a 'significant impact' on the environment.
4   Of 41 core MEAs, UNEP provides the secretariats of 22, which include 12 of the 18 global MEAs and 10 of the 22 regional MEAs.
5   Voluntary initiatives are non-legislatively required commitments or obligations agreed to by one or more organizations, often by companies making commitments to improve their environmental performance beyond legal requirements (see OECD, 1999, and Utting, 2000, pp29–32).

Chapter 6

Locating the Government's Bottom Line

Jonathon Porritt

Any book about triple bottom line (TBL) reporting is going to have to take stock of the ongoing usefulness of the concept of the triple bottom line and the way in which the government is helping to frame both legislative frameworks and the broader 'political discourse' to embed TBL thinking across society as a whole. Though this whole agenda is *not* driven exclusively by government interventions, the role of government in promoting the kind of sustainable, responsible wealth creation that triple bottom line thinking points to is absolutely crucial. I will return to that area of concern in the second half of this chapter.

Historically, as a business-friendly rhetorical device, there's no doubt that it has played an extremely important role in encouraging companies to rethink performance management and reporting techniques (at a technical level), as well as to explore the role of business in society more broadly (at a strategic level). It has sensitized business leaders and senior managers to the idea that all sorts of different people and organizations (or 'stakeholders') have all sorts of different expectations of business, and that it makes good business sense to address these expectations proactively and rigorously. Any interim summary of the catalytic role of TBL in establishing and 'popularizing' the concept of responsible and sustainable business practice would therefore be a positive one.

So much for the past. As to the present, it is still widely used in business circles, often in informal, unsystematic ways, to convey general support for the idea of more responsible and sustainable business practices. And sometimes it is used as a formal performance management and reporting framework. Operationally, it therefore remains useful to a lot of companies (and commentators in the media), not least because of its accessibility (people just 'get it' without necessarily understanding what an environmental bottom line might look like, let alone a social one!), and plasticity (wisely, no attempt has been made to standardize TBL performance management or reporting methodologies as such).

Its role in the future, however, is a different story. Among many of the companies with which Forum for the Future works, there is a sense that TBL has had its day, and is already being superseded by a number of alternative concepts and frameworks (such as the Global Reporting Initiative or GRI, the 'Five Capitals Framework' and SIGMA used by Forum for the Future), as well as customized adaptations that are moving well beyond the original concept. What's more, the investment community would appear to have found TBL reporting to be of limited usefulness, continuing to focus predominantly on the financial bottom line (for perfectly sound reasons within today's capital markets), discounting data on the environmental and social bits as immaterial (at best) or entirely irrelevant (at worst).

As it happens, these strictures could be levelled against *any* integrated reporting practice as far as the investment community is concerned. So, it may well be worth asking the heretical question: will it ever be any different? Indeed, *should* it ever be any different?

It's becoming increasingly apparent to me that all of the good endeavours of many organizations (including the Forum for the Future's own Centre for Sustainable Investment) to demonstrate to analysts and fund managers that the business case for sustainable development is a great deal stronger than it is currently perceived to be are up against much more fearsome barriers than might at first have been apparent. 'Culture clash' may be an overused concept; but the experience of protagonists on both sides of this particular fence (the investment community and the sustainable development community) has predominantly been one of mutual incomprehension, conceptual disconnection and flawed discourse.

Notwithstanding some important attitudinal shifts in more recent times (not least because of the 2001 Pensions Act requiring pension fund trustees to declare their policy on taking proper account of the environmental, social and ethical aspects of their investment decisions), advocates for more responsible business still can't understand why the City doesn't take all of these issues a great deal more seriously, and people in the City still can't understand what they're all banging on about.

But is that so surprising? After all, despite the mystique with which some people imbue their job, analysts are just glorified number-crunchers, shifting huge volumes of financial data to make judgements about the future prospects – from a strictly financial point of view – of one company relative to other companies in their sector, and in the market as a whole. They lay claim to considerable expertise in the exercise of that task, though any objective analysis of their performance in that regard leaves one wondering quite how they command such eye-wateringly generous recompense.

Be that as it may, they operate in a pragmatic and narrow-focus way in the fundamentally amoral milieu of the City. They are not required to make judgements about a company's moral worth (unless, for some reason, the quality of a company's senior management team or chief executive officer is under scrutiny because of some perceived moral – rather than legal or financial – failings) and are expected to be familiar with a company's environmental and social performance only in so far as it has a material influence on financial performance.

This influence may be *direct*, affecting bottom line performance in terms of costs saved (through eco-efficiency measures, for example) or additional costs incurred (through liability claims on issues such as asbestos or other pollution impacts), or *indirect*, affecting reputation or brand value in some way that would negatively impact future shareholder value.

But materiality is a harsh taskmaster, and most analysts remain unpersuaded that even the most conscientious quantification of benefits derived from more environmentally and socially responsible behaviour will come up with a set of figures that bears materially on overall financial performance. For very large companies, even eco-efficiency savings of tens of millions of pounds over time will, in themselves, fall below the usual materiality threshold that analysts will be working to in that sector. They may well have a secondary 'proxy' value to analysts in as much as they can be interpreted as indicative of consistent quality leadership in the company. However, analysts may well choose to use other proxies with which they are much more familiar, rather than drawing conclusions from a proxy measure about which they themselves feel so uncertain.

This may explain why most companies seem to take little trouble to calculate the financial benefits arising from their endeavours to perform more sustainably. Explicitly or implicitly, they deem the tangible benefits to be too small to bother with, and the intangible benefits too vague or 'subjective' to persuade analysts that they are going to make a real difference to future earnings, although the different case studies referred to by Rupert Howes in Chapter 10 demonstrate just how powerful a practice this can be in terms of reinforcing the business case. More work clearly needs to be done on demonstrating the linkage between the intangible benefits of operating more sustainably and competitive advantage, this being the 'missing link' that is most likely to make analysts engage more systematically.

At the moment, however, even when such efforts are made, companies know all too well that the vast majority of analysts are insufficiently expert in their own understanding of social responsibility or environmental sustainability to make any useful judgements as to materiality. It may well be true that those intangibles all come down to 'reputation, reputation, reputation'; but what special skills do analysts have to assess those societal factors that influence corporate reputation? They were hardly appointed on the basis of that particular skill set, after all. And their track record in this area (Enron, British Energy and so on) is more or less laughable.

Beyond that, does it actually make sense to try and assess the value of a company's contribution to sustainable development through the narrow lens of its impact on future earnings? That, it seems to me, is the conundrum now facing the Corporate Reporting Group set up by Patricia Hewitt to offer guidance on precisely this question of materiality. Having bottled out of mandating social and environmental reporting for all large companies, the Department of Trade and Industry (DTI) is now stipulating that companies will need to demonstrate that they have taken 'proper account of factors material to an assessment of the business's future prospects'. To which the first (and most important) question is material to whom?

The proportion of any sustainability-related benefit that accrues to a company's shareholders may be tiny in comparison to the proportion that accrues to society as a whole, or to the communities in which that company is based, or even to such remote stakeholders as future generations or other life forms. Reducing that broad societal value into the narrow monetized coinage used by financial analysts is surely a self-defeating exercise?

That's the paradox. Due to a lack of any equivalent grouping of social analysts or environmental analysts or ethical analysts, using equivalent levels of expertise in these areas to compare relative company performance, huge efforts are made to convert what are essentially 'public societal goods' into the metric of 'essentially private financial benefits'. That doesn't in any way invalidate the importance of demonstrating the real business benefits of engaging proactively in more sustainable and socially responsible behaviour – without which companies will continue to find it almost impossible to move as fast as they now need to; but it does put even the most powerful business case for sustainable development in a more appropriate framework.

So, is that where initiatives such as Business in the Environment's (BIE's) Index of Corporate Engagement, the FTSE4Good and the Dow Jones Sustainability Indices come into play? Only to a limited extent. People don't invest in companies primarily to help create a better world; they make those investments primarily to make money. If data about relative social and environmental performance help investors to make money with fewer negative externalities, so much the better. But notwithstanding the enormously encouraging growth in ethical and socially responsible investment (SRI) funds, it seems improbable that the rather limited pressure from investors that this represents is going to be the deciding factor in transforming business behaviour.

And that may well have something to do with some rather common misperceptions of what it means to invest in equity markets. Capital is not really being allocated to companies for wealth creation (through direct investments in those companies), but for capital accumulation through the shares of those companies. According to figures from the Federal Reserve in the US, about US$1 in US$100 trading on Wall Street actually reaches companies. The other US$99 is all speculatively invested. In 1999, the value of new stock sold was US$106 billion; the value of all shares traded was US$20.4 trillion.

Analysts do, of course, have a critical role to play in this business of capital accumulation (and can just as easily get it right or wrong); but they are only marginally influencing the flow of capital into 'good' or 'bad' corporate behaviour, as such. In that respect, if not in every respect, the description of today's capital markets as a 'casino economy' is a reasonable one, populated as they are by a large number of gamblers, hedgers and speculators, out to make as fast an honest (and occasionally dishonest) buck as they can. In which case, isn't it perhaps a little bizarre to look to this particular set of relationships (focused as they are on legitimate but essentially speculative financial gain) to drive more responsible business behaviours through the inherently inadequate device of TBL reporting?

To which, I suspect, the answer is both 'yes' and 'no'. 'Yes', if people put too much faith in it as a driver (when, in reality, it's just one driver among many, and relatively less important than some of the other drivers); but 'no' if it helps to bridge the divide between the business of creating wealth and the imperative of finding ways of living sustainably on this planet. And 'no', again, if governments are thinking creatively about using this driver (as I alluded to at the start of this chapter) to get things done more effectively via this particular route rather than via any other.

It is my firm belief that they aren't. In *Government's Business: Enabling Corporate Sustainability* (Cowe and Porritt, 2002), we identified all sorts of ways in which the UK government is falling short not just on this narrow front, but across the whole terrain of corporate social responsibility. The 'mosaic of intervention' available to it is, as yet, used hesitantly, uncreatively and with no real sense of any overarching vision of what 'sustainable wealth creation' might really mean.

It is ludicrous to deny the importance of consistent leadership from government in such matters – as is argued by many right-wing commentators on the grounds that less fettered markets provide much clearer signals of what is asked of business or the investment community by consumers and investors. Unfortunately, the price we pay for things in those markets does not reflect the true cost of bringing them to market; in the face of such imperfect information and systemic market failure, governments have no choice but to intervene in framing the parameters within which the investment community and business, in general, must operate.

BOX 6.1 UK GOVERNMENT QUALITY OF LIFE INDICATORS

Economic

H1 Economic Output
GDP per head (UK)
H2 Investment
Total and social investment (UK)
H3 Employment
Percentage of people of working age in work (UK)

Social

H4 Poverty and Social Exclusion
Selected indicators of poverty and social exclusion
H5 Education
Level 2 qualifications at age 19 (UK)
H6 Health
Expectancy of good or fairly good health (Great Britain)
H7 Housing Conditions
Households in non-decent housing (England)
H8 Crime
Recorded crime (England and Wales)

Environment

H9 Climate Change
Emissions of greenhouse gases (UK)
H10 Air Quality
Days when pollution is moderate or higher (UK)
H11 Road Traffic
Road traffic (Great Britain)
H12 River Water Quality
Rivers of good or fair chemical quality (UK)
H13 Wildlife
Populations of wild birds (UK)
H14 Land Use
Homes built on previously developed land (England)
H15 Waste
Household waste (England and Wales)

Source: DEFRA (1999)

It may be helpful to look, first, at the government's own approach to TBL reporting on its own performance in order to understand why it's unlikely to be championing anything terribly radical for the business community. At one level, the UK government has a seriously good story to tell. It was the first to develop a properly integrated framework for bringing together the key economic, environmental and social elements of sustainable development, and having published its strategy for sustainable development (*A Better Quality of Life*) in

1999. It has issued three annual reports since then (the latest in February 2003) demonstrating progress against 15 headline indicators, comprising its 'quality of life barometer' (see Box 6.1).

No other government does it quite like this – and no government does it quite as well. Sustainable development pundits may quibble about the choice of indicators; but it would be hard to dispute that some simple TBL practice has been introduced into government thinking via this particular mechanism.

But how seriously is it taken? If one looks at the four objectives that underpin the government's sustainable development strategy and 15 headline indicators, a different but closely related materiality issue begins to emerge:

- social progress that meets the needs of everyone;
- effective protection of the environment;
- prudent use of natural resources;
- maintenance of high and stable levels of economic growth and employment.

While the majority of people in government, business, academia and, indeed, society at large are perfectly comfortable with the pursuit of 'high and stable levels of economic growth', and have no reason to suppose that there is any fundamental incompatibility between this and the other three objectives, a vocal, durable minority see in that wording ambiguity, intellectual incoherence and a continuing failure to properly understand the essence of sustainable development and the impact of economic growth as it is measured today.

No one denies that securing the benefits that economic growth brings simultaneously generates both social and environmental externalities of varying kinds and severity. Beyond a certain threshold, those negative externalities effectively reduce economic well-being. Environmentalists argue that they are now so grave (in terms of impact on ecosystems, resource depletion, climate change, biodiversity and so on) as to imperil nature's self-regenerating capacities – and, in the process, imperil humankind's own capacity to improve our quality of life. While ministers are quick to distance themselves from the apocalyptic rhetoric of such an analysis, they now regularly acknowledge the seriousness of the situation and deploy a range of policy levers in an attempt to limit the impact of these externalities – principally through the achievement of increased resource productivity.

But at the heart of today's worsening ecological crisis lies a systemic misperception about the relationship between the Earth and the global economy that has expanded so dramatically over the last 50 years. For most economists and politicians, the global economy has become the centre of reality, *the* overarching system within which all else is subsumed. Human societies, communities, ecosystems and habitats are all seen as sub-systems of that overarching system. As such, there is no inherent reason why that overarching economic system shouldn't go on expanding indefinitely, with constant increases in the throughput of both energy and matter. In an extraordinarily perverse way, the negative externalities that arise from this pattern of growth are seen as more or less 'immaterial' – as being of lesser or zero concern in comparison to the imperative of generating exponential economic growth.

In terms of today's prevailing political economy, such a worldview is not all that surprising. Unfortunately, it ignores both the basic laws of thermodynamics and the natural laws on which all life support systems depend. It also flies in the face of biological reality. However persuasive and dynamic it may be, the global economy is in the first instance a sub-system of human society, which is in itself a sub-system of the totality of life on Earth.

This means that the majority of economists (and the politicians whom they advise) choose to ignore the fact that as an open sub-system of the much larger but essentially closed ecosystem, it is the physical limits of that ecosystem that constrain the speed and scale at which the economic sub-system can expand. In the long run, it *cannot* grow beyond the capacity of the surrounding ecosystem to sustain that growth – and the planet (or overarching ecosystem) cannot grow. What we have is what we've got. Come what may, therefore, the scale of the economic sub-system will eventually be determined by the overall scale of the ecosystem, by its ability to provide high-grade resources and absorb low-grade waste, and by the interdependency of all interlocking elements within that ecosystem.

This does not make all economic growth inherently unsustainable – far from it. But it does mean that we need to fundamentally rethink the dominance of economic growth as *the* driving force in the modern political economy, and to be far more rigorous in distinguishing between the kind of economic growth that is compatible with the transition to a genuinely sustainable society and the kind that absolutely isn't. Optimists here tend to point to the so-called 'invisible environmental hand', where economic growth can actually help to reduce pollution if it accelerates resource productivity at a faster rate than both resource consumption and population growth. Wilfred Beckerman, for instance, asserts that, in the longer run, the surest way to improve your environment is to become rich. The pessimists promptly point to the 'rebound effect' (whereby any additional 'environmental space' created by increased resource efficiency is immediately offset by additional consumption), and simply invite people to re-examine the irrefutable empirical evidence of continuing and worsening ecological damage, much of it at the hands of the richest nations on Earth.

What makes this so hard to read is that our single most important indicator of economic prosperity – namely, gross domestic product (GDP) – obscures the reality of what is actually happening. The standard aggregated index of GDP is used to capture all marketed exchanges and government expenditures, and therefore measures the increase in the economic value of overall production – but *not* decoupled from levels of biophysical throughput that generate increased economic value. So, as we eat up our 'natural capital', or degrade the ecosystem's capacity to renew the kind of natural services upon which we depend, we persist in counting all that destructive economic activity as current (benign) income. At the same time, we also count in many so-called 'defensive expenditures', caused by having to deal with some of the externalities of economic growth, be they environmental (environmental protection and restoration, damage compensation, etc) or social (car accidents, poor health, rising crime, etc).

A number of efforts have been made to come up with a better way of measuring well-being, perhaps the best known of which is the Index of Sustainable Economic Welfare (ISEW). ISEW is an attempt to make a better measure of welfare than GDP by adding to it some measure of untraded benefits, such as unpaid domestic work; by subtracting the value of activities that are traded but do not contribute to human welfare, such as the treatment of pollution-related illnesses; and by correcting for income inequality. The UK's ISEW rose until the mid 1970s, then stayed level, and then began to decline again (while per capita GDP continued to rise). ISEWs calculated for several other developed countries all show the same overall pattern of levelling off and then declining. This overall shape is robust over a wide range of weightings of the contributory factors – a partial answer to valid criticisms that ISEW is a methodological mongrel, made by arbitrarily aggregating incommensurable (and often individually questionable) indicators of very different kinds of things.

It is hard to validate the ISEW curve against comprehensive studies of perceptions of quality of life, since the few surveys that have been done measure changes in people's views of their well-being. However, the accumulated data from many quantitative and qualitative studies that have examined aspects of quality of life do, indeed, suggest that the ISEW's picture of a sizeable gap between GDP per capita measures of welfare, on the one hand, and 'real life' welfare, on the other, is on the right lines.

However, the prospects for this or any other alternative approach (all of which are, essentially, addressing questions of materiality in a radically different way from that which is embedded in today's dominant economic paradigm) getting real purchase in today's political economy are questionable. People have become so accustomed to the notion that 'economic growth solves all' (albeit on the patently inadequate grounds that a bigger overall 'economic cake' means there's more to spread around, or at least more crumbs to trickle down) that to disabuse them of the thermodynamic impossibility of this would exact a heavy political price. Better by far to deny the physically impossible (that biophysical throughput can keep on growing indefinitely) than face the political 'impossibility' of selling in the alternatives.

That is *not* to say that the government doesn't take key social issues (such as health, education and crime) seriously. It does take them very seriously, indeed. To a lesser, but still significant, extent, it has also started to take environmental issues much more seriously. But nothing is taken quite so seriously – deemed to be quite so 'material' – as the pursuit of increased economic growth.

Interestingly, this is not because the concept of sustainability is alien to economists, as many environmental critics have claimed. In fact, the basic understanding of sustainability is inherent within one of the seminal texts of contemporary economics – namely, the work of J R Hicks in 1946 in which he coined the definition of income that has been standard since then: 'the maximum amount that a community can consume over some time period and still be as well off at the end of that period as at the beginning' (Hicks, 1946). In that respect, 'as well off' was explained by Hicks as having the same capacity to generate income during the next year – that is, maintaining capital intact.

Unfortunately, economists then proceeded to ignore stocks of *natural* capital (largely on the grounds that it was either not scarce or could not command a market value as it came to us 'for free') and focused exclusively on the different aspects of human-made capital.

Even when it began to dawn on economists (at the persistent prompting of pioneers such as Herman Daly and David Pearce) that this was unwise, the key issue of substitutability still had to be confronted. Wealth creation is a process that judiciously combines the different kinds of capital to produce the goods and services that people want (and therefore value). There is obviously some scope for substitution between the different forms of capital; but there is a world of difference between maintaining the *sum* of different kinds of capital, in aggregate, and maintaining each stock of capital in its own right. The former position (still dominant in contemporary economics) holds that it's fine to substitute one form of capital for another, and that in most cases there will be no problem about liquidating natural capital just so long as one then invests to create equivalent value in human-made stocks of capital. Exponents of the latter position argue that natural capital and human-made capital are complementary but, increasingly, non-substitutable, or at least only substitutable at the margins.

A basic lack of understanding of how natural systems work lies at the heart of most politicians' and economists' ecological illiteracy, compounded by the fact that disaster would, until now, appear to have been averted. But ecosystems often remain productive even as their resilience continues to decline, masking the inevitability of future collapse unless those systems are allowed to regenerate properly. Though some changes are reversible, many are not. And given our relative ignorance as to the workings of nature, especially when exposed to the impact of exponential economic growth, a much more precautionary approach is clearly advisable. But this is in itself problematic to those intent on maximizing the value to be derived from the conversion or liquidation of natural resources.

With such a yawning conceptual gap at the heart of this – and every other OECD government's thinking – interpretations of materiality in both accounting and political terms are bound to be skewed. It's hardly surprising that the government's genuinely innovative and significant quality-of-life barometer has so little knock-on benefit in terms of enabling both politicians and their electorates to get a better handle on sustainability. By the same token, given their own difficulties in this area, it's hardly surprising that their efforts to promote anything other than rather primitive TBL practice and reporting in business have been so limited.

But I do not believe that this should unduly dishearten us. Awareness always precedes action and, over the last ten years, levels of awareness both within government and the business community (and latterly even within the investment community) have increased markedly. Prime Minister Blair's first-ever speech on sustainable development, at the launch of the *Quality of Life Report* on 24 February 2003, gave ample evidence of just how far things have moved on since the Earth Summit in Rio de Janeiro in 1992. His words certainly give voice to a proper sense of the *materiality* of learning to live sustainably on this planet – even if there is a mighty long way to go before that becomes embedded both across government as a whole and within the business community.

In that broader context, the concept of the triple bottom line would really seem to have come to the end of its useful life, a bold pioneer that struck out into new territory at exactly the right time, made great inroads into the collective corporate consciousness, but should now be generously pensioned off!

Chapter 7

Towards Reporting on the Triple Bottom Line: Mirages, Methods and Myths

Rob Gray and Markus Milne

Introduction

Are individual companies sustainable? Are they contributing to or detracting from the planet's ability to sustain life and to provide fair access to environmental resources for both current and future generations? Are we to believe them when they say, for example, that they place the principles of sustainable development and/or social responsibility at the heart of their strategy? Who could really know?

What we *do* tend to know about organizations – with a fairly high degree of reliability – is the extent to which they are acting with appropriate financial probity. And we know this because organizations are required to provide full statements about their financial performance and these statements are subject to a usually fairly rigorous audit. Only when most organizations of substance are equally required to produce complete, competent and complex statements about their social, environmental and sustainability performance will society be in a position to answer our opening questions. Until that time, we will remain almost entirely ignorant of the extent to which (if at all) organizations are performing to the highest standards of social and environmental stewardship and are being truthful with their claims to probity and propriety.[1]

Thus, in this chapter we wish to briefly address three aspects of the triple bottom line (TBL) debate. Firstly, we wish to consider why reporting and real accountability are essential and why this will require legislation, not voluntary action. Secondly, we want to explore what triple bottom line reporting really should be aiming for – a sort of first pass at what it would look like. Finally, we want to explain why TBL and sustainability reporting are *not* synonyms and thus speculate on some of the things that will be necessary if sustainability reporting is to develop.

Voluntary? Reporting?

The idea of social and environmental reporting is certainly not a new one.[2] However, not only was there very little systematic social and/or environmental reporting by organizations less than two decades ago, but companies, in particular, were actively keen to prevent such issues from being discussed.

The exceptional and innovative upsurge of environmental reporting during the early 1990s (and the less enthusiastic re-emergence of social reporting from about the mid 1990s)[3] provided a platform (albeit a partial and shaky platform) on which moves towards TBL and/or sustainability reporting could be built.[4] The developments in reporting brought very significant changes with them. It became fairly commonplace to hear chief executive officers (CEOs) and boards discussing social responsibility, sustainability, triple bottom line sustainability and so on. So much so that one could almost believe that we have arrived in the promised land – a land where the very highest goals of human aspiration (justice, decency and the maintenance and respect for the planet) are at one with the very core values of leading capitalistic enterprises. Without detracting from the achievements of the leading reporting organizations – and, indeed, without detracting from the well-deserved accolades that they have received – there are a number of reasons why such a conclusion would, we suggest, be more than a little premature.

Firstly, companies have successfully opposed the introduction of mandatory social and environmental reporting (for example, in the UK during the 1970s and in New Zealand during the 1990s). They can just as successfully withdraw their support now should current fashion for 'stakeholders' change (see, for example, Mayhew, 1997; Beder, 1997). This is because reporting is currently a voluntary phenomenon in most countries.[5] Voluntary regimes of reporting only achieve widespread high-quality and permanent changes if the volunteers include most of the population and can be relied upon to remain fully and permanently committed (we are unaware of any evidence to encourage such optimism); or the regulatory authorities – whether governments, stock exchange authorities or even accounting regulators – can be relied upon to bring substantive regulation into being if the voluntary initiative fails.[6] There is little persuasive evidence of this either.

Secondly, while we very properly celebrate and reward the leading reporters on a worldwide basis, such reporting is only maintained as a regular (annual or biannual event) by very few companies. The total number of companies that have reported at all remains relatively small. The vast majority of companies simply do not report and (all the evidence suggests) will not do so until a firm and substantial regulatory framework is in place – preferably through law. Voluntary systems are only best if, and only if, everybody is willing to volunteer.

Thirdly, the quality – and, especially, the *completeness* – of such social, environmental and sustainability reporting as exists has remained, with a few notable exceptions, fairly low. Environmental reporting has mostly remained partial in scope, rarely covering matters such as ecological footprint, total resource use and so on. The leading edge of reporting has not advanced much beyond the standards set by the pioneers in 1990.[7] Modern (post-1990) social reports cover few stakeholders, tend to cherry-pick elements of news and generally ignore the major social issues that arise from corporate activity, such as lobbying, advertising, increased consumption, distributions of wealth and so on.[8] And, as we shall discuss below, sustainability reports have long had the principal failing that they say little – or, more usually, nothing – about sustainability.

Poor standards of reporting mean that a reader cannot assess to what extent – if at all – an organization has discharged its responsibilities to the environment and to society. Indeed, such reports are, in fact, misleading and certainly do not discharge accountability.

In fact, matters are worse still as reports ignore issues of complexity and context. In other words, the 'social responsibility' of an organization makes no sense taken out of the context of capitalism, local laws and culture. Equally, environmental performance only really makes *environmental* sense in the context of the state and the functioning of wider environmental systems. Current forms of reporting can verge on the meaningless as they are both too simple and devoid of context.

So that, fourthly, and finally, when we hear CEOs and boards openly discussing issues of social responsibility, accountability and sustainability, for example, we are forced to ask: why should anybody believe such statements, claims and assertions? And what is in the mind of people – what do they actually *mean* – when they use these words?

The belief factor is important. Industrial society sensibly regulates companies, directors and, especially, financial reporting and disclosure. It requires the reporting to be subject to an expert attestation. Even so, financial information can prove to be misleading, unreliable or just plain lies. A sensible society would not, therefore, necessarily accept the directors' word when they talk of social or environmental matters. Careful and thorough regulation and auditing of social and environmental information is no less crucial than for financial information. Yet, the evidence is that the quality of attestation normally applied to social and environmental reports (usually voluntarily) is significantly weaker than that applied to financial reports (see, for example, Ball et al, 2000; Milne et al, 2001; Owen et al, 1997; 2000; 2001).[9]

Responsibility, accountability and meaning

So, what *do* organizations mean when they talk of 'responsibility', 'accountability', 'sustainability' and so on?

Social responsibility has proven to be an exceptionally elusive concept for many years (see, for example, Frederick, 1986; McGee, 1998). In essence, if it is defined in a way that suits business (for example, according to what is possible within the current activities and goals of business), it ends up fairly trivial or tautological. If it is defined as an individual would understand it, the concept is clearly unattainable by a financially successful business because responsibility runs against the principles of self-interest upon which most notions of business are predicated. Indeed, it is of note that the two greatest students of capitalism, Karl Marx and Milton Friedman, were in fairly close agreement on this: companies *cannot be* socially responsible. It is, in all probability, entirely unreasonable to ask companies to act in socially responsible ways – they operate in a system (capitalism) that largely penalises non-economic (socially responsible) action when that socially responsible action is in conflict with economic dictates. It is only through the use of laws passed by a civilized society that the organs of capitalism are made to act in 'responsible' ways. Complying with a sensible set of laws then becomes (as Milton Friedman so famously noted) the principal responsibility of business. However, such a restricted sense of responsibility only makes sense if, *and only if,* the companies themselves have little or no influence on the legal process. It is hardly a responsibility worthy of admiration if the organs of capitalism are proud to comply with the rules that they, themselves, established.

The same is true of sustainability. It looks exceptionally likely that the current form of capitalism is not sustainable – it is, after all, based on private property rights, growth and expansion, competition, maximizing consumption of non-essentials, maximizing returns to shareholders and directors and so on (see, for example, Gladwin et al, 1997). These are not the characteristics of a sustainable economic system in the Brundtland (UNWCED, 1987) sense of the word. It seems profoundly implausible that an individual company could be sustainable (or responsible) in an unsustainable (or irresponsible) system (see, for example, Thielemann, 2000).

This is where accountability comes into play in such an important manner. Accountability is the principle of providing to society the information about which it has a right to know. Society has a right to know about the extent to which its principles and tenets are being complied with and how its environmental resources are being looked after. These are fairly basic rights in any democracy. However, organizations, in general, and business, in particular, by making claims that, for example, they are acting in entirely responsible ways and/or that society and the environment are safe in their hands, are challenging society's right to legislate over these issues. In doing so, businesses are, by default, establishing that society has a right to know the extent to which these claims are valid ones.

Reporting – and especially triple bottom line reporting and sustainability reporting – is about the discharge of that accountability. Such reporting, *most importantly*, will allow society – and the stakeholders, in particular – to judge the extent to which large organizations, in particular, are meeting the duties placed upon the organization (typically the law) and the extent to which they are – or *are not* – meeting the standards that they set for themselves or claim for themselves. Social and environmental accountability will demonstrate the extent to which large organizations *cannot be* socially or environmentally responsible or sustainable as a result of, for example, a conflict between moral and financial criteria.

Few organizations are willing, voluntarily, to undertake this sort of reporting. However, without such reporting, it is not at all obvious that society can sensibly re-examine its laws in order to reconsider whether the system – the rules of the game – are, indeed, those that produce a just society.

Triple bottom line

The triple bottom line (Elkington, 1997) captures a simple but important idea: if an organization is, indeed, a social and environmental entity, as well as an economic/financial entity, then it needs to report upon (if not control) its social and environmental activities in the same way as it reports upon its financial activities. The result of a real TBL report would be an annual report of a company comprising equal sections on financial, social and environmental accountability – giving the social and environmental interactions equal billing with the financial.

At the heart of the idea of TBL reporting is a subtle tension: it is virtually impossible to imagine many situations in which a conflict of interests between financial expedience and social or environmental responsibility will result in the social or environmental being given precedence over the financial. Indeed, an organization in modern capitalism is designed to follow the financial; to the extent that it does not, it will be 'penalised by the market'. Fineman (1994; 1996; 1997), for example, examines how corporate executives in the automotive, chemical, power and supermarket sectors are dealing with environmental issues.

He suggests that the bureaucracy of corporations translates environmental issues into public relations issues, engineering problems, legal challenges, matters for accounting or marketing projects. The environment in the corporation is 'everywhere and nowhere'. He concludes that:

> *Corporate environmentalism as an ethically green cultural response is largely a myth. It fits uneasily into the current realities of trading and corporate governance. 'Business and the environment' is often a gloss that disguises practices which are more like 'business or the environment'* (Fineman, 1994, p2).

A company must be managed for the financial bottom line, otherwise there will be no company and the well-intentioned directors will be looking for another job. The social and environmental dimensions of the business will be – and, indeed, can be – introduced only within:

- zones of discretion;[10]
- where there is no apparent conflict with the financial; or
- where social and/or environmental issues actually have positive financial benefits (the win–win situations; Walley and Whitehead, 1994).

A TBL report that was honest and complete would expose this tension and the fact that the financial does – and must – dominate.

So, a triple bottom line report – to be worth anything at all beyond public relations puff – must contain a substantial and believable social report and a full and audited environmental report.[11] Only in this way can these conflicts and trade-offs be exposed and, ultimately, their causes explored and solutions considered.

A *full* social report can be approximated through the stakeholder model. It has been argued elsewhere (see, for example, Gray et al, 1997) that it is relatively easy to make an initial specification of an organization's potential accountabilities through the application of the stakeholder model. Then, for each organization–stakeholder relationship identified, several levels of information are required to approach a full accountability. These levels are, at their simplest:

- descriptive information about the relationship between the organization and the stakeholder (for example, numbers and categories of employees);
- the accountability that society requires through law and quasi-law (for example, health and safety data);
- the accountability that the business wishes to express (for example, the activities of employees outside work); and, finally,

- the accountability that the stakeholders themselves wish to see (for example, the state of those made redundant).

Each party – company, society and stakeholder – is thus given a voice in the process.

A *full* environmental report can be approximated through the application of a broad eco-balance to the reporting organization. This records all inflows, outflows and leakages and thus captures most – if not all – environmental interactions. Coupled with the reporting of ecological footprints (see, for example, Wackernagel and Rees, 1996), this will provide a fairly substantial picture of the organization's environmental stewardship.[12]

Such reports, together with the traditional (or possibly even simplified)[13] financial statements, would, we believe, bring us as close to triple bottom line accountability as we can currently achieve.

The TBL remains an ideal that shows us where real accountability – so widely discussed – might actually lie. Unfortunately, the TBL report remains something of a mirage, and will continue to be so as long as the debate about, and the practice of, social and environmental reporting continue to owe more to rhetoric and ignorance than to practice and transparency.

Sustainability? Reporting?

What social and environmental reporting, TBL or otherwise, cannot tell us is the extent to which the organization is contributing to, or detracting from, sustainability. A full social report might indicate stakeholders' preferences for dialogue, for example; but it does not tell us to what extent the organization has increased or decreased income inequality, freedom of access to environmental resources and so on. Equally, a full environmental report may tell us about the overall footprint of the organization; but while this may give us a clue, it does not tell us directly about whether or not environmental sustainability is better or worse off as a result of the organization's activities for the year.

A TBL report may be a necessary condition for sustainability reporting; but it is not a sufficient condition. It can only be the most oblique approximation of a sustainability report.

Elsewhere (Gray and Milne, 2002) we have argued that sustainability reporting requires a systems level of thinking and analysis that most economically driven organizations will find impossible to accomplish. Sustainability, as we understand the concept, implies the need to consider the scale of development relative to the available resource base; the fairness with which access is provided to those resources and the outputs from them, both among current generations and between current and future generations; and the efficiency with which resources are used (see, for example, Daly, 1992; Wackernagel and Rees, 1996). While organizations can adapt to issues such as eco-efficiency (for example, resource management), they find it much more difficult – even impossible – to address issues of equity, social justice (Gray and Bebbington, 2000) and the scale of their development.

As Paul Hawken (2002) illustrates with reference to the Global Reporting Initiative (GRI) report from McDonald's Foods:

> *The question we have to ask is what is enough? Is it enough that one in five meals in the US is a fast food meal? Does that satisfy McDonald's?... Does McDonald's want to see the rest of the world drink the equivalent of 550 cans of soda pop as do Americans?... They won't answer those questions because that is exactly their corporate mission... A valid report on sustainability and social responsibility must ask the question: what if everybody did it? What would be the ecological footprint... What is McDonald's footprint now? The report carefully avoids the corporation's real environmental impacts. It talked about water use at the outlets, but failed to note that every quarter-pounder requires 600 gallons of water... An honest report would tell stakeholders how much it truly costs society to support a corporation like McDonald's.*

A serious sustainability report would have to include a report on the organization's contribution to/detraction from environmental sustainability; and a report on the organization's contribution to/detraction from social sustainability.

The work of Bebbington and the Centre for Social and Environmental Accounting Research (CSEAR) (Bebbington et al, 2001; Bebbington and Gray, 2001; Gray and Bebbington, 2001; Bebbington, 2001) and, more recently, Forum for the Future (Howes, 2001), for example, has shown real progress towards measures that can be used to estimate the degree of environmental *un*sustainability of an organization's activities. Although such methods expose the difficulties inherent in attempts to measure something this complex and, indeed, suggest that succinct, single-point estimates of such measures are unlikely to be possible, they do demonstrate what we more or less knew – companies are not currently sustainable and probably cannot be sustainable under the current system of economic and financial organization.

Social sustainability is altogether more difficult to conceptualize and estimate. It is also a great deal more obviously political as it rests on nothing less than interpretations and explanations of the relationships between modern capitalist activity and social justice – the probability of a consensus on this area seems slim, indeed. Nevertheless, it is just such fundamental relationships that need to be explored and discussed if sustainability is ever to be a serious goal.[14]

There is a more basic problem, though, in that there must be some doubt over the extent to which the concept of sustainability can actually be applied at the organizational level.

Sustainability is primarily a global concept – to isolate the contribution to/detraction from that state by individual economic units – although reflecting the current nexus of power and control requires a calculus of such awesome complexity as to rather defy belief. It may well be that we can think of sustainability, to a degree at least, as relevant at local ecosystem level and examine factory/site and organizational impact at that level. But such excursions must be, at best, crude estimates. More significantly, it is, of course, not the impact of individual organizations that matters but the interactions and total impacts that a range of organizations has on an ecosystem's carrying capacity. This requires a level of analysis that is quite different from the analysis assumed by organizational reporting, and one that requires decision-taking and action to be operable at, for example, local, ecosystem and/or national level – not at the level of organization itself.

This means that if sustainability is really our goal, then the place for the principal control over resources, their use and their distribution is *not* the company or other organization, but some other geographic or community level. There is currently no political will or wherewithal to set about wresting power from corporations and returning it to communities and ecosystems! Consequently, we do well to remember that while we may, eventually, be able to account at the organizational level for elements of *un*sustainability and for contributions to/detractions from social justice, a full account of sustainability may simply make no sense at an organization level.

Conclusions

We live in exciting, if confusing, times. This is not least because we are involved (or we hope we are involved) in the great experiment to make modern, European-based, capitalist societies less unsustainable and, if the gods smile upon us, to make our ways of economic and financial organization sustainable.

In terms of social and environmental TBL and sustainability reporting, we conclude that there are five developments that would advance the cause of sustainability and accountability through, primarily, seeking to match the level of informed discussion and the level of activity with the level of hopeful rhetoric and optimistic assertion.

In the first place, we need to develop a more analytical and sceptical understanding of what is meant by 'social responsibility', 'environmental stewardship' and 'sustainability'. Until reporting organizations use these, and related, terms in the ways in which they are more commonly understood, hubris, confusion and just plain deception will dominate over transparency and clarity.

Secondly, we need firm, sensible and comprehensive legislation requiring all large organizations to report fully and honestly. This will take the burden off the few leading-edge companies and make comparable and reliable social and environmental reporting the norm as opposed to the exception.

Thirdly, we need to formally recognize that TBL reporting is a potentially achievable – but very rarely achieved – goal. We now know enough to define what a first pass at a TBL report would look like. But progress towards this goal is not helped by empty rhetoric. Only when the practice of TBL reporting becomes widespread will we learn about the substance of the reporting issues and the challenges that such a development will make on regulators, reporters and stakeholders.

Fourthly, there is good work being done in trying to establish some of the parameters of sustainability at the organization level. This 'good' work contrasts crucially with other, entirely misleading, work that has no connection with any concept of sustainability with which we are familiar.[15] Such capture and emasculation of sustainability is a crucial impediment to any real progress. More commentators need to explicitly recognize this distinction and keep it to the fore of all discussions of social and TBL reporting.

Finally, we need to learn that sustainability is a systems – not an organizational – concept. Our current systems of financial and economic organization lead us to try and relate all important matters to the level of current organizations because it is here that power and decision-making seem to lie. But nature and ecology know nothing of our companies and institutions. If we are to return to some notion of harmony with our ecological roots, we will need to reconceptualize our decision-making and probably our institutions and organizations along ecological lines. Ecology, clearly, will not reconfigure along our modern institutional lines.

Above all, we need to try for more clarity and more honesty, and (for this to happen) we need to start to regulate our economies in ways that privilege life, justice and the environment and to see economics and finance only as a means, not as the end. Because if we don't, they will be!

Notes

1   Most prominent among these claims are, *inter alia*, the World Business Council for Sustainable Development (WBCSD) and the Dow Jones Sustainability Index, which invariably seem to suggest that not only is reporting in good shape, but that regulation of such reporting would be an entirely unnecessary infringement of the wealth-making activities of business. Such suggestions are not just misleading; they are also dangerous in that they can lull stakeholders, society and regulators into a

false sense of complacency – when there is, by definition, no evidence on which to base such a complacency! To illustrate the point, consider the following quotes taken (and not out of context) from the *Dow Jones Sustainability Group Indexes Report Quarterly 3/99*:

> *The performance of companies implementing sustainability principles is superior because sustainability is a catalyst for enlightened and disciplined management... The concept of corporate sustainability has long been very attractive to investors because of its aim to increase long-term shareholder value.*

These statements are perniciously, outrageously and blatantly untrue; but there they are, out in the public domain, in a widely distributed and widely followed and admired indexing system. The statements seem to be accepted when, at best, there is no evidence to support them and, at worst, they are breathtakingly untrue.

2   ASSC (1975) and see Gray et al (1996) for a summary.

3   See ACCA (2002). For an historical overview, see Gray and Bebbington (2001) or Gray et al (1996).

4   See, for example, Gray et al (1995) and Hackston and Milne (1996) for reviews of reporting developments.

5   See UNNGLS and UNRISD (2002) for more detail on developments in regulation.

6   This is a sceptical view of voluntary regimes that suggests that their success should not be measured in changes in reporting practice but in changes in the *appearance* of reporting practice and in their ability to persuade regulators that regulation is not necessary.

7   See, in particular, the ACCA reporting awards and the *Report of the Judges, 2001*, on the *ACCA and Sustainability* CD-ROM published in 2002.

8   This is one of the major difficulties that the GRI has failed to overcome. Most social reports are not social reports at all, they are 'employee reports' or, in some cases, 'employee, consumer and local community reports'. (See, for example, Owen et al, 1997; 2000; 2001).

9   Social and environmental attestation fees are only rarely disclosed, so we have to rely on circumstantial and hearsay evidence to understand the work levels that are undertaken. Consultants, in addition to being untrained, are probably not sufficiently remunerated to undertake appropriate levels of work within the organization.

10   Where there is sufficient economic 'elbow room' to take 'uneconomic' choices. These will often be very small relative to the organization as a whole, and smaller for quoted companies.

11   Audit is a necessary, but not sufficient, condition for a reliable report. The fact that financial audit and the current state of social and environmental report 'verification' are poor simply tells us about the quality of auditing, not the principles of auditing (see, for example, Ball et al, 2000).

12   A related concept is the 'carbon footprint', whose reporting is becoming more common.

13   Increasing the importance of social and environmental statements may involve reducing the importance of – and emphasis given to – financial statements.

14   See Henriques (2001) for one approach.

15   Paul Hawken (2002) is especially expansive on this point in relation to McDonald's and the GRI.

Chapter 8

Good Intentions – Bad Outcomes? The Broken Promise of CSR Reporting

Deborah Doane

The promise behind corporate social responsibility (CSR) is a broken one. Conventional wisdom holds that 'what's good for business is good for society'. But not only has CSR failed to bring us the vision of leadership we expected, it has also fallen short in delivering more sustainable companies.

The New Economics Foundation (NEF) was a pioneer in the field of social auditing and reporting during the early 1990s, with a view that it would ultimately lead to companies that considered their social and environmental impact to be as important as their financial outcomes. 'The challenge is to create the conditions where social and environmental benefits go hand in hand with competitive advantage', remarked NEF in a study for the Association of Chartered Certified Accountants (ACCA) on the subject during the late 1990s (Gonella et al, 1998). Certainly, over the past couple of years – especially since the establishment of the pensions legislation two years ago – we've witnessed the conditions under which reporting appears to have taken off. From fewer than 25 reporters in the UK just two years ago, consultancy group Econtext reports that there are now 103 reporters from the FTSE250 (Saltbaxter and Context, 2002), and SustainAbility finds 234 reporters globally. But the quantity says very little about quality. Repeated studies, including SustainAbility's *Global Reporters Survey* released in November 2002, confirms that there is little meaningful reporting out there that really grapples with the triple bottom line (TBL) question (SustainAbility and UNEP, 2002a).

Perhaps this has been due to the limitations of CSR. Its incentives are the market, and market incentives will mean that a company uses certain levers, such as reputation, as the leading driver. Consequently, rather than NEF's (and others') original aim of seeing companies rewarded for making a more positive contribution to society and the environment, the results of reporting have, instead, brought us a litany of oxymorons: British American Tobacco is being considered part of the Dow Jones Sustainability Index, in part because it issues a social report. Apparently, the long-term impacts of tobacco on health are good for society. In a similar vein, British Petroleum is hailed as the most socially responsible oil company – despite its strong-arming the Turkish government to develop an oil pipeline and despite the fact that it aims to increase oil production and sees no immediate profitability in renewable energy.

Most absurd is that British Aerospace (BAE) is now trying to be the world's most responsible arms manufacturer, having just issued its first social and environmental report. In it, it talks about exemplary environmental initiatives – for example, reducing harmful chemicals on guns. At the same time, a new advertising campaign touts its remote bomb-dropping technology (named 'Nora', or 'nagging Nora', to the fighter pilots) as just one of the ways in which BAE makes the world a safer place. This isn't just silly: it's absurd.

Corporate social reporting was not about trying to mask the negative impacts of a company by turning them into a 'good' – that is, a safe war; it was about trying to ensure that we hold companies to account for their wider impacts and, in the long run, about rewarding those companies who genuinely contribute to a sustainable society.

Yet, in spite of the increasing uptake in reporting, we have not exactly been led down the so-called 'virtuous path'. In fact, we appear to be going in the opposite direction. Certainly, a plethora of CSR initiatives have been introduced since reporting was in its infancy, and the consultancy basis for CSR programmes and triple bottom line reporting is growing. But while the number of papers, programmes, seminars, conferences and consultancies on the subject grows in size, the depth of these approaches has not kept pace. Sadly, reporting remains an exercise in managing public perceptions of a company, with the outcome being a company 'doing what it can', rather than 'what it should'.

It should be no surprise, then, that civil society groups, among others, are getting impatient and not waiting for the market to deliver quality reports. Thus, 2002 saw the launch of the Corporate Responsibility Coalition (CORE), calling for mandatory social and environmental reporting of all top businesses. Since early in 2003, around 40 leading organizations, from Amnesty International UK, to Christian Aid, Friends of the Earth and the New Economics Foundation, support the coalition, while 287 MPs signed an early day motion (EDM) supporting CORE's aims.

But while legislation is certainly a way to facilitate more meaningful triple bottom line reporting, it will likely only go so far in terms of delivering sustainable development. It's time that we asked ourselves: does business really have the power to change behaviour, or are we caught in an endless cycle that more often rewards bad outcomes over good?

Business being business

When we see an increasing number of companies wanting to report openly on their impacts, joining initiatives such as the UN Global Compact or the UK's Business in the Community benchmarking club, we assume, rightly or wrongly, that the market is working. Indeed, in some cases, the market is managing to bring about more active consciousness about CSR, as with B&Q's sustainable wood products. But while the market delivers consciousness, it does so within the confines of 'shareholder value'. Thus, it rewards behaviour that will have a direct impact on profitability. Companies that can deliver a business case for CSR are far more likely to invest in sustainability programmes, including transparent and honest reporting.

But the outcomes of this can often be perverse. Public relations-driven incentives – which the business case tends to lean towards – may not actually result in real changes in behaviour, as per a few of the examples cited earlier. And we should be wary of assuming that consumers will make decisions based simply on the transparency commitment of a company, let alone their ethical stance. Most research on 'ethical consumption' shows that while a minority of consumers are active in their purchasing decisions, the vast majority are relatively passive – and most are generally only concerned with price. The 2002 Ethical Purchasing Index does confirm that 'deep green' and ethical businesses are growing at a faster rate than the overall market; but they still continue to capture less than 1 per cent of the market in key areas (Co-operative Bank and New Economics Foundation, 2002). A recent study by the Institute of Grocery Distribution shows that 70 per cent of food shoppers base their purchasing decisions on price, taste and sell-by date (Mason and Jones, 2002).

Socially responsible investment (SRI) is also a growing field. But the trend towards 'ethics-lite' investment – investing in the 'best of the baddies' – is increasingly common, and consumers don't generally look below the SRI surface. The recent inclusion of British American Tobacco in the Dow Jones Sustainability Index makes a mockery of CSR and gives evidence to the fact that, at the end of the day, triple bottom line is more like a pyramid scheme, with profit firmly ensconced at the top. Even SRI funds that aim to keep closer to the intentions of socially responsible investment are limited in the companies that they have to choose from. Thus, banking and mobile phones become the norm for many of the leading SRI funds. But the mobile phone industry has yet to come to grips with the health concerns of mobile phone masts and the use of handsets, taking a defensive stance that is reminiscent of the tobacco industry not too long ago. And banking investments only mean that investment in non-sustainable industries is one step removed – with the banks themselves holding investments in companies that the SRI industry would most likely shun. A handful of companies are trying to get to grips with these issues. Morley's Asset Management issued its sustainability matrix recently, which aims to differentiate between those companies who positively contribute to major social or environmental issues, versus those that are more reactive in this area (Morley Vision, 'Socially Responsible Investing', at www.morleyfm.com). But they still continue to be limited in what they can do from a sustainable development perspective. Cable and Wireless is considered one of the top sustainability performers within Morley's matrix. But they're currently being dragged over the coals as they risk losing monopoly-power concessions in developing countries who have held poor people at ransom, but delivered substantial profits to investors. So, investors are pulling out (John, 2002).

The problem is that the short-term incentives of the stock market are simply not compatible with the long-term objectives of sustainability. Consistent drives for quarterly profit figures won't reward companies who are prepared to make long-term and, indeed, expensive investments in things such as poverty eradication or sustainable energy. Nestlé is taking the Ethiopian government to court for US$6 million in spite of the country's current famine crisis. Nestlé's chief executive has in the past, however, vowed to contribute as a business to sustainable development (Crooks, 2002).

Companies themselves are not necessarily to blame. The limitations of the market-based model to deliver are, quite simply, inadequate. We've been led to believe that there is an immediate business case for CSR and real triple bottom line reporting; but the business case extends little beyond arguments that result in gloss over substance. Thus, SustainAbility's findings confirm that while the size of reporting has increased, companies have yet to take on board the more critical triple bottom line issues (SustainAbility and UNEP, 2002a).

Government limitations

A level playing field would certainly make a measurable difference in the way in which companies report on and manage these issues. In the UK, the Company Law Review and its subsequent output, the Government White Paper on Company Law, attempted to reach a compromise on the issue of non-financial reporting. By calling for companies of a certain size to report on social and environmental issues, where it is 'material' to a company's operations, it argues that adequate pressure will be brought to bear on companies to fully disclose their impacts.

But not only would this approach be limited in terms of delivering more sustainable impacts (what is material to business is not commensurate with what is material to society); international pressure, and certainly business pressure from various industry lobby groups, would make it difficult for government to go any further. Perceptions about 'red tape' and yet another layer of bureaucracy see government consistently leaning towards the lowest common denominator approach to regulation on corporate accountability. This is in spite of the fears over repetitions of the various US-style corporate debacles of the past year.

The dance of the slaves

In summary, we're locked into a pattern for which there doesn't appear to be an immediate exit. Government is reluctant to regulate in favour of mandatory reporting and is insistent that business should only report on those impacts that are 'material' to the business. Furthermore, none of the leading CSR-practising companies are prepared to break ranks with their Confederation of British Industry counterparts to support the introduction of a level, accountable playing field to encourage more honest reporting that could ultimately lead to more sustainable performance of business.

The SRI industry can only influence behaviour to a limited extent because it has to make reasonable returns on our investments. And consumers will always only be active for a small part of the time; certainly, the motivations of consumers rarely fall within the altruistic realm. Tony Golding, a leading writer on the City, calls this the 'chain of pressure' (Golding, 2003). I call this a 'dance of slaves', where no one is prepared to take the lead.

Breaking ranks

The failure of CSR reporting to lead to any measurable change is partly a problem of design; reporting has been about process, rather than performance. We also have to continuously remind ourselves that reporting itself is not an end – it is a means. While the CORE campaign advocates for mandatory reporting and stakeholder accountability, people have wrongly assumed that this has led the argument astray. People who are really concerned about the quality of reporting are more concerned about what businesses and others do with this information, once out there. Will they hold the company to account for its actions? Will the behaviour and outputs actually change? Or is it just a discursive method of belying the truth?

The real reason for the current failure of CSR is that we've been fudging the case for triple bottom line reporting. We have to be honest and 'fess up', as they say. It's time that we openly acknowledge that corporate social reporting, and, indeed, CSR as a whole, is about a *public good* outcome – not necessarily a business outcome. While these two may occasionally align themselves, this will not always be the case.

Thus, for any reporting to be meaningful, there has to be some commensurate accountability mechanisms in place to hold company reporting in check. Civil society groups and other stakeholders should be able to ensure that companies don't overstate their claims and, similarly, include issues that may just be a little bit uncomfortable for the company to accept. Public policy – certainly on mandatory reporting – is one way that would immediately deliver more informed, transparent and honest reporting. Perhaps this shouldn't be linked to business reporting ('the business case'); it should be about something wider.

More boldly, it seems, we should return to our original reason for developing reporting in the first place: to tackle big global problems, rather than see business being more 'profitable' by 'doing good'. And with this in mind, one could argue that the reporting prescription itself has led us down a myopic approach that aims to minimize business impacts on society, rather than having more marked effects on the way that businesses operate. To this end, perhaps triple bottom line reporting could only enable us to support 'best in class' of the baddies, rather than anything more.

The corporate social responsibility agenda should be looking to provoke a far more challenging new agenda for business in society. The real question is: what kind of business and institutions do we need in the 21st century to deliver sustainable development? Public concerns – from poverty to health and the environment – become the master, rather than the servant, to business. In asking this question, we are led down an entirely different road than either the hard-nosed approach to regulation or the process-driven reporting prescriptions of the last decade that have become 'CSR'. Not only would such an examination revolutionize our investment in certain types of industries, it could alter the very incentives we use to reward business today. Different forms of corporate governance would most likely emerge, and the monolithic multinational-sized company could well become obsolete.

Critical qualities for sustainable business would be the following:

Transparent and accountable

By transparent and accountable, I'm not referring to the issuing of a 'glossy' report, for which business may mask its negative impacts simply through excluding information from a report. British Petroleum (BP) engaged in an arguably transparent and accountable 'stakeholder dialogue' in Indonesia, regarding the Tangguh liquefied natural gas project. In the stakeholder analysis, comments such as 'We were forced and tricked into selling our land' and 'The potential for BP to benefit is much greater than that for villagers' came up; yet, any negative feedback from the exercise is eliminated from BP's environmental and social report (2001) and there is no opportunity for stakeholders to actually challenge the outcome of the analysis. The project is expected to proceed.

Equally important is for meaningful and accessible information to be made available to all stakeholders, from minor shareholders to communities. If the outcome of a 'stakeholder dialogue' is, on balance, a negative one, and not in the interests of the wider community, then we should be able to hold business to account for this. Yes, profits and shareholders should be taken into consideration, but not at the expense of others with less power.

At the same time, accountability should also extend to business being willing to hold itself open to the appropriate checks and balances entailed in regulation – not simply letting the market work for itself. Business must recognize that if it is to balance the needs of wider stakeholders, a level playing field and a role for government is, indeed, legitimate.

Trustworthy

A trustworthy business is an extension of the transparent and accountable company. But 'trust' isn't something that's done; it is earned. Immediate and honest responses to disasters or product failure are more likely to build trust and retain customers than defensive actions or ones that hide the truth. If a company finds out that it has 'done harm', as in the case of Unilever in India in 2001, then it should immediately disclose the information and aim to mitigate against negative impacts (Corporate Watch, 2001). Of course, more and more, businesses are recognizing this to be the case; but there remains a plethora of examples where the opposite holds true.

Social and environmental goods versus financial ones

I'm not arguing that business shouldn't be profitable; but profits should not be made off the backs of products and services that aren't delivering sustainable outcomes. Sustainable business is not about minimizing the 'bads'; it's about producing 'goods'. Yes, we need an energy company. No, we don't need, in the long run, those that are harmful to the environment. Yes, we need pharmaceutical innovations. No, we don't need those that are only accessible to a small minority, while excluding the majority.

Companies would require having a much more integrated understanding of how their business impacts upon the outside world – and, in turn, how they can have a positive impact on outcomes. To do this requires a real shift in how we measure intangible assets and how we 'internalize' our 'externalities'. Are companies, consumers and government prepared to give equivalent value to non-financial returns? Is this the real triple bottom line? And can we penalize companies who don't? One way is for us to break down our intangible asset base and include 'tangible' social and environmental measures that would see us moving more towards triple bottom line decision-making, rewards and returns.

Stakeholder driven

A radical redefinition of the 'stakeholder' company would seem to be in order. Companies are now operating based on the primary concerns of shareholders. Although the Centre for Tomorrow's Company tried to redefine this by arguing that those companies who considered their stakeholders would ultimately benefit the shareholder, it would seem that the 'enlightened shareholder value' approach continues to produce limited results when it comes to more sustainable outcomes. We don't want companies who just listen to stakeholder concerns, but dismiss these when it contradicts the shareholder value model; we want companies who are prepared to make difficult choices – real trade-offs between financial and social outcomes. Companies must, therefore, be governed by a wider set of stakeholders. But our current form of corporate governance doesn't yet provide for this and directors' duties continue to be focused primarily on the singular bottom line.

Conclusions: corporate social responsibility and sustainable development

With the public's trust in business increasingly on the decline (MacGillivray, 2002), there seems to be an urgent need to restore not only our faith in business, but in the ability of leaders to address the larger sustainable development problems of our time. However, the current deadlock between individual businesses, financial markets, government and, indeed, consumers is unlikely to bring about a change in the way forward.

Two things are essential. Firstly, leading businesses need to break ranks with the lowest common denominator and give government the green light to bring about relevant legislation that would facilitate more rapid change in this area, from encouraging real transparency and reporting to paying for the full costs of environmental and social degradation. Secondly, and perhaps more importantly, business should turn its strategic thinking regarding corporate social responsibility on its head and ask the question: what are the kinds of businesses we need in the 21st century to deliver sustainable development? And in asking that question, business should be shaped in such a way as to really provide the most positive outcomes, as mapped out above. In short, the 21st century needs companies that lead the future – so that others may share in it.

Chapter 9

What a Fine Mess! Moving Beyond Simple Puzzle-solving for Sustainable Development

Rupesh Shah

Introduction

In 1991, the development director of a small UK-based non-governmental organization (NGO) called Living Earth approached Shell International to discuss concerns over the company's operations in South America. Living Earth worked on environmental education initiatives, primarily in the UK. After some time together, the company set up a relationship with the director of Living Earth, using him as a sounding board and consultant to help manage environmental and community issues. This advisory relationship was maintained over Shell's encounters in Brent Spar in the North Sea and in Ogoniland in Nigeria during 1995, when the company was rocked by outrage and criticism of its handling of the environmental and social implications of its operations.

Eventually, the two parties agreed to collaborate on a community development initiative in the Niger Delta of Nigeria. One of the reasons Shell began to engage with NGOs was because of the high esteem in which society

BOX 9.1 LIFE EXPECTANCY IN AFRICA

Life expectancy across Africa is, on average, 45.89 years. In Senegal, where 3 in every 10 children die before their 5th birthday, it is 37 years. In Europe or North America, average life expectancy is just over 75.

Source: The Guardian (2002)

held them (Shah, 2000). However, the specific context in Nigeria also led Shell to recognize the importance of working with NGOs as a conduit in their bond with local communities. Meanwhile, they also felt that their 'licence to operate' had been lost in the region due to an unprecedented level of community disturbance in their oil-producing regions.

In 1999 I was able to engage with Living Earth and Shell as part of my PhD research. My intention was to work with both organizations to bring about some reflection on their partnership in the Niger Delta (and to do the fieldwork required for my PhD). In this chapter I explore the network of relationships between Shell, Living Earth, the communities of the Delta and myself. I relate how these interactions seem, initially, to have had highly managerial and control-oriented dimensions. Such a technocratic approach seems quite often to be the starting point for attempts at addressing the problems of ecologically and economically unsustainable and socially unjust human development. I go on to suggest that by themselves such *technocratic responses* are insufficient for creating a more people-centred and ecologically grounded form of development.

First steps

In its annual report, Shell Nigeria highlighted its relationship with Living Earth as an opportunity for 'partnering for development' (SPDC, 1997, p17). At the outset, I read this and other documentation that was available and had some initial conversations with individuals from the two organizations. With some naivety I thought that the relationship had been a wonderful example of collaboration between NGOs and business, aimed at fostering change and opening the space for more sustainable forms of development.

At the time, other research was beginning to explore the relationships between NGOs and business (Murphy and Bendell, 1997; Long and Arnold, 1995), and I was excited by the chance to document the learning on such a talismanic issue as Shell's community relations in the Niger Delta.

Over the course of a year I spent time with both organizations in the UK and Nigeria and developed a 'learning history' (Roth and Kleiner, 1995; 1998; Bradbury and Lichtenstein, 2000) of their relationship. Through the engagement with both organizations and the communities in the Delta, I

BOX 9.2 CONSUMPTION PATTERNS

There are approximately 14 million species on the planet, one of which consumes 40 per cent of 'potential net primary productivity' (essentially photosynthetic activity).

Source: Vitousek and Ehrlich (1986)

BOX 9.3 MIGRATION INTO GUANGDON PROVINCE

Between 100 and 150 million people are estimated to be moving from rural provinces of China into Guangdon province, a region that now reportedly makes one in three of all shoes sold in the world. This is the greatest migration in human history, in part resulting from consumer demand for cheap manufactured products.

Source: UK Radio 4, July 2002[1]

---

became aware of the difference between the formal external presentation of the partnership and the far more messy realities of the relationship between the company, NGOs and the community in Niger Delta.

Shell's responses to its problems in the Delta were manifold and ongoing. At one level, for example, they initially increased spending on community development activities from approximately US$10 million to US$35 million between 1992 and 1996. Later on the response included the recruitment by Shell of community development experts. Shell Nigeria brought in a number of development professionals from the World Bank and other aid agencies with a remit to help with easing the tensions between the company and communities in the area where the company operated. As Shell attempted to respond to the situation it re-labelled 'community engagement' initiatives within the Delta as 'Shell Partners for Development in the Community' as a way of indicating a shift from 'community assistance' to 'community development'.

Despite such activity, the problems of community disturbance and unrest continued to threaten Shell's ability to operate in one of its most profitable regions. At present, Shell, as well as other Western oil companies operating in the region, continues to put more money into community development activities in order to maintain its 'licence to operate'. Shell and the other oil companies have been shifting the emphasis of their operations from inland oil extraction towards offshore extraction, one implication being the reduced need to interact with communities. However, Shell is still confronted by numerous problems of separation from the communities, alongside whom it operates in the Delta. Recent reports have emerged from the Delta that community disturbance has caused various oil companies to shut down operations in the region and has resulted in a loss of 29 per cent of output.[2]

Straight lines and emerging messes

It seems to me that Shell – an organization with considerable 'engineering' success and expertise – was first minded to respond to the situation in the Delta by considering the simple technical issues that might have been causing the

---

BOX 9.4 RESOURCE DISTRIBUTION

1.2 billion people currently lack clean drinking water. Daily water consumption in Tanzania costs 5.7 per cent of the daily wage; in the US the cost is 0.006 per cent.

US$170 billion would be required to provide clean and healthy sewerage systems for all individuals worldwide. US$350 billion is spent on farm subsidies, primarily in the US, Europe and Japan.

Source: The Guardian (2002)

---

situation. For example, one angle the company took was to respond to what it perceived as the needs of the 'community' by increasing the quantity of community investment. Thus, from a level of approximately US$0.3 million in 1989, Shell's community spending in the Delta rose to US$42.6 million in 1998. From an initial focus upon agricultural extension-type development activities, the new money was channelled into a variety of infrastructure projects, such as the building of schools, hospitals and roads.

This extra money was being spent with the same attitude and culture that had marked the company's engagement with the communities to date. The company's perception of 'community' was understood through a technical and separatist cultural frame that had, arguably, contributed to the conditions for conflict. So, for example, those areas of the Delta in which Shell maintained operations were defined as 'oil-producing communities'; and it was towards these areas that Shell focused virtually all of its initial increased spending. This categorization seems to reveal a set of assumptions that 'community' can be understood as corresponding to discrete pockets of people on plots of land. This can be contrasted to appreciating and working from a more fluid, complex, emergent and 'power-aware' understanding of community. The highly technical nature of the interpretation and initial response to the 'community' is remarkably similar to the way in which oil exploration and extraction areas are separated into discrete 'concessions', without attention to bio-regions or local ecological processes.

I can also see a cultural pattern of a technical and mechanistic attitude in the use of isolated and outside advisers and consultants, such as the community relations department in Shell Nigeria. By maintaining a focus upon changing its relationship with the communities through the work of the community relations department within Shell Nigeria, the majority of the organization (including operational staff) remained excluded from co-constructing the change process. Meanwhile, the use of outside 'experts', such as Living Earth and me, enabled the company to maintain an attempt to separate itself from the activities of the communities.

The overriding flavour of the company's response that I tasted was of a technical approach to managing the situation. The response pattern matched the organization's skill in solving the outward manifestation of problems using its current frames of reference. Moreover, much of Shell's subsequent response to the agenda of sustainability has also been in line with a technical, problem-solving mind-set. Yet, there are suggestions that the culture was shifting, becoming more open to another, less reductionist, mind-set. For example, by attempting to shift the foci towards 'partnership with the communities', there was some sense that mutual interdependencies were present. There was a sense that a *relational attitude* could be more effective than the previously separatist attitude and culture. It suggested that there might be some understanding of the fluid and power-infused aspects of its relations with the communities and wider society. However, the game of changing culture seems to be a difficult one, with many false starts, numerous regressions and considerable uncertainty.

Philosophy, psychology and the triple bottom line

I do not think that Shell's response pattern to the questions posed by current unsustainable development is unique. There is a sense that this technocratic and separatist orientation towards puzzle-solving is deeply cultural and systemic in nature – marking out our language, ways of talking, our institutions and our ways of organizing since the time of the Enlightenment in 18th-century Europe.

In this chapter I have begun to wonder whether a purely technocratic approach to developing responsible business practices is sufficient to address some 'facts and figures' about sustainability issues of our time (see Boxes 9.1 to 9.4).

Given the ever-increasing rate of the emergence of environmental and social problems, the call to find action-oriented solutions (Brown et al, 1997; 1999) has, indeed, been one of sustainable development's loudest and most resonant calls. In this sense the pragmatic responses of business can be applauded and encouraged.

If you understand sustainable development to merely be a call to the 'technocratic management of planet Earth' (McAfee, 1999; Purser, 1994; Shiva, 1989), then perhaps these actions are enough. However, sustainable development has sought out and elicited other voices calling for deeper changes in human societies and systems. In this context, I think we need to find spaces for beginning to explore the issue of *what we think we know*. This is something that comes from our current worldview. These are issues of truths and power that offer to take us beyond simple technocratic fixes towards an appreciation of the deeper systemic and cultural changes that are also required for human development to take on more ecologically sustainable and people-centred dimensions.

Transforming the patterns of 'puzzle-solving' (Kuhn, 1996)

As the example of Shell in Nigeria suggests, unsustainable development can severely threaten business. At the same time, extreme global inequalities have been suggested to offer business with new markets and significant product development opportunities (Cairncross, 1991; Prahalad and Hart, 2001; Schmidheiny, 1992). Since the challenge of changing the currently unsustainable patterns of human development has emerged, parts of the business community, such as Shell, have responded in a variety of practical ways. While various academic communities have devoted considerable attention to the meaning and vision underlying the notion of sustainable development (Ayres, 1998; Murphy, 1996; Nieto and Durbin, 1995; Pezzey, 1992), businesses have been confronted with some of the immediate implications of ecologically unsustainable and inequitable forms of development. They have become busy trying to deal with the issues. Businesses have engaged in measures for eco-efficiency (Shrivastava, 1995), collaborated with environmental and development NGOs (Long and Arnold, 1995; Shah, 2001), sought to source, produce and market ethically and environmentally labelled products and services (Elkington and Hailes, 1988; Hartman and Stafford, 1996), produced reports (Wheeler and Elkington, 2001) and employed auditors to measure and legitimize environmental and social performance (Raynard, Sillanpää and Gonella, 2001). Corporate responsibility departments have been created and various manifestations of professional practice have emerged.

The overriding pattern of these initial moves has been a technocratic orientation that accords with the worldview that has dominated social processes since the Enlightenment. Since that time in 18th-century Europe, a technocratic approach to organizing and understanding has marked out human social processes (Harman, 1996; Tarnas, 1991). This technocratic approach – built upon a patriarchal and mechanical view of the world and a culture of dividing and separating our world in various ways – has been hugely successful in delivering power over the material world. For example, in our language and ways of organizing facts that are separated from and promoted over values, man is separated and elevated from nature, male power is separated from female and the 'Occident' is separated from the 'Orient'. In addition, the 'mechanistic metaphor' maintains an overriding sense of the need and ability for complete control, certainty and mastery of the material conditions of life for human happiness and development.

However, for me and many others, what is required is other than 'images of economists and policy experts sitting in a computerized control room, coolly pushing buttons and pulling levers, guiding the planet to something called sustainable growth' (Orr, 1992, p53). It requires something more than pictures of businessmen assuming new ways of controlling the ecological and social conditions of life. These problems are more than a call for simply solving the next puzzle since they also require culturally oriented transformations in our current ways of thinking, being and knowing. They involve changing how we look at puzzle-solving and changing the puzzles that we are interested in solving. Such attempts to change culture require some form of investigation into the assumptions about *what we think we know*, assumptions that are automatically and continually affecting all of our actions and interactions.

'There is nothing so practical as a good theory' (Kurt Lewin)

We are not terribly comfortable dealing with issues of truth and power. I was warned by one of the editors of this book to avoid 'too heavy a philosophical stance' in this chapter for fear that readers would skip over it; this is a practical book for managers that must offer them ways forward.

I can appreciate the perspective. When I read such figures as I have cited in Boxes 9.1 to 9.4, I often feel a call to arms to get busy and make an immediate impact upon such apparently disturbing realities. However, after some time spent wondering about the meaning of the figures, I find the call to pragmatism is accompanied by another, deeper rumbling noise. This evokes the systemic, mental and cultural patterns of the issues. It asks for time spent with myself and others, enquiring into how we make sense of, and give meaning to, our lives, our spirituality, our humanity and our values, and how we are trying to live with them. This must compete with the sharp cry, above all, to be practical and provide solutions that people can implement. Whatever you do, don't talk about theories and philosophy.

However, we are continually working with philosophy, metaphysics and our theories about the world. It is just that, for the most part, we are not aware of the influence that our assumptions about truth, knowledge and power have upon our actions. Therefore, an attempt to look at the theories we use in our lives and where they come from is a task of some considerable significance.

For instance, I could look back at the figures and wonder about how I had read the information. Perhaps, I could ask myself: 'How can I be clear that there is no agenda behind this information?' or 'Who provided these messages and why?' I may, with some more focused energy, notice the silent way in which I integrate certain messages from the information within my way of looking at and interpreting the world. I may find that I stick to interpretations that comfort my ideas about the world, rather than turning towards possible interpretations that cause discomfort and challenge. These are marshy lands where the clear call to pragmatic action that I initially heard becomes dulled by a fog of doubt and uncertainty.

It seems to be far easier to revert to yet more *monstrous* forms of technocratic puzzle-solving – particularly when cultural messages, institutions and patterns of social organization are currently repeating the *value* of this way of sense-making. Yet, increasingly we find that truth and power are both troubled and troubling issues for us. We need to begin to learn how to play with them in order to transform them, our puzzle-solving activity and ourselves.

Puzzle-solving 'in here'

The scientist, the scholar, the missionary, the trader or the soldier was in, or thought about, the Orient because he could be there, or could think about it, with very little resistance from the Orient's part (Said, 1978, p7).

While I was in the Nigeria I had two conversations that particularly affected me. One was with Miriam Isoun, director of the Niger Delta Wetlands Centre (NDWC). During our conversation she criticized the approach taken by Living Earth and the control that oil companies effected in their community development work. She was also the first person who talked to me about the ethnic and racial conflicts in Nigeria, the issues of resource control and local land rights and how this all filtered through to the community development work of Living Earth, Shell and the relationship between the two organizations.

During our conversation she showed me a cartoon (see Figure 9.1). As she presented it to me I could see how, in some ways, I was another man placed in that line-up of external 'experts', expecting/hoping/wanting to be of assistance to someone further down the line. I became clear that I was constructing a story of the situation in the Delta based upon my particular gender, position, role, needs and history. I had read the books and had adopted a language of participation, ownership and collaborative engagement. Despite this, I was largely working only from the technocratic puzzle-solving frame of mind where it was possible to 'get things right'.

When I was visiting the communities in the Delta I spent some time at Opume village. This village is within 3 kilometres of Shell's and Nigeria's first discovery of commercial quantities of oil. It also sits within some of the most stunning ecology that I have experienced. At Opume I talked to the village chiefs for 40 minutes or so. Towards the end of the conversation one of the younger members of the group, Authority, asked me what I thought of Nigeria. I responded that I thought Lagos was a noisy, polluted and overcrowded city, but that the Delta was truly remarkable, peaceful and beautiful. When I told him this, he said that I had offended them. Stunned, I asked him 'why'. He said that

So much has been done <u>in the name of the Niger Delta</u> ;
what has been done '<u>for</u>' the Niger Delta?

Source: adapted from *Spore*, 1995

Figure 9.1 *In the name of the Niger Delta*

I had chosen to come into the Delta; but equally and immediately I could *choose* to leave and return to all the conveniences of my lifestyle in England. They did not have this choice and, therefore, what I had seen as the beauty of the environment failed to take into account the conditions of underdevelopment and lack of running water, proper sanitation and electricity that people were living under.

I have since spent much time wondering about the message in Figure 9.1 and the conversations that I was able to have with Miriam and Authority. I began to appreciate that, in part, I was present in the Delta because of my role in a research community and academia. I noticed that my PhD and my professional development as a researcher had some influence upon my research work. In part, I needed to exert some form of control in the situation. I needed a good enough story to tell that could increase my chances of the research being legitimated by the professional academic community. And this professional community formed by the dominant culture of our time created a separatist and control-oriented environment for my engagement. For example, while the academic community could assess and reward my technical growth as a professional researcher, it had to separate this from any attempt to understand my personal psychological growth as a spiritual being, the outcomes for communities in the Niger Delta or the ecological and cultural impact of my presence there. It had to ignore these things, not because academia deems them unimportant, but because it does not know how to make sense of their combined and changing complexity.

Because there is no business-as-usual case

Walk forward questioning.[3]

The diagrams and conversations continue to evoke colourful questions in my attitude towards change and the role of business in sustainable development. For example, is everyone in that 'line' always only there for his or her own sake? Are some of the well-paid development experts brought in by the oil companies looking to benefit the proverbial (and real) woman worker at the end of the line? If outside agents did not come in, how would change be effected?

And even my telling of these stories about my experiences can be further interrogated – after all, neither Authority nor Miriam were invited to write a chapter for this book. My voice is here for many reasons, at least part of which comes from my own position of power and a desire/need to keep myself professionally employed. I find it very easy to turn away from this and focus upon being busier in my job, writing more articles and avoiding the need to challenge the ways in which I make sense of my world.

I cannot ignore the call to contribute to changes in the way that we are acting today. However, I remain aware that there is a limit to how far our current puzzle-solving activity can take us. Another game must be played that seeks transformation of what we perceive as truthful, valuable and powerful. This game seeks to transform the puzzles themselves and how we look at puzzle-solving activity.

So, for me, reflective questioning and action go on. I try to increase my attention to the ways that I frame, understand and talk about people, ecology and the world. I move towards paying more attention to how I speak to people – where I am looking for individual control – to appreciating the people and things I don't respond to. This is not paid work for me; it is spiritual play. There is no pragmatic, business-as-usual case. The play cannot be rewarded or measured through professional development, performance assessment or academic careering. The world (the one we are trying to change) does not yet have the ability to understand it, value it and sell it, so we must go on ahead of the world.

Notes

1 BBC Radio 4 (2002) 'Crossing Continents', July 2002
2 *This Day* (2003) 'Warri: NNPC Oil Chiefs Hold Emergency Meeting', *This Day*, Lagos, 25 March 2003
3 From Zapatista's movement against the oppression of neo-liberalism in the Chiapas region of Mexico.

Chapter 10

Environmental Cost Accounting: Coming of Age? Tracking Organizational Performance Towards Environmental Sustainability

Rupert Howes

Introduction

This chapter provides an overview of the dynamic subject of corporate environmental accounting. It outlines the business case and rationale for engaging in environmental accounting and illustrates how leading UK companies are already adding value and reducing risk through the use of innovative environmental accounting techniques and methodologies. The two broad focus areas of environmental accounting are discussed. The first is concerned with accounting for 'internal' environmental-related expenditure – expenditure already incurred and captured within a company's accounting system but perhaps lost in general overheads. The misallocation of environmental costs in this way can lead to internal price distortions within companies and can result in sub-optimal decisions: wasted resources and lower profits. The second is concerned with 'external cost accounting' (the internalization of environmental externalities).

The main part of the chapter provides an overview of an external environmental accounting methodology developed by the sustainable development organization Forum for the Future that is now being used by a growing number of international companies and organizations to assess their progress to (or from) 'environmental sustainability'. These include AWG (formally Anglian Water); Bulmers; Marks and Spencer; UPM Kymenne (the world's largest manufacturer of newsprint); Interface Europe, part of Interface Inc (the world's largest manufacturer of floor coverings); Wessex Water; and CIS (the insurance division of the newly formed Co-operative Financial Services or CFS). Its starting point is the recognition that our current systems of industrial production and consumption are unsustainable. The evidence is all too pervasive: current patterns of economic development are overwhelming and destroying the productive capacity of the planet and the life-support systems upon which all life on Earth, let alone economic activity, depends (see Box 10.1).

While there may be uncertainty over what constitutes a sustainable level of economic activity, one thing is certain: the transition towards a more sustainable economy will require a dramatic increase in the level of resource productivity, perhaps by a factor of four or more. We will need to produce more from less and dramatically decrease the amount of waste – solid, gaseous and liquid wastes – generated within our industrial economies. The external cost-accounting methodology attempts to apply this notion of ecological limits when determining the appropriate sustainability targets for individual companies' impact- and emission-reduction targets. In effect, it provides an attempt to operationalize the environmental (natural capital) component of Forum for the Future's 'Five Capitals Framework' at the company level and provides organizations with a practical tool that can help them to quantify potential contingent liabilities (and assess their materiality), add value and reduce business risk.[1]

While this chapter focuses on environmental sustainability, Forum for the Future has developed the work and methodologies outlined in the following sections to incorporate aspects of an organization's social performance. This work on sustainability accounting is outlined in Chapter 4 by Julie Richardson.

What is environmental accounting?

For the purposes of this chapter, environmental accounting has been defined as the generation, analysis and use of monetarized environmentally related information in order to improve corporate environmental and economic performance. While this definition may seem a little dull, environmental accounting is not. It is all about making the link between environmental and financial performance more visible, getting 'environmental sustainability' embedded within an organization's culture and operations and providing decision-makers with the sort of information that can help them to reduce costs and business risk and to add value.

It is a new area, with no hard-and-fast rules or standards. However, a growing number of companies are now beginning to actively engage in environmental accounting as the professional accounting bodies, financial analysts and other stakeholders demand greater disclosure and reporting of environmentally related financial data to enable them to distinguish between good and bad performers. This transition is being pushed along by several recent developments, including the Company Law Review, the amendment to the 1995 Pensions Act, the Turnbull report on internal controls and the recent Association of British Insurers' (ABI's) guidelines on socially responsible investments (SRIs). The UK government is also applying further pressure on companies to improve and report on their environmental, ethical and social policy through a policy of 'naming and shaming' FTSE250 companies that are currently not reporting. The disclosure of environmentally related financial data is actively being encouraged, and mandatory environmental reporting has been threatened and seems inevitable in the absence of more widespread and comprehensive reporting by UK companies. It has recently been introduced in France and is already in place in several other European countries.

If a company is seriously committed to the idea of decreasing its environmental footprint (the damage caused by its activities and operations), it needs to manage and control both its internal environmental costs (such as the costs relating to waste management and energy consumption) and reduce the external environmental costs resulting from its activities. These external costs are currently borne by the rest of society and represent 'value extracted' by the company, but not paid for. The following sections provide more detail on these two aspects of environmental accounting. The sections draw on practical UK case study examples to illustrate how leading companies are already incorporating environmental accounting techniques and methodologies within their management information systems.

Internal environmental cost accounting

For a company embarking on environmental accounting, the identification of internal environmental costs provides a useful starting point. These costs can include the following:

- costs of monitoring emissions;
- licence, permits and authorization costs;
- special insurance fees to cover the use of hazardous chemicals;
- payment of fines and charges;
- costs of operating an environmental department; and
- capital spending with an environmental component.

There is no one definition of what constitutes environmentally related expenditure, and the importance of various categories will clearly vary depending upon the nature of the company and its principal activities. A more

BOX 10.1 THE MAINTENANCE OF NATURAL CAPITAL: SOMETHING IS MISSING FROM CORPORATE ACCOUNTS

Can wealth creation and environmental sustainability ever be reconciled, or is there an inherent conflict between profits and the environment? Much of the business school rhetoric, from the late 1980s to the present day, would suggest that there is no conflict. The talk is all of 'win–win' or 'double dividend' opportunities, measures that bring reduced environmental impact and enhanced profitability. Clean and efficient industries, it is said, will produce new products and technologies without environmental destruction. But despite their obvious appeal, the adoption of clean technology, waste minimization and the pursuit of energy and eco-efficiency in isolation will never be enough. While these activities need to be encouraged and actively promoted, given the magnitude of the environmental challenges we face, it would be naive to rely on what industry deems to be win–win to deliver necessary environmental improvements. Producing more from less is not the same as sustainable industrial production.

The role of natural capital

The problem, in part, stems from the failure of accounting systems – at the national and corporate levels – to fully account for 'natural' capital. While companies account for the depreciation of manufactured capital to ensure that productive capacity and, hence, the ability to generate future returns and income is maintained, no account is made for the degradation of natural capital when calculating corporate profits. Natural capital can be thought of as the exploitable resources of the Earth's ecosystem – its oceans, forests, mountains and plains – that provide the raw material inputs, resources and flows of energy into our production processes. It also consists of a range of 'ecosystem services'. These services include the provision of an atmosphere and a stable climate, a protective ozone layer, and the absorptive capacities to disperse, neutralize and recycle the material outputs and pollution generated in ever-increasing quantities from our global economic activities. While some account is taken of the depletion of resources, no account is taken of the degradation of what has been described as 'critical natural capital': the essential ecosystem services without which no life, let alone economic activity, would exist.

Evidence of this incomplete accounting is abundant. For example, while companies may account for the timber (the actual resource) that they extract from a forest, they do not account for the ecosystem services provided by that forest. These include water storage, soil stability, habitat and the regulation of the atmosphere and climate. Unfortunately, the cost of these essential ecosystem services becomes all too apparent when they start to break down. In China's Yangtze basin in 1998, for example, deforestation triggered flooding that killed 3700 people, dislocated 223 million and inundated 24 million hectares of farmland. This US$30 billion disaster forced a logging moratorium and a US$12 billion emergency reforestation programme (Hawken, Lovins et al, 1999). Similarly, external costs of global climate change are beginning to become more obvious. Storm and extreme weather event-related damage (global climate change is expected to increase the frequency and severity of such events) caused upwards of US$90 billion of damage in 1998 alone. This represents more weather-related damage destruction than was reported during the entire decade of the 1980s (Hawken, Lovins et al, 1999).

The key to resolving the conflict between profits and the environment, as many have pointed out, lies in getting the prices right. Businesses (and consumers) should pay for the external costs of their activities. Farmers should pay for the contamination of groundwater (and not be subsidized to pollute the water in the first place); timber companies should pay for the destruction of water catchments; and industry should pay for its myriad external environmental impacts. These include industry's contribution to global climate change; its impact on poor and declining urban air quality; loss of agricultural production and productivity as a result of aqueous and gaseous emissions and direct impacts; and disposal of waste to land. Until this happens, the conflict will remain. Only when these costs have been internalized will profits, as reported in financial accounts, approximate to what can be regarded as environmentally *sustainable* profits. One way of getting the prices right is through the process of ecological tax reform (ETR): moving taxes from the 'goods', such as employment and profits, to the 'bads' of resource use and pollution. The UK's landfill tax and the climate change levy are examples of ETR. The revenues raised from these taxes are redistributed back into the economy by reducing employers' national insurance (NI) contributions. However, neither of these taxes fully reflects the full extent of the external impacts resulting from the disposal of waste or the business use of fossil fuel-derived energy.

In the absence of the political will to establish a comprehensive and radical ETR programme, companies committed to improving their environmental performance need to move beyond simple corporate environmental reporting, to begin to account more completely and transparently for both their internal environmental costs and their external impacts. In effect, they need to begin to account for the depreciation of 'natural capital' in the same way that accounting rules and standards require them to account for the depreciation of manufactured capital. Once these costs are internalized, everything changes: prices, costs and what is or is not profitable.

Source: Howes (2000)

rigorous allocation of these costs can bring many benefits in itself. Often, environmental costs are hidden in overheads or allocated somewhat arbitrarily across departments/cost centres. Studies such as those undertaken by the World Resources Institute (Ditz et al, 1995) have shown that these costs can be substantial. The six case studies presented in the WRI study show that, for certain products and facilities, environmental costs can account for 20 per cent of total costs.

When environmental costs are this significant, tighter and more transparent accounting can more than pay for itself. Traditional cost allocation methods (on the basis of machine hours, output or, perhaps, headcount) can lead to a situation where products with relatively low environmental costs subsidize those with higher costs. This results in poor product-pricing decisions as managers respond to distorted internal 'price signals'. The case of Spectrum Glass, one of the companies reviewed in the WRI study, illustrates this point. Their principal environmental concern was the use of the colourant cadmium oxide, a chemical used for only one product: 'ruby red' glass. This product was responsible for the bulk of the hazardous waste produced by the company. At the time of the WRI study, with environmental costs being allocated across all products, 'ruby red' glass appeared profitable. In reality, it was actually making a loss.

Spectrum Glass may not be typical of the ease with which environmental costs are directly attributable to particular products. But it is indicative of how internal subsidies, created through a misallocation of costs, can lead to inappropriate pricing and product-mix decisions. With more transparent and complete accounting, firms are more likely to be able to identify cost-saving opportunities, make better decisions with regard to product mix and pricing, and also be able to avoid future costs through inappropriate investment decisions. At the very least, making the link between environmental and financial performance more apparent can make it easier to win support for further environmental initiatives.

One way of presenting how value can be added through environmental investments and initiatives is through the preparation and reporting of a company-wide environmental financial statement (EFS). The EFS is a periodic financial statement that attempts to collate and report, in a single statement, total environmental expenditure and any associated financial savings achieved as a result of that expenditure over the particular accounting period under review. The statement aims to capture all relevant items of environmentally related expenditure, irrespective of which department or cost centre incurred them, and to match the expenditure, on a line-by-line basis, where appropriate, with its associated financial benefits or savings. A pro-forma EFS is shown in Table 10.1.

Until recently, only one company, Baxter Healthcare Corporation, a US company, has attempted to produce and report a company-wide EFS. Baxter spent several years developing the EFS methodology and recognizes that the process and procedure have evolved and developed considerably since it first engaged in corporate environmental accounting during the early 1990s. When cumulative savings brought forward are taken into account, Baxter's have found that savings and avoided costs from environmental investments actually exceed environmentally related expenditure. As noted on the company's website in 1999, environmental investments instituted in prior years back to 1992 yielded approximately US$86 million in savings and cost avoidance – a powerful bottom line argument for environmentally responsible corporate behaviour (www.baxter.com). In the reporting year 1999, savings of US$12 million equated to 80 per cent of the costs of the basic environmental programme. One of Forum for the Future's business partners has used the EFS methodology to identify cumulative annual cost savings and avoided costs in the region of 5 to 10 per cent of post-tax profits. This clearly provides a very powerful signal to the board to initiate further sustainability investments and to replicate identified good practice across the organization.

However, eco-efficiency savings are only one part of the overall business case for sustainable development. More value is likely to be associated with the intangible benefits associated with greater corporate social and environmental responsibility. These include the impact on brand value and reputation, the ability to attract and retain the best people, higher productivity from a motivated and inspired workforce, access to new markets (and maintenance of existing markets) and so on. These are benefits that environmental and sustainability accounting tools and methodologies are beginning to try to quantify. Innovative

Table 10.1 *Pro-forma environmental financial statement (EFS)*

	2002 £	2000 £
Environmental Costs		
Costs of basic programme		
Environmental services (percentage of)	✗	✗
Environmental/energy coordinators, etc	✗	✗
Business unit environmental programmes and initiatives (including personnel costs/professional fees, etc)	✗	✗
Waste minimization and pollution prevention – operations and maintenance	✗	✗
Waste minimization and pollution prevention – capital costs	✗	✗
Total cost of basic programme		
Remediation, waste and other costs[2]		
Fines and prosecutions	✗	✗
Waste disposal costs	✗	✗
Environmental taxes – eg landfill, climate levy	✗	✗
Remediation/clean-up costs	✗	✗
Other costs, etc	✗	✗
Total remediation, waste and other costs	✗	✗
Total environmental costs		
Environmental savings		
Income, savings and cost avoidance from report year		
Reduced insurance from avoidance of hazardous materials	✗	✗
Reduced landfill tax and other waste disposal costs	✗	✗
Energy conservation savings	✗	✗
Water conservation savings	✗	✗
Reduced packaging savings	✗	✗
Income from sale of recovered and recycled materials	✗	✗
Other savings, etc	✗	✗
Total environmental savings	✗	✗
As a percentage of environmental costs	✗%	✗%
Summary of savings	✗	✗
Savings in report year	✗	✗
Savings brought forward from initiatives in prior years	✗	✗
Total income, savings and cost avoidance	✗	✗

work by the Co-operative Bank, for example, is investigating the link between its ethical policies and the bank's overall profitability. During the reporting year 2000, 15 to 18 per cent of the bank's pre-tax profits were attributed to the Co-operative Bank's brand and reputation.

Internal costs, however, are just one part of the equation. The next essential step for a company committed to moving towards environmental sustainability is to begin to account for its external environmental impacts. The rationale for *internalizing* these externalities and the business case for doing so are presented below.

External cost accounting: internalizing environmental externalities

While companies 'add value' through their activities, they also extract value for which they do not pay. Their activities and operations give rise to external environmental impacts, such as the contamination of groundwater, traffic congestion, poor urban air quality and so on. The costs of these external impacts are picked up by the rest of society; prices do not reflect costs and, as such, companies (and individuals) do not pay the full costs of their production and consumption decisions. Instead, sub-optimal and inefficient decisions are made as producers and consumers respond to imperfect price signals. At the level of an individual company, this means that profits as reported may not be environmentally sustainable. The degree to which the company is genuinely 'adding value' through its activities remains uncertain, and if the company was to pay a dividend, the payment could end up being made out of *natural* capital rather than income – a situation that is clearly unsustainable over the long term. The assumption that the company is a 'going concern' may also no longer be valid.

For a company committed to moving towards environmental sustainability, the challenge is to try and determine/estimate what its environmentally sustainable profits may be and, hence, to gauge to what extent it is really adding value and making the transition to becoming a more environmentally sustainable enterprise. The development of more complete, transparent and integrated accounts/accounting systems – systems that specifically take into account the most significant external environmental impacts resulting from a company's operations – is a prerequisite to enabling a company to be able to do this. As noted, several UK companies, including AWG, Wessex Water, Marks and Spencer and Bulmers, have already embarked on developing such systems.

The business case

The long-term future and sustainability of individual corporations is inescapably linked to their ability to reduce their environmental impacts and to continuously improve their overall environmental (and social) performance. Leading companies recognize this. For example, Wessex Water, in their 2001 annual review and accounts, state that 'in the long term, the "bottom line" is that all economic value flows from products and services provided by the environment (natural capital) and people (human capital) themselves. These resources should not be eroded; instead, a sustainable society would live off what can provided year after year.'[3] Similarly, in their 2001 sustainable development report *Transforming Our World* (www.awg.com), AWG states that the integration of sustainable development within a company's activities and operations will bring advantages to the business, as well as to the environment and the communities within which that business is operating.[4]

What were once external costs can quickly become internalized through environmental regulation and taxes. The landfill tax, climate change levy and aggregates taxes provide recent examples of such legislation. Governments throughout Europe are committed to the increased use of such policy instruments. Customer and local community expectations and demands for responsible corporate environmental governance are also increasing and the consequences of corporate 'environmental and/or social failure' (for example, Shell with the disposal of the Brent Spar and Nike with child labour) have become all too apparent.

Financial stakeholders are also showing more interest in assessing corporate environmental performance. While investor/financial market pressure has historically been limited to concern over legal liabilities and to negative risk factors, recent legislative changes and emerging evidence of the link between earnings and environmental management have encouraged analysts to consider the more positive aspects of corporate environmental performance. Increasingly, the quality of a company's environmental management is being seen as an indicator to the outside world of the overall quality of its management – a key investment/stock selection consideration. Analysts are being urged to demand new forms of data and information to measure this more positive aspect of corporate environmental governance. A number of commercial environmental risk-rating methodologies and several new financial products based on an assessment of environmental/sustainability performance (such as the FTSE4Good indices, the Dow Jones Sustainability Group Index and others) have been launched in response to this demand. The ability to compare and benchmark performance is becoming increasingly important. Environmental accounting, involving the monetarization/valuation of environmental impacts and their integration within mainstream corporate accounting, could, potentially, be one of the tools/methodologies to enable such comparisons to be made.

Being aware of their environmental costs (and benefits) – that is, the company's exposure to potential environmental problems (before they become issues) – can assist the company's management in its forward/strategic planning and, consequently, help to reduce the company's exposure to future environmental risks and liabilities. Without adequate and appropriate systems to identify and account for such costs, it is unlikely that companies will be able to meet the future expectations of their customers, shareholders and the requirements of a more stringent regulatory environment and environmentally aware City.[5] 'First movers' will clearly have an advantage.

Aims and objectives of the methodology

The methodology described below provides a tool to estimate, within narrow system boundaries, the environmental sustainability of a company's activities and operations – in effect, the environmental sustainability of its economic activity. By linking monetarized environmental performance data to the company's mainstream financial and management accounting systems, it attempts to quantify what could be considered, again within the narrow system boundaries adopted, as the organization's environmentally sustainable profits. These are the profits (or loss) that would remain at the end of an accounting period after provision has been made, or expenditure incurred, to restore or avoid the most significant external environmental impacts resulting from the company's activities and operations. In essence, the aim is to estimate the profit level that would remain if the company endeavoured to leave the environment in a similar state at the end of the accounting period as it had been at the beginning of that period.[6]

The four main stages in developing a set of external cost accounts are as follows:

- identification of the most significant/major environmental impacts resulting from the company's activities and operations;
- estimation/determination of what a sustainable level of emissions/impacts may be (the determination of relevant sustainability targets);
- valuation of those impacts;
- development of a set of environmental accounts incorporating these values and subsequent estimation of the company's sustainability cost and environmentally sustainable profits.

Wessex Water's external cost accounts, published alongside its conventional financial statements in its 2001 annual review and accounts, are shown in Table 10.2. The headings used in the accounts reflect recommendations on sustainability reporting detailed in the latest version of the Global Reporting Initiative (GRI) guidelines and include impacts to air, land and water.

Methodologically difficult areas included the issue of where to draw the system boundaries – that is, to what degree the life cycle impacts should be taken into account in determining a company's sustainability cost. Depending upon the nature of the company, these cut-off considerations could significantly affect the magnitude of the estimated *sustainability cost* of the company's operations. However, given the objective of the investigation – to estimate an individual company's sustainability cost – fairly narrow system boundaries have been used. Only direct or first-level impacts (those environmental impacts that the company was directly responsible for and had greatest ability to control), plus the second-level impacts resulting from the consumption of electricity, have been accounted for. In effect, the approach taken amounts to an attempt to apply the polluter pays principle to an individual company.

Sustainability targets have been determined by reference to the latest scientific thinking or understanding on the particular impact in question. For example, when estimating the sustainability target for carbon emissions, a 60 per cent reduction target has been used. Both the UK's Royal Commission on Environmental Pollution and the Inter-governmental Panel on Climate Change (the IPCC) have suggested that emission cuts of this order are required to avoid dangerous anthropogenic interference with the Earth's climate systems. Targets for non-carbon-based transport emissions have been determined according to World Health Organization estimates to bring urban air quality within health-based guidelines. In reality, no one really knows what a sustainable level of impacts or emissions may be and, consequently, it is necessary to take a fairly pragmatic approach when setting targets.

Once impacts and targets have been established, the individual sustainability cost estimates are valued, as far as possible, on the basis of their avoidance or restoration costs – that is, on the basis of what the organization would need to spend in order to either avoid the impacts in the first place or to restore the environmental damage caused by its activities and operations if they are unavoidable. Costs, as far as possible, are based on 'real' or market-based prices. For example, emissions of carbon dioxide, nitrogen oxides and sulphur dioxide from electricity production/use can largely be avoided by switching to some form of renewable energy tariff. Hence, the appropriate avoidance cost to use would be any resulting premium charged. Transport-related emissions of hydrocarbons and particulate matter from large vehicles can largely be avoided by the retro-fitting of continuously regenerating traps (CRTs). These actually reduce emissions by about 90 per cent and again provide an example of a market-based avoidance cost. Other valuations can be harder to identify and determine.

The main purpose of the estimation is to illustrate what a given/stated improvement in environmental quality would cost. The estimation simply represents the cost of achieving a given improvement in environmental quality based on current (and available) technology. In this 'pure' form, the sustainability cost estimate (to achieve consistent standards or improvements in environmental quality) will only change for two reasons: changes in absolute emissions/impacts (that will, hopefully, be decreasing) or changes in abatement technology (and the price of that technology). The sustainability cost can, therefore, provide a powerful indicator of a company's progress towards (or away from) environmental sustainability (for a more detailed review of the methodology and practical guidance on how to produce external cost accounts, see Howes (2002a)).

Table 10.2 *Wessex Water Services' external environmental cost accounts, 31 March 2001*

Emissions/Impacts	UK£000s Emissions (tonnes)	Sustainability gap. Reduction target (tonnes)	Avoidance and restoration costs. Unit cost £ (where relevant)	Total avoidance and restoration costs UK£000s
Impacts to air				
Direct energy				
Electricity consumption 195.1 million kWh				
CO$_2$	86,325	51,741	—	
NO$_x$	234	140	—	
SO$_2$	488	293	—	
Total (avoidance)				1950
Natural gas consumption 11.07 million kWh (CO$_2$ only)	2103	1262	6	8
Diesel oil – 18.91 million litres CO$_2$ only	4728	2837	6	17
Production relation emissions	91,140 (expressed as CO$_2$ equivalent)	54,684	6	328
Methane (CH$_4$) emissions from wastewater treatment				
Transport				
Company cars (petrol and diesel) 13.2 million kilometres				
CO$_2$	403	241	6	2
NO$_x$, HCs and PM	1	<1	14,000	8
Commercial vehicles (petrol and diesel) 13.2 million kilometres				
CO$_2$	3918	2381	6	14
NO$_x$, HCs and PM	30.5	17	7200–14,000	323
Commuting and private car use 8.3 million kilometres				
CO$_2$	2294	1377	6	9
NO$_x$, HCs and PM	16	8	7200–14,000	100
Contractors 11.4 million kilometres				
CO$_2$	2500	1500	6	10
NO$_x$, HCs and PM	37	17	7200–14,000	282

Table 10.2 (continued)

Emissions/Impacts	UK£000s Emissions (tonnes)	Sustainability gap. Reduction target (tonnes)	Avoidance and restoration costs. Unit cost £ (where relevant)	Total avoidance and restoration costs UK£000s
Impacts to land *Contaminated land (restoration of sacrificial and dedicated land)*	–	–	6000–9000	120
Impacts to water *Abstraction at vulnerable sites – provision of alternative supplies*	–	–	–	5170
Total sustainability cost				**8341**
Profit after tax per the financial accounts				**72,000**
Environmentally sustainable/ adjusted profit				**63,659**

Conclusions

Needless to say, external cost accounting is still evolving. Consequently, the accounting framework outlined above is likely to undergo some changes as more companies begin to engage and experiment with the methodology. It has, after all, taken us several centuries to develop the current, and still dynamic, framework of financial accounting and reporting standards. However, the broad approach is likely to remain constant – namely, to identify where a company is in terms of its environmental impacts, to determine appropriate 'sustainability' targets or standards to aim for, and to work out the most cost-effective way for the company to close that 'sustainability gap'. Greater understanding of environmental sustainability and improvements in scientific understanding will lead to more appropriate and generally higher targets being set. In any event, it seems likely, as Bulmers Group Financial Manager Dave Marshall noted in a recent article, that eventually every company will have to make these calculations as part of routine accounting and reporting requirements – particularly as investors begin to ask questions about the cost of unsustainable business. As Marshall commented: 'There is something to be said for being prepared.'[7]

Notes

1   See www.forumforthefuture.org.uk for more information on the 'Five Capitals Framework'.
2   Proactive environmental action will clearly minimize these costs and, hence, reduce the 'cost' side of the statement.
3   *Wessex Water Services Ltd Annual Review and Accounts 2001*, 'Tap into your water source', p61. The external cost accounts can help companies to define what can be provided year after year – that is, to define these limits and to identify the options that are available to the company, enabling them to reduce their external footprint and begin to make the transition towards environmental sustainability.
4   AWG (2001) *Transforming Our World: Sustainable Development Report 2001*. The report defines these advantages as follows: winning business by creating additional advantages and opportunities; reducing costs by introducing efficiencies that directly reduce our consumption of resources and are attractive to the investment community; reducing risk – developing and contributing to sustainable regulation and competition, and becoming even better managers of corporate risk, while making the business grow; and developing and applying new technology.
5   By identifying external environmental risks, and the opportunities open to the company to avoid or reduce them, external cost accounting can also contribute to helping companies meet their obligations under the combined code to establish adequate systems of internal control.
6   The sustainability cost approach is one of three ways identified by Rob Gray and Jan Bebbington to enable organizations to begin to account for sustainability (Gray et al, 1993). Forum for the Future's external cost accounting work draws on this concept in developing a methodology that could be employed by companies to account for the external environmental impacts resulting from their activities. It also draws on the pioneering work on environmental accounting undertaken by BSO Origin, the Dutch management consultancy company.
7   *Green Futures* (2001) 'In the Black, Red or Green', 27 (March–April), pp60–61

Sustainability Assessment Model: Modelling Economic, Resource, Environmental and Social Flows of a Project

Tom Baxter, Jan Bebbington and David Cutteridge

Introduction

This chapter describes the development by British Petroleum (BP) (in collaboration with others) of an accounting tool for 'making sense' of the extent to which its operations could be said to be in accordance with the principles of sustainable development (SD). The accounting tool that has been developed is called the Sustainability Assessment Model (SAM). In brief, SAM seeks to track significant economic, resource, environmental and social impacts of a project over its full life cycle and then to translate these impacts into a common measurement basis – that of money. The outcome of this process is to produce both a graphical representation of the positive and negative impacts (we call this the SAM 'signature'), as well as the construction of an indicator (the SAM*i*) of how well the particular project performs (which itself could be used to benchmark different projects). This information may then be fed back into project evaluation processes, either to inform the (re)design of the project or to feed into future project planning processes.

The SAM is a form of full-cost accounting (FCA; see Bebbington, Gray et al, 2001, for a summary of FCA) and attempts to identify all of the internal and external costs and benefits associated with a particular project. FCA involves a generic four-step approach (see Box 11.1), and how the SAM operationalizes each of the four steps in FCA is outlined below.

BOX 11.1 STEPS IN FULL-COST ACCOUNTING (FCA)

1 Define the focus of the costing exercise (which may be, for example, a product, production process, waste disposal option, project, part of an economic entity, an entire entity or an industry).

2 Specify the scope or limits of analysis (that is, what sub-set of all possible externalities is to be identified).

3 Identify and measure external impact (which involves making the link between a cost objective and the externalities arising from the cost objective).

4 Cost external impact (monetization of the externalities, or determination of the fuller costs that are associated with, but that are not already captured, by the current accounting for a cost objective).

Sustainability Assessment Model (SAM)[1]

In the first instance, SAM defines the cost objective as being a discrete project – in this case, a 'typical' oil and gas field development. The project focus has been specifically adopted because we believe that this gives visibility to the significant contributions to SD from a particular project and is useful where organizations organize their activities on a project basis.

Secondly, the boundaries of the SAM exercise have been defined widely. SAM tracks the SD impacts of a project over its full life cycle. In the case of an oil and gas development, phases include exploratory drilling, the design of, for example, a drilling and production platform, the construction, installation and commissioning of the platform, the production of oil and gas and the eventual decommissioning of the platform. These parts of an oil and gas development are usually directly within the control of the project. SAM, however, extends the analysis beyond the extraction of oil and gas and traces the external impacts from refining, the manufacture of products from oil and gas and eventual product use. Thus, SAM examines cradle-to-grave impacts of an oil and gas project.

The extension of the modelling to impacts that are outside of the direct control of the business raises problems. For example, some may argue that given that an impact is uncontrollable by a specific business (for example, the use of oil and gas is not within the control of oil and gas producers), the business cannot be held accountable for its impact. While this may be the case, we were keen to provide a cradle-to-grave model so that the impact of the activity on SD from society's perspective would be clear. The question of responsibility for impacts is a secondary, albeit a crucial, issue.

The third aspect of SAM has been to identify and measure the impact of the project. We have organized the impacts under the generic headings of economic, resource, environmental and social. The activity data used in the SAM was drawn from operational data for a particular oil and gas project. This data includes hours worked on the project, number of people employed, number of barrels of oil produced, amount of water used, amount of raw materials used in fabrication, waste produced, as well as financial data for the project itself. The links between this array of activities and economic, resource, environmental and social impacts have been derived. The type of data that is produced at this stage is very similar to that which many organizations produce in their social and environmental reports.

The final step undertaken has been to monetize the externalities identified as arising from the development of the oil and gas field. Monetization is the most difficult and contentious element of FCA for both practical and philosophical reasons. Firstly, for many people, the problems that SD seeks to address arise from fundamental structural and spiritual problems within society. The 'deep Greens' would suggest that a belief that one can reduce 'the environment', for example, to a monetary figure is what has caused the environmental crisis in the first place. Hence, to seek to remedy the problem by adding more of the very thing (economic calculative rationalism) that caused the problem in the first place is, at best, misguided. The second set of reservations over monetization of external impacts arises from the difficulty of obtaining a single uncontested figure for monetization. The main approaches to monetization (the maintenance cost approach and the variety of approaches that come under the broader heading of the damage cost approach) may yield significantly different measures of externalities. As a result, knowing what the resulting figures mean is often very difficult (we will return to this issue below when we consider how SAM may be used). In the case of SAM, we have primarily used damage cost estimates to monetize externalities. The application of these principles resulted in the following specification of the SAM.

The economic flows around an oil and gas development are taken as the starting point for analysis. These flows are derived from the allocation of total income from the field to various categories of expenditure (split within the model into taxes, dividends, reinvestment, social investment and money to contractors). The total of the economic flows is, therefore, the number of barrels that the field will produce, multiplied by the oil price at a point in time (a long-run average expected price is estimated). The economic flows, in turn, reflect actual movements in physical and social resources that are captured in the other sub-categories. In addition, an initial focus on traditional financial measures of activity is necessary in order to divide the impacts into those that are captured within the operator's accounting systems (that is, internal costs) and those costs that are external to the operator. The remaining cost and benefits identified by SAM relate to external costs and benefits.

The resource use flows identified by SAM attempt to capture the inherent values of the resources used in the development of an oil and gas field (to the extent that payments made and captured under economic flows do not capture these values). These resources include natural consumable resources, as well as intellectual capital and infrastructure. The figures for resource use are drawn primarily from the open literature (for example, the figure for the value of oil and gas used is drawn from the UK environmental accounts).

The tracking of external environmental impact flows that arise from business activities is what is most usually associated with FCA exercises (see, for example, Chapter 10). In this category, four sub-elements of environmental impact are identified: pollution impacts (primarily from combusting fossil fuels); nuisance impacts (such as noise, odour and visual impact); footprint (around any facility and/or pipeline); and waste impacts (to the extent that costs have not been captured in waste disposal costs). A variety of sources (both the open literature and BP's own work) were reviewed in order to obtain damage costs for the environmental impacts.

The final sub-category examined relates to external social impacts of oil and gas field development. The impact under this category has been estimated using three elements. Firstly, the value generated from direct jobs is estimated and the health and safety impacts of these jobs are quantified. This element thus includes both positive and negative values. The socially beneficial impacts arising from direct jobs consist of the multiplier effect that jobs generate in an economy. This figure estimates how much economic activity is generated from wages paid.

The second element in the social externalities category seeks to establish a link between the project and less directly tangible social impacts arising from the project. This was the most difficult element within the model development. When the project team attempted to define what broader social impacts arose from a project, it quickly became apparent that each individual had their own conception of what social sustainability was and how economic activity impacted upon their vision of a sustainable society. Some common ground was therefore sought. The UK government's SD priorities were selected as representing the UK's best estimate of which social aspects are the most relevant in achieving social sustainability. As a result, SAM seeks to link the impacts of a project to the UK government's strategy for sustainable development. The most direct financial link between project and the government is through taxation.

As a result, the second element of the social impacts of a project takes as its base the tax paid over the project life. The taxes paid are split on a pro-rata basis according to the UK government's spending patterns. The next step is to estimate what social benefit arises from tax spend in each category. For example, if UK£1 of tax is spent on education or health, what (on average) is the social benefit from that spend? As a result, a series of tax multiplier factors has been estimated. The pro-rata tax spend is then multiplied by the factor.

The final element in the social impacts category requires an estimate of the external benefits of oil and gas products. Three products are generated from a

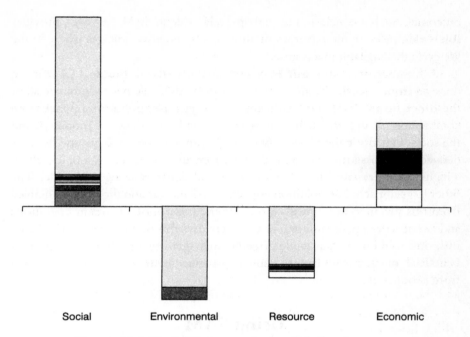

Figure 11.1 *The SAM signature for a typical oil and gas project*

typical oil and gas field: mobility (via refined fuel), heating (which is either a direct result of combusting oil-based products or comes via the use of oil and gas in power supply) and oil-based products (which include the likes of pharmaceuticals, plastics and other chemicals). SAM attempts to estimate the benefits that are derived from these items. The need to identify the positive externalities that arise over and above the income derived from the sale of crude is necessary to ensure that all positive and negative externalities are captured in the model. In particular, if the negative environmental impact from fuel combustion is within the model, the benefit derived by society from the product should also be included.

Clearly, a series of choices has been made in order to develop data for SAM. Wherever possible, we have used data that is in the public domain; but we have had to estimate data in several places (thus the information can only be used as a guide to possible full life-cycle impacts). The data has been graphed by sub-category to produce a pattern of monetary quantified positive and negative impacts that arise from a 'typical' oil and gas development. We term this pattern the SAM 'signature' (see Figure 11.1). Where the bars are above the horizontal, a net benefit is produced in the capital sub-category. Where the bars are below the horizontal, a net dis-benefit is produced in the capital sub-category. In brief, the signature suggests that in order to generate social and economic positive outcomes, there have been negative resource and environmental impact outcomes. Such a conclusion is, perhaps, self-evident. SAM, however, provides some indication of the quantum of those costs and also indicates where in the life cycle the largest impacts arise.

A number of points can be made on the basis of Figure 11.1. Firstly, drawing from a sensitivity analysis of the model, three elements dominate all of the other flows. These elements are oil and gas use; pollution impact from combusting oil and gas (as it is used to provide heating and/or mobility); and the social benefit of the product (which is, again, heating, mobility and benefits derived from fossil fuel-based products). From an upstream position, therefore, a higher recovery rate will yield a better overall signature using this model. The other large impacts (the pollution impacts of oil and gas and the benefits derived from this product) are, however, outside the control of upstream operations and are heavily dependent upon how society uses this particular resource. From this, one could infer that while effective management of offshore impacts is beneficial, much greater benefit could be obtained by managing impacts arising from product use.

Using SAM

Developing the SAM signature is only the first step in evaluating a project. In order to use SAM to evaluate whether or not a project is 'sustainable', some operational definition of SD is necessary. In particular, a view has to be taken as to whether one needs to sustain total capital in order to be deemed sustainable or whether or not each sub-group of capital (economic, resource, environmental or social) need be sustained. This decision rests, at least in part, on the assumptions that may be made about the substitutability of different capital groups. Further elaboration on this point is required.

In SAM we noted that there were both positive and negative outcomes from a development. It would, therefore, be reasonable to assume that where the number is positive, that type of capital has been sustained, and where the number is negative, that type of capital has not been sustained. Furthermore, the extent to which these capital sub-categories could be combined depends upon the extent to which you believe that capital is substitutable. There is a spectrum of views on this matter and these views will affect how the various elements could be treated and when a project could be called sustainable. For example:

1   If all capital is substitutable and if the total of all the categories of capital is positive, the development is sustainable.
2   If all capital is substitutable except critical natural capital ('things' that we only have one of), and if the total of all the categories of capital is positive,

and if there is no loss of critical natural capital (for example, no species extinction), the development is sustainable.

3   If capital is not substitutable outside of its own capital sub-category, but there can be substitution within a category (for example, the creation of jobs in one location can be substituted for the loss of jobs in another), and if the total of any one of the capital categories is negative, then moves will have to be taken to remedy the negative impact on that capital until a neutral or positive position is created; or re-design the development to remove this impact. In order for a project to be sustainable under these conditions, all capital sub-categories would have to have a positive value.

4   If no loss in any capital is permissible, then any negative impact in any of the categories of capital (regardless of whether the total impact of the category is positive or negative) cannot be allowed. All negative impacts would, therefore, need to be remedied or designed out of the project in order for a project to be sustainable.

None of the above positions can be deemed to be 'right' in any predetermined manner. The third option, however, is a reasonably 'mainstream' view on capital substitution, and it is this assumption that has been tentatively adopted in the use of SAM.

While the signature provides an elegant visual presentation of the internal (under economic) and external (under the remaining categories) impacts of an oil and gas development, it is difficult to make sense of the graph in isolation. As a result, we propose that the data be converted into a ratio that would provide an indication of nearness to a sustainable position. We have termed this ratio the SAM*i* (the Sustainability Assessment Model indicator).

The SAM*i* combines the numbers into an overall measure, is premised on the third option regarding capital substitution and provides an indication of how 'sustainable' a project could be said to be. In the example used within this chapter, we get a SAM*i* of 25 per cent. A 'score' of 100 per cent would indicate that a project was a SD – that is, with no negative aspects in any capital sub-category. A score of greater than 100 per cent would indicate that the project contributed to SD.

Conclusions

In brief, this chapter has outlined a novel and visionary FCA tool – the SAM. SAM has been developed as a project evaluation tool that provides a sketch of how developing an oil and gas field impacts on economic, resource, environmental and social capital. The pattern of impacts in the SAM signature is used to calculate SAM*i*. SAM*i* itself attempts to indicate the SD performance of a particular project. We believe, however, that SAM could also be used to make detailed design decisions, as well as for assessing the performance of a company or industry sector. Finally, we suggest that SAM offers a potentially valuable (but not unique) way of conceptualizing the impact that activities have on the goal of SD. As such, SAM could be transferable to other industries and locations. It is likely that SAM will prompt different insights into SD in these industries.

Notes

1   This section draws from Baxter et al (2002).

Chapter 12

Social Capital at Work: A Manager's Guide

Alex MacGillivray

Introduction

This chapter explains the importance of 'social capital' to business. Social capital is the stock of networks, stakeholder relationships and shared rules that help organizations and their surrounding communities work more effectively. In short, it is creative trust.

A well-known example is New York's diamond traders, who work in a tight network with minimal transaction costs due to their high levels of trust and common norms. It is also widely accepted that business soon becomes impossible when such networks and norms disappear – as has happened recently in Argentina, for example. What is not yet well enough understood is what role business can play in building and maintaining social capital.

Social capital has, until recently, been studied by sociologists, especially in the US. It is now becoming a more familiar term to the business audience because it is a crucial part of the triple bottom line (TBL) – where economic, environmental and social balance sheets must all be in the black for a business to be sustainable.

Sustainability managers are familiar with the need to manage four types of capital successfully. These are well described by Hawken et al (1999):

- natural capital, made up of resources, living systems and ecosystem services;
- manufactured capital, including infrastructure, machines, tools and factories;
- financial capital, consisting of cash, investments and monetary instruments; and
- human capital, in the form of labour and intelligence, culture and organization.

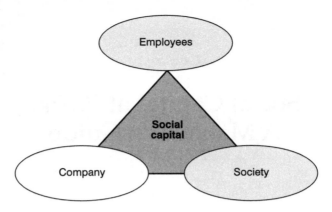

Figure 12.1 *The role of social capital*

By common consent, the last form of capital is the hardest to manage, with no key performance indicators and with responsibility split between human resources (HR), information technology (IT), corporate responsibility and communications departments. Business writers have talked about intellectual or emotional capital, and about the need for hard indicators or warm anecdotes, often in conflicting terms.

However, social capital or creative trust is the glue that binds together the individual skills and intelligence of the work force with the organization's collective memory and ability to innovate. It also cements these assets to the goodwill of the surrounding community, suppliers, customers, regulators and other stakeholders. The role of social capital as glue binding employees, the company and external stakeholders together is shown in Figure 12.1.

Like all forms of capital, social capital can be put to bad uses in business. Old boys' networks, unspoken cartels, and, at the extreme, the mafia, are all examples. But, in general, businesses benefit from high levels of social capital because it helps them to innovate and build trust. Since innovation and trust both tend to be in short supply in business, managing social capital is an important part of the sustainability manager's task.

Social capital is not unmanageable, but nor should it be taken for granted. It can be *built* by proactive staff, supplier, customer and community policies. For example, in 2002, creative newcomer Nokia ousted long-established Colgate as Europe's most trusted brand. It can also be rapidly depleted. Enron was considered in 2001 to be a 'great place to work' and was admired for its innovations by business gurus.

Social capital consists of the *bonds* between employees within a business, and also of the *bridges* the business builds with its surrounding communities. Both are necessary for social capital to be effective. Too much bonding leads to an

Table 12.1 *A four-way matrix for social capital*

	Bonding	Bridging
Creativity	Innovation 'at work', in tight teams, using sweat equity and incentives	Brainwaves in 'the third place', among friends and strangers, for the fun of it
Trust	Building the brand through shared ethos, mission, morale, story-telling, gossip	Marketing the brand by example and reputation, rooted in the community

introspective company that misses opportunities. Too much bridging leads to high staff turnover and lack of focus.

Understanding and measuring the bonds and bridges between an individual business and its stakeholders (suppliers, customers and host communities) is not straightforward. Although there is a handful of management books now available, there is still not much guidance on how to measure your company's social capital. Areas such as community engagement have not yet been tackled systematically by sustainability projects such as the Global Reporting Initiative (GRI, 2002). Only a few companies are reporting on their experiences.

This chapter sets out a framework for understanding and measuring social capital, breaking it down into four components, as shown in Table 12.1.

At the end of the chapter, a number of possible indicators are supplied for the framework. With these, managers can begin to measure social capital as an important first step to managing this intangible asset.

Defining social capital

Although it is a comparatively new term in the business literature, there are already numerous definitions of social capital, as shown in Table 12.2.

There are almost as many definitions of social capital as there are of sustainability. A recent study from the UK Department of Trade and Industry (DTI) found no less than seven types of intangible assets: relationships; knowledge; leadership and communication; culture and values; reputation and trust; skills and competencies; and processes and systems (DTI, 2001, p4). There are two consistent findings from this recent work, though. The first is the importance to the triple bottom line of trust and creativity, elusive though they may be. The second is the difficulty of getting a management handle on creative trust, which is used in this chapter as a working definition of social capital (MacGillivray, 2002).

Table 12.2 *Various definitions of social capital*

Author	Definition
Leenders and Gabbay (1999)	The set of resources, tangible or virtual, that accrue to a corporate player through the player's social relationships, facilitating the attainment of goals.
Hüppi and Seeman (2000)	As business evolves, increasingly what sets companies apart is how well they manage their intangible assets – their people and their people's skills, knowledge, energy and creativity. And that, in turn, depends upon how well these people work together. Those relationships – the processes by which information and ideas are exchanged – are a firm's social capital.
Cohen and Prusak (2001)	Social capital consists of the stock of active connections among people: the trust, mutual understanding and shared values and behaviour that bind the members of human networks and communities and make cooperative action possible.
Putnam (2001)	Features of social life – networks, norms and trust – that enable participants to act together more effectively to pursue shared objectives.
SIGMA (2001)	The value added to any activity or economic process by human relationships and cooperation. Social capital takes the form of structures or institutions which enable individuals to maintain and develop their human capital in partnership with others, and includes families, communities, businesses, trade unions, schools and voluntary organizations.
Global Reporting Initiative (2002)	Innovative partnerships with stakeholders around environmental or social aspects of products or markets can lead to product differentiation and brand enhancement. Indeed, some view strong stakeholder relationships as an intangible asset in its own right.

The business benefits of creative trust

Business innovation or creativity is often portrayed in the business literature as the work of a lonely genius or a small tight-knit team working all hours in the lab (or the garage). The stories told about Hewlett Packard, Apple Mac or Dyson all fuel this myth. Meanwhile, business critics such as Naomi Klein claim that brand value and trust is 'engineered' by manipulative advertising and cynical community relations.

In fact, creativity and trust are both usually the result of multiple social interactions between staff, suppliers, customers, family, friends and competitors. To demonstrate how firms and community can interconnect effectively, we will look first at the humble Post-It note, then at Tupelo, Mississippi, the birthplace of Elvis.

3M employee Art Fry dreamed up a use for a failed batch of not-sticky-enough carpet adhesive as he sat pondering how not to ruin the hymn books in his choir group. After being told by superiors that his semi-sticky paper pads

---

Box 12.1 TURNING TUPELO AROUND

Not even the birth of Elvis Presley in January 1935 could lift Tupelo, Mississippi, from being one of the most depressed small cities in the US. The Great Depression was capped in 1936 by a devastating tornado and the closure of its only factory the following year. Tupelo had hit rock bottom.

But then things started to change. Local sociologist turned newspaperman George McLean was one of many who, over 50 years, have rebuilt civic life in the city. A crucial breakthrough for Tupelo was the disbanding of the elitist, business-focused chamber of commerce and its replacement with a broader community development foundation open to all. The foundation worked hard to improve social services, and made ambitious social demands on incoming businesses. Another cornerstone was the Tupelo Community Concert Association, which has anchored the city's cultural life.

Today, Lee County has excellent schools, including a state-of-the-art high school campus, and one of the country's most well-respected healthcare complexes, which has attracted hundreds of millions of dollars in inward investment. Tupelo has low unemployment and high social inclusion. It is a dynamic place, honoured by the National Civic League as an 'all American city' in 1967, 1989 and again in 1999. It has been listed as 'one of the best towns in America' for quality of life, while Mississippi, as a whole, is ranked 48th out of 49 US states for social capital.

The investment in social capital that brought these economic benefits was not a one-off activity. The city's commitment to a vibrant civic life is ongoing. For example, the Tupelo Artist Guild Gallery, a public arts gallery, was opened in 1985 in the original People's Bank and Trust Company. More recently came the Pied Piper Playhouse, opened in 1992, and which relies upon funding and services donated by local businesses.

Has all of this civic-mindedness been a big burden on local business? In fact, Tupelo is an economic success story. The region is now the largest producer of upholstered furniture and the second largest manufacturer of all furniture sold in the world. More than 4400 Lee County residents are employed in furniture manufacturing, with a 'cluster' of more than 100 companies producing related goods.

According to Harvard professor Robert Putnam, 'residents invested in social capital – networks of cooperation and mutual trust – and reaped tangible economic returns'.

Source: www.tupelo.net/welcome.html; Putnam (2001, pp323–324)

---

would be too expensive to make and have no market, he made up samples at home and distributed them to friendly secretaries, who quickly found that they were ideal for sticking important messages on computer monitors.

So was born the Post-It note, just one of 3M's 525 US patents to date. The company is consistently ranked top for innovation, and has paid a dividend every quarter since 1916. 3M actively manages its social capital – for example, with the '15 per cent rule'. Technical employees are urged to spend up to 15 per cent of their work time – one day in seven – pursuing ideas of their own choosing, including those outside of their normal responsibilities. 'You can't be innovative', according to William Coyne, senior vice-president for research and development, 'if you only do what your boss tells you to do' (www.3m.com/about3m/century/3M_COI_Book.pdf).

Business writers Sumantra Ghoshal and Christopher Bartlett emphasize that trust and creativity are intertwined at 3M: 'On the organizational trapeze, individuals will take the entrepreneurial leap only if they believe that there will be a strong and supportive pair of hands at the other end to catch them' (www.3m.com; Cohen and Prusak, 2001, pp119–120).

3M is a good example of social capital seen from the company's perspective. In Box 12.1 we move from Minnesota to Mississippi to see it from the wider community's viewpoint.

These two stories are, admittedly, anecdotal, as much of the literature on social capital tends to be. For example, authors Cohen and Prusak (2001) (a duo from IBM's Institute for Knowledge Management) are rare in that they address the full range of social capital issues rather than the narrower and more company-centric concept of intellectual capital. So, they focus on informal networks, story-telling, gossip and open-office design, as well as technical networks and knowledge-management systems. In their view, 'the subject of organizational social capital is too new to have generated much [statistical] evidence... Our focus reflects the fact that social capital resides in the daily life of organizations' (Cohen and Prusak, 2001).

However, there is an emerging body of evidence of the importance of creative trust to business (MacGillivray and Doane, 2001). Recent examples include the following:

- A study of entrepreneurs in North Carolina showed that individuals with a more diverse set of network contacts are more likely to start businesses than those without such networks (Renzulli et al, 2000).
- A US Department of Labor study of eight large firms found that over 80 per cent of workplace learning occurs informally. A specific study for Corning found that 80 per cent of engineers' ideas came from face-to-face contact, but that they would only stray about 30 metres from their own desks to bounce ideas around informally (Cohen and Prusak, 2001).
- Networks – word of mouth, friends of friends – helped about 50 per cent of people, especially disadvantaged groups, enter the US job market (Putnam, 2001). Active participation is more common in smaller, informal business networks than in large ones (Davis and Aldrich, 2000).
- San Francisco has higher social capital than Boston – which has been linked to the economic success of the Silicon Valley high-tech cluster over its East Coast rival. There is also UK evidence that social capital correlates with enterprise formation (Saxenian, 1996; MacGillivray, 2002).
- UK inner-city enterprises with strong community links have higher turnover growth rates than those with weak links (MacGillivray, Potts et al, 2002).

We have reviewed the evidence that creative trust is good for business. How does it work?

Social capital at work: bridging and bonding

There are two different ways in which businesses can build capital. 'Bonding' occurs within homogeneous, like-minded groups (such as among a company's sales reps), while 'bridging' occurs between heterogeneous groups (such as when senior management meets community activists). 'Bonding social capital', says Robert Putnam, 'constitutes a kind of sociological super glue, whereas bridging social capital provides a sociological WD 40' (Putnam, 2001).

An example of the two types of social capital at work is the Co-operative Bank. The Co-op's well-known ethical stance is, according to the bank's regular partnership report, popular with staff. The vast majority of staff say that they are proud to work for the company, which benefits from low staff turnover for the sector. The ethical position is also believed to be the main attraction for a third of the bank's current account customers. The Co-op's ethical position, therefore, builds social capital twice: bonding with bank staff and bridging to customers. The bank's ethical stance has even made an impact on the behaviour of some of its suppliers – though not all.

Another example of social capital at work is at British Airways (BA). When discussing social capital with BA in 2000, we found that some aspects of social capital were flying high: the highest level of employee share ownership in the UK and a very low staff turnover rate of 3 per cent. On the other hand, the company had strong departmental cultures, which makes 'bridging' a challenge. Pilots, in particular, were said to be 'cliquey' and did not mix with cabin crew.

BA has invested heavily in social capital in the form of its new Waterside headquarters. This is a complex of buildings arranged along a bustling thoroughfare; a café, bank, shops and restaurant, intermingled with trees and fountains, give a light, spacious feel even on a typical overcast West London day. Bridges, glass-sided elevators and open atriums let people see the public area as they move through the headquarters. 'This not only increases the chances that people will find someone they want to talk to', say Don Cohen and Laurence Prusak, 'it helps make the collective life of the organization visible. It shows that the organization has a collective life, a fact that the elevators and mazes of walls and cubicles of a high-rise building can strip it of its reality' (Cohen and Prusak, 2001, pp89–91).

A third example of a company that has invested in social capital as part of its drive for sustainability is Marks and Spencer (M&S). During the early 2000s, only 45 per cent of people surveyed by the Future Foundation said that M&S was open in providing details, and customers were deserting in droves. It was losing its creative trust. Nigel Robertson, head of change, identified the need 'to be more honest and challenging with each other. That's something we've found very difficult in the past'.[1] M&S is planning major improvements in the way that it talks to the public – and has been considering setting up a stakeholder council. Even more importantly, M&S has committed itself to being 'the most trusted retailer wherever we trade by demonstrating a clear sense of social responsibility and consistency in our decision-making and behaviour'.

'Marks and Spencer is strong enough to survive', says Robert Jones of Wolff Olins (Jones, 2000, p145):

> *Integrity – honest trading – is a big enough idea. It just needs reinterpretation in a way that undermines the old autocratic culture of 'closing ranks'. One option – and the company is already doing lots in this area – is to be the retailer that's best at organic foods, at products free of genetically modified ingredients, at ensuring fair wages for its third-world clothing workers, at reducing unnecessary packaging, at cutting the energy its stores use up, and so on. This, after all, is the new respectability: and it's ideal territory for Marks and Spencer.*

So much for successes; what about problems? One example is Kodak, which during the early 1990s had 23 different groups working to develop applications for digital scanners, linking well to the outside research community but unable to collaborate effectively with each other. Another example is Johnson & Johnson, which was said to have had 150 people working – largely independently – on preparing its IT systems for Y2K (Cohen and Prusak, 2001).

A third example is the sample of UK firms recently surveyed by the Design Council. Under half of them said that design, innovation and creativity had contributed to increased profits during the past three years, and only 37 per cent of the companies said that they had developed or introduced any new product or service during that period (Design Council, 2001).

Bridging and bonding are both needed to boost creativity and build trust. Too much bridging on its own leads to lack of focus; too much bonding leads to complacency. It is not hard to think of recent examples of companies depleting their social capital by getting this wrong. The question is how to manage it better.

How to manage and measure social capital

When it comes to measuring social capital, we can learn from the experience of other forms of capital such as intellectual capital. *Fortune* journalist Thomas Stewart insisted that 'intellectual capitalism desperately needs a practical language...or it will be mired in a quicksand of meaningless verbal goo'

Table 12.3 *Framework and indicators for managing social capital*

	Bonding	Bridging
Creativity	*Key words*: Innovation 'at work', in tight teams, using sweat equity and incentives	*Key words*: Brainwaves in 'the third place', among friends and strangers, for the fun of it
	Examples: Xerox, BT, Shell	*Examples*: 3M, Grameen Bank, Dyson
	Indicators: Time spent on innovation/ investments in R&D (eg 3M) 'Rookie Index' (average years of service) (eg Celemi) Number/ratio of project ideas accepted/rejected	*Indicators*: New products as percentage of total turnover (eg Hewlett Packard) Staff serving on committees of local organizations Percentage of staff who have worked for competitors
Trust	*Key words*: Building the brand through shared ethos, mission, morale, story-telling, gossip	*Key words*: Marketing the brand by example and reputation, rooted in the community
	Examples: Hewlett Packard, Co-op Bank, Marks and Spencer	*Examples*: Nokia, Amazon, Virgin
	Indicators: Length and quality of relationship with suppliers and clients Employee share ownership and retention rates (eg BA) Existence of independent enthusiasts' clubs/websites (eg Harley Owners Group)	*Indicators*: Reputation/trust in company (eg BT) Brand value/reputation as place to work (eg Interbrand) Level and scope of local community engagement (eg GRI)

(Stewart, 1998). On the other hand, business writer Charles Leadbeater warned that companies could be 'heading down the cul-de-sac of collecting endless inventories of often irrelevant data suggested by new accounting tools' (Leadbeater, 2000).

The experience of Scandinavian companies such as Cowi, Skandia, Nokia Tyres and Celemi with intellectual capital has been that measurement is a useful way to manage new forms of capital so long as it is kept in proportion (Nordika, 2001). More recently, British Telecom (BT) has been measuring reputation; Zurich Financial Services makes a social capital statement; and the Nationwide Building Society is asking itself what trust is worth to its business (MacGillivray, 2002).

Despite these specific examples, however, there is still no generic guidance on how to measure social capital in business. To generate a coherent framework that would allow this, social capital can be broken down into four components: creativity, trust, bonding and bridging. These components interact, as is shown in Table 12.3.

Each element in Table 12.3 has key words to explain the nature of the interaction, along with some business examples and some possible indicators (primarily taken from existing company measurement projects) to help measure and manage the interactions.

In total, Table 12.3 contains 12 possible indicators, some of which are easy to measure, others harder. If consistently measured over time, they would lead to a dynamic understanding of social capital and of how to build it. Of course, many other measurements are possible; but these 12 would make a useful start in what is still a new area for management. The alternative – to do nothing – would risk losing creativity and trust.

Notes

1   *On Your Marks* (2000), issue 8, www2.marksandspencer.com/the company/ ourcommitmenttosociety/index.shtm

Chapter 13

What if Business as Usual Won't Work?

Ros Oakley and Ian Buckland

The role of standards in corporate sustainability performance

There is a growing sense that organizations must recognize that they have a wider responsibility than their own profitability and returns to shareholders. They must take responsibility for their wider economic, social and environmental impact. But there is a lack of consensus about what organizations should be doing to contribute to sustainable development, or what constitutes corporate social responsibility. Corporate sustainability standards have a key role to play in establishing this consensus.

Emerging standards for sustainability and corporate citizenship serve two purposes. In part, they are about circumscription, practical guidance and measurement that allow good practice to be understood and repeated. This coincides with the familiar definition of a standard as a measure of quality, an approved example or model for imitation, and a mark of integrity and honesty. But standards are also about providing focus for this still-developing movement. This is consistent with another meaning of a standard as a distinctive emblem used as a rallying point of an army or movement. Corporate sustainability standards provide a vehicle to articulate what organizations of the 21st century should be about. Indeed, the very process of developing standards is as important as the resulting standards themselves; it is a mechanism for drawing in the views of different stakeholders.

It is possible to draw distinctions between codes, guidelines and standards, particularly whether they are mandatory or voluntary and their level of formality.

This, however, is not the focus of this chapter and we will use standard here in a wide sense that encompasses codes and guidelines. We use the term standard to mean a written statement that seeks to influence practice so that it is repeatable.

The growth and scope of corporate sustainability standards

Take-up of voluntary standards continues to grow. Research by the Institute of Business Ethics (Smith, 2002) found that 'in August 2001, 73 of the companies listed in the FTSE100 either had a code of business ethics or had one in preparation. There has been a rising trend among FTSE500 companies to have such codes rising from 33 per cent in 1993 to 57 per cent in 1997.' Probably the most widely accepted standard is the International Organization for Standardization's (ISO's) ISO14001, which by the end of 2001 had been taken up by over 37,000 organizations in 112 territories.

The spectrum of standards has also been expanding to cover all areas of the sustainability agenda. However, research in 2000 by the Organisation for Economic Co-operation and Development (OECD) on 246 voluntary corporate codes found that most were concerned with the environment and labour agendas. It is also noticeable that codes of conduct tend to be concentrated in certain sectors. OECD found that codes were concentrated in trade, textiles, chemicals and extractive industries. Codes addressing labour issues tend to be concentrated in sectors such as garments, footwear, sports goods, toys and retailing, whereas environmental codes are more likely to be found in chemicals, forestry, oil and mining.

Do we need corporate sustainability standards? Given the growing resources being devoted to developing and adopting standards, it is worth asking do we need them at all? What benefits do they offer and what are the drawbacks?

Benefits of sustainability standards

Standards:

- Allow good practice to be codified and shared. A recent OECD report (OECD, 2001) argues that private codes help to change business behaviour and help to develop intangible resources, notably expertise and consensus.
- Reduce the learning cycle that each organization must go through, allowing previous experience to be shared and built upon. The Global Reporting Initiative (GRI), for example, provides a ready-made framework of appropriate indicators for organizations wishing to report their social performance.

- Allow professionalization. The development of AA1000, for example, has given rise to a recognized set of skills and practitioners in the field of social auditing and stakeholder dialogue.
- Help drive out bad practice. The development of clear reporting guidelines and management systems will help to counter the problem of manipulation by corporate public relations (PR) departments to put the best possible light on corporate performance.
- Provide a mechanism for recognizing those who commit to follow them. The recognition of achievement helps consumers to reward those companies that reach agreed standards and, in turn, provides some incentive for companies.
- Help consolidation and focus – a standard picks out the essential elements. This helps organizations to overcome complexity and focus limited resources. It is noticeable that some actors are involved in several standards initiatives, bringing with them shared frames of reference. Sometimes standards refer directly to others. The FTSE4Good, for example, takes account of compliance with a diverse range of standards as evidence of meeting its criteria. These include elements of ISO14000; the UN Global Compact; the International Labour Organization's (ILO's) core labour standards; the Environmental Management and Auditing System (EMAS); Social Accountability 8000 (SA8000); and the World Health Organization (WHO)/ United Nations Children's Fund (UNICEF) international code on the marketing of breast-milk substitutes.
- Allow comparison: from comparison comes learning. Comparison also underpins accountability, allowing, for example, the benchmarking of comparable activities.
- Can reduce entry and transaction costs by providing ready-made templates and management systems, and can make those costs easier to forecast.

Concerns about sustainability standards

Standards can create problems too, of course. Dangers include:

- Promoting accepted practice rather than best practice. The QWERTY keyboard is now the *de facto* standard for keyboard layouts, despite the fact that it is not the best design ergonomically. As this example shows, standardization even around an inferior standard can still be better than no standard at all.
- Inhibiting innovation. Companies may choose to follow standards rather than develop their own practices. The existence of a standard can make it harder for new practices to be accepted.

- Being seen as an irrelevance, that they are not taken up or are inappropriately applied. It is true that in the area of voluntary standards companies may choose those that are easy to comply with, and ignore those that are really most relevant to their operations.
- Promoting the lowest common denominator. Of course, standards can be pitched so low that they may give stakeholders a false sense of reassurance. But, over time, the understanding of standards and what they mean will grow. It is easier to campaign to change a specific standard than investigate and campaign to change the practice of each individual company.
- Being too rigid or too flexible. Drafting a universally applicable standard runs the danger of being insensitive to a whole host of diversity issues. Does a ban on child labour preclude children delivering newspapers in the UK? If not rigid enough, does it leave the standard open to endless interpretation?

In our view, there is no doubt that the benefits outweigh the potential problems. The development of standards is essential to agreeing the parameters of organizational responsibility and evaluating organizational performance. But what type of standards do we need?

Approaches to standards

As we have seen, the number of standards is proliferating. Despite their variety, they can be grouped into a series of approaches.

Principles-based standards

These set out broad principles of behaviour but do not specify how they are to be achieved or how conformity with them can be assessed.

The pros of these standards are that they help to identify the scope of issues with which an organization should be concerned. They provide opportunities for external alignment for an organization.

The cons are that they often lack details as to how they are to be implemented, and compliance is often difficult to establish.

Performance standards

Performance standards are concerned with what the organization actually achieves. These may vary from very specific targets, to outlining indicators against which organizations should report and then tracking their performance historically or against a suitable external benchmark.

The pros of these standards are that they help to provide transparency about what is actually being achieved.

Table 13.1 *Approaches to standards*

Principle-based standards	Process standards	Performance standards	Hybrid standards
UN Global Compact	AA1000	SA8000	FTSE4Good SIGMA
OECD Guidelines for Multinational Enterprises	ISO14000 ISO9000	Global Reporting Initiative	London Stock Exchange Combined Code
Caux Roundtable Principles for Business			Winning with Integrity (Business in the Community)

The cons include the difficulty of establishing generally applicable targets that are sufficiently sensitive to different operating contexts – for example, different industries, countries and scale of operation – and of ensuring that like is compared with like. Such standards may have a narrow scope. Their predefined scope may miss the issues that are most important to a given company and its stakeholders.

Process standards

These standards outline processes that an organization should follow in order to improve its performance. While performance is not directly addressed, the standards may include processes to identify appropriate performance targets – for example, in consultation with stakeholders or by reference to external codes.

The pros of these standards are that they provide practical guidance to organizations and help to establish repeatable processes and behaviours.

The cons are that they do not prescribe performance levels, and may be over-bureaucratic.

Hybrid standards

Some standards combine elements of the three other approaches as illustrated in Table 13.1.

Principles-based standards, while strong on values, are weak at suggesting how they should be operationalized by business. In contrast, performance and process standards are often more detailed. One criticism sometimes made is that there is too much emphasis on process and not enough on performance-based standards. But performance standards tend to rest on process. Process standards, with their emphasis on defining concepts and prescribing activities, are part of the process of building the infrastructure for ever-improving levels of performance. We need to take care not to dismiss process standards simply

---

Box 13.1 ISO14001 AND THE PROCESS/PERFORMANCE PARADOX

The Environment Agency of England and Wales sponsored research during 2002 into whether the environmental performance of ISO14001-certified sites was superior to those without the standard. The results found that while the standard was associated with better procedures, these procedures were not associated with better performance (fewer incidents, complaints or non-compliance events) (Environment Agency, 2002). Critics seize on such evidence to dismiss ISO14001 or process standards. But we need to be wary of judging process standards directly for performance – we don't condemn the existence of financial management systems when we discover poor performance. We use the management system to help identify and understand the problem. If the system is also hindering performance, then we improve the process. Our financial accounting system has evolved in just such a way, constantly modified in the light of new understanding. Despite its failings and its indirect relationship with financial outcomes, it plays an essential supporting role. In the corporate sustainability field we are still building this necessary infrastructure.

---

because they do not directly address performance. Likewise, a certain degree of consensus needs to be achieved about what is to be done before you can measure how well it is being performed and the impact that it has. A case in point for many practitioners today is to agree on ways to measure new intangibles such as social performance in order to set performance targets (see Box 13.1 for a discussion of the process/performance paradox relating to ISO14001).

And, so, it is all too easy to get into a sterile debate about which of these types of standards is best. In reality, each of the different approaches has something to offer. One single approach cannot provide all that is needed. We need an architecture of standards that together combines the best of the different approaches and provides:

- a framework of principles;
- practical workable guidance on what is to be done; and
- the ability to assess actual performance.

The diverse format of standards

We find further diversity in the format of different standards. They vary from *de facto* practice, to loose guidelines, to specifiable standards and formally recognized standards developed through nationally and internationally agreed mechanisms – for example, the British Standards Institution (BSI) or the ISO. Similarly monitoring and enforcement mechanisms range from none at all to self-regulation, or the use of transparency mechanisms – for example, public reports – through to formal independent auditing and verification. Codes concerned with broad principles tend to have a less prescriptive format and looser enforcement mechanisms. Performance-based codes tend to have tighter monitoring procedures. SA8000, which is concerned with labour standards, for example, requires certification by an SA8000-accredited body. The certificate is renewed every three years and requires six-monthly surveillance audits. Process codes tend to be quite prescriptive in their format – for example, the ISO14001 standard sets out clear steps to be followed, which can be audited. The variety of formats reflects the different audiences for whom they are written, their intended uses and their authorship.

Who are the standard-makers?

As Table 13.2 illustrates, there are many different actors involved in crafting standards. Companies are able to write organization-specific codes that are relevant to them and their context, and which they are committed to uphold. But there is nothing to stop a company from avoiding difficult issues and resisting external challenges. A company code in isolation is vulnerable to the accusation of being simply a PR exercise. Industry codes can be particularly helpful in identifying relevant dimensions of performance and laying the foundations for comparable data. A potential concern is that standards forged in an industry forum such as a trade association may result in a lowest common denominator approach and result in weaker standards.

Business-led standards may lack credibility with civil society, especially because of the need to reconsider the boundaries of companies' responsibilities and to whom they are accountable. Conversely, non-governmental organization (NGO)-led standards are sometimes charged with lack of realism, and may be viewed with suspicion by business. As for traditional standard-making bodies such as the BSI and ISO, some argue that their processes are not sufficiently transparent and are ill equipped to properly represent the voices of civil society and the developing world.

Governments are, of course, key players, responsible for the United Nations declarations and capable of moving from voluntary to mandatory standards. But governments of different hues have, to date, been hesitant to take the lead, nor is there universal agreement that this is what is needed.

In response to the shortcomings of standards led by a single stakeholder group, there has been a developing trend to involve diverse stakeholders (such as the GRI as illustrated in Box 13.3). Such multi-stakeholder initiatives can be challenging and complex to manage. Nor are they immune to criticism. They, too, must consider to whom they are accountable and how they reflect the views of different stakeholders fairly, particularly Southern perspectives; but the outcome of multi-stakeholder dialogue is more likely to have widespread credibility. Table 13.2 illustrates a sample of standards by different authors. Box 13.2 provides more detailed illustration of Responsible Care as an example of an industry standard.

Table 13.2 *Sample of standards by authorship*

Authorship type	Example
Single company	Allied Domecq; Levi Strauss; Nike; Bradford and Bingley
Industry	FORGE2 (banking and insurance); Responsible Care Programme (Chemical Industries Association)
Commercial-rating agency	FTSE4Good; Dow Jones Sustainability Index
Business grouping	Caux Roundtable
NGO	Amnesty International's Human Rights Guidelines for Companies; Principles for Global Corporate Responsibility by the Interfaith Center for Corporate Responsibility; Ecumenical Council for Corporate Responsibility(Great Britain); Task Force on the Churches and Corporate Responsibility(Canada)
Standards-making body	ISO9000; ISO14000
Government	European Union's Eco-Management and Audit Scheme
International institution	UN Declaration of Human Rights; ILO conventions; OECD Guidelines for Multinational Enterprises
Multi-stakeholder	GRI; AccountAbility 1000 series; Social Accountability International SA8000; SIGMA; Ethical Trading Initiative Base Code

---

BOX 13.2 RESPONSIBLE CARE – AN INDUSTRY STANDARD

Responsible Care was started by the Canadian Chemical Producers Association during the mid 1980s and now operates in 46 countries as a means for the chemical industry to express its commitment to continual improvement in all aspects of health, safety and environmental performance. In the UK, the Responsible Care Programme is operated by the Chemical Industry Association (CIA), which represents 75 per cent of the chemical industry, including companies such as Bayer, AstraZeneca, Johnson Matthey and Kodak. At the heart of Responsible Care are ten guiding principles covering such areas as product stewardship; resource conservation; policy; process safety; and employee involvement. In 1998, the CIA published a Responsible Care guidance manual that includes a management system and mandatory self-assessment. Take-up of these elements has been high; but interest in voluntary third-party certification has not been as strong. Responsible Care contains a number of initiatives to help struggling members. Poor performers are offered peer support through a system of local 'cells' and consultancy best practice packages paid for by the CIA. As with many sectoral standards, Responsible Care does not exclude individual companies from operating their own codes or attaining other cross-sectoral standards.

BOX 13.3 GLOBAL REPORTING INITIATIVE (GRI)

The Global Reporting Initiative (GRI) is one of the better-known standards. A long-term multi-stakeholder international undertaking, GRI's mission is to develop and disseminate globally applicable sustainability reporting guidelines for voluntary use by organizations reporting on the economic, environmental and social dimensions of their activities, products and services. The guidelines set out five principles for reporting. GRI was originally sponsored by the Coalition for Environmentally Responsible Economies (CERES) – a coalition of environmental groups, socially responsible investors and public pension administrators – but then received United Nations (UN) support. In 2002 it became a permanent institution. Organizations that adopt GRI produce reports on their financial, social and environmental information. GRI takes an integrated approach to performance measurement. It includes cross-cutting indicators that straddle traditional issues-based demarcations. By the time of its August 2002 review, over 140 organizations had prepared reports based on GRI, attracted, in part, by its comprehensive and easy-to-understand guidelines on non-financial reporting. The GRI August 2002 release sought to build in ease of benchmarking over time and between organizations; however, its growing complexity may deter less committed users. It does not a specify a rigid format, preferring a guidelines approach that allows organizations to report 'in accordance'. GRI does not police reporting claims made in its name.

What makes for successful sustainability standards?

Existing sustainability standards are already contributing to understanding and practice. The diversity of approaches helps to provide flexibility. But there is a need for some consolidation, even if only to reduce the sheer number of standards and resulting confusion. What characteristics are required of successful corporate sustainability standards for the future?

Credibility with a wide range of stakeholders

As already indicated, taking a multi-stakeholder approach is essential to building credibility and acceptance.

Integrated management

Many companies are managing the three elements of the triple bottom line (TBL) separately; but, increasingly, the three elements need to be managed in a way that recognizes their interrelationships. Such a strategic approach is also important to making breakthrough rather than incremental change. Fewer integrated standards may also encourage take-up by companies for whom the number of standards has been a deterrent to action.

Practically focused

Many businesses are looking for practical guidance on what they should do.

Flexibility

Standards need to reflect the circumstances and context in which they are applied, where this is appropriate. It is unlikely that a single standard can provide all that is needed. It may be appropriate to have a company code to reflect corporate values and circumstances, a sector code to address specific issues, as well as a more generic standard that is externally recognized and validated. The way in which standards interact will play an important part in achieving flexibility.

Proven effectiveness

It is important to show evidence of organizational improvement over time. As more companies report, particularly to agreed standards, we are likely to see more benchmarking and league tables being published. It is also likely that we will see more industry-specific measures being developed.

Drivers for corporate sustainability standards

There are a number of drivers for increasing standardization. A succession of different opinion surveys suggests that the public expect higher levels of non-financial corporate performance. At the same time, the surveys also suggest declining trust in companies. The investment community is showing increasing interest in corporate sustainability performance and is looking for ways to assess it, evidenced by the development of specific indices such as the FTSE4Good.

Governments are also showing increasing interest. We are seeing more examples of legislation touching on the social and environmental behaviour of companies. In the UK, the 1999 amendment to the 1995 Pensions Act requires trustees of pension funds to declare a statement of investment principles, including the extent to which social and environmental issues are considered. In France, a new law has been published requiring reporting by French corporations. The European Union (EU) has issued first a Green and then a White Paper on corporate social responsibility (CSR). It has concluded, so far, that a voluntary approach is preferable.

ISO, the international standards-making body, is also showing increasing interest in this area. In June 2002 its Consumer Policy Committee considered the desirability and feasibility of a CSR standard and recommended the establishment of a working party. It has mentioned the sustainability integrated guidelines for

---

BOX 13.4 SUSTAINABILITY INTEGRATED GUIDELINES FOR MANAGEMENT (SIGMA)

The SIGMA project is led by AccountAbility, the BSI and Forum for the Future, and is backed by the UK government's Department of Trade and Industry (DTI). SIGMA aims to develop an integrated approach for organizations to manage sustainability issues in order to improve their social, economic and environmental performance.

SIGMA builds on existing standards such as AA1000 and the Global Reporting Initiative (GRI), but seeks to pull them together in an integrated framework. Via its project steering group, SIGMA involves a wide range of stakeholders, including the Confederation of British Industry, the Association of Chartered Certified Accountants (ACCA), Traidcraft, and the World Wide Fund For Nature (WWF). In addition, it is actively piloting its work with leading companies and public-sector organizations to test out what actually works. The SIGMA guidelines consist of a set of principles, a management framework and a toolkit of practical approaches. The guidelines provide a process for organizations to improve their performance.

---

management (SIGMA) (see Box 13.4) as an example of what a corporate responsibility management system might look like. Discussions within ISO about whether a standard is needed and the form it should take are ongoing.

Some argue for voluntary standards, seeing them as a substitute for legislation and mandatory standards. That is, if business regulates itself and secures its licence to operate, it will stave off the prospect of governmental interference. An alternative view is that voluntary standards are a precursor of legislation. Here the existence of agreed concepts and approaches makes the legislators' job much easier and thereby brings legislation closer.

Conclusion

Standards are no panacea. There are real problems in crafting standards that are general enough to be widely relevant; specific enough to be actionable; flexible enough to endure; and stringent enough to secure improvement. The standards we currently have may not do enough, but they are capable of evolution. Standards do have a crucial role to play. They provide a vital part of the infrastructure to improve corporate performance. They enable learning, allow comparison, set thresholds and provide an example for others to follow. The development of standards is also important in a second sense. It provides a rallying point to focus on the fundamental nature of corporate performance, how it is to be achieved and how it should be evaluated. Crafting new and ever-more challenging standards is an essential endeavour. Standards of different types will help to give greater definition to the concept of the triple bottom line and, most crucially, will help to ensure that it is effectively translated into action.

Chapter 14

Put Up or Shut Up

Paul Monaghan

Introduction

Whether matters progress over months, years or decades, the drivers for social and environmental disclosure seem set to increase. For large companies based in the developed world, the question seems not to be *whether* to report, but *when* and in *what manner*.

Based on the example of the Co-operative Bank, which has been recognized as a world leader in both the pursuit of sustainable development and its translation into profitable performance, this chapter explores the *whys* and *hows* of producing a leading-edge sustainability report.

It looks like CSR is around for the duration

In 2002, the FTSE100 index fell by 25 per cent – the third consecutive year in which the London stock exchange finished lower than it began. In Japan, the Nikkei 225 index fared even worse, finishing lower than it had at any time during the preceding two decades. On Wall Street, the Dow Jones fell by 17 per cent in 2002, its worst performance for 28 years. Taken together, this represented the most severe bear market since the Great Depression, more than 70 years ago.

The prophets of doom and gloom would surely now be vindicated; the fragile shoots of corporate social responsibility (CSR) and ethical consumerism would wither under the pressure of an economic downturn. The markets and consumers would reassert themselves along more neo-classical, value-devoid lines and we would be back to the situation where 'the business of business is business'. But no, the precise opposite has happened. CSR has gone from strength to strength, and ethical consumerism is slowly growing! The proponents of CSR have found that their ideas are falling on ever-more fertile ground. Doors that had remained firmly closed are now somewhat ajar. An increasing number of blue chip companies are taking a triple bottom line (TBL) or sustainability approach to management. At the centre of this revolution is enhanced corporate governance, more rigorous risk management and internal control, much improved accounting and reporting, and a complete overhaul of independent audit and assurance. How has the situation come to pass?

There are many reasons, not least the reverberations of the collapse of Enron in November 2001. Prior to this, the markets had pulled away from their post-11 September lows and many investors were in bullish mood. What followed was an avalanche of profit warnings and tales of boardroom misbehaviour. June 2002 saw not only the biggest corporate failure in history, WorldCom, but also the discovery of a potential UK£2 billion accounting fraud at Xerox. Now it was not just the public and non-governmental organizations (NGOs) who were taking corporate utterances with a pinch of salt, but also financial analysts and investors. The deputy chairman of Credit Suisse Asset Management recently commented: 'Investors are fed up with being misled by companies which claim they're performing; but it turns out they are not. Companies that do not have perfect corporate governance will underperform.'[1] In order to counter US investors' lack of trust, the Sarbanes-Oxley Act was hurriedly cobbled together in 2002 and serves to remind chief executives that they should present a true picture of their companies' financial state and personally vouch for it. Across most of the world, the rules governing those who watch over business – from auditors to non-executive directors – are being tightened. And shareholders are now much more willing to question corporate actions and the way in which they are rewarded.

Of course, this 'revolution' is currently little more than ethics with a small 'e', and while it may assuage investors, it will do little to tackle the wider lack of trust in business among the general public. Much more can be done, and done profitably. This chapter examines why trust in business is rightly so low and offers some straightforward and inexpensive suggestions for those businesses that wish to maintain or build on stakeholder trust. Use is made of the UK-based Co-operative Bank, which has won many plaudits across the world for both its sustainability reporting and the manner in which good ethical and ecological performance has contributed to improving profitability.

Trust in business is low and falling

It is common wisdom to observe that the public's trust in organizations and institutions of *all* types is deteriorating. However, if one looks at the research a little closer, it transpires that, arguably, there is only one occupation where there has been a persistent deterioration over the last decade in trust: business. Since the early 1980s, opinion pollsters MORI have researched levels of trust among the UK's different occupations. They have found that over the period of 1993 to 2002, trust in 'doctors' and 'teachers' has increased and that these professions are trusted by more than 80 per cent of those polled. In comparison, 'business leaders' is the only occupation to show a persistent decrease in trust over the same period, and trust in the utterances of this profession is now only just over 20 per cent and only marginally better than for journalists and politicians.

Research by MORI has found that the proportion of the UK public who feel that industry and commerce does not pay enough attention to its responsibilities has increased from 68 per cent in 1997 to 73 per cent in 2002, and that the number of people able or willing to name any company that contributes to society and the community has remained static at 33 to 34 per cent.[2] Such trends are particularly worrying for business when one also considers that, compared with five years ago, the proportion of consumers saying that corporate responsibility is very important in their purchasing has almost doubled, from a quarter (24 per cent) in 1997 to more than two in five (44 per cent) in 2002 (MORI, 2002).

The need for transparency and third-party assurance

Not long ago it was assumed that environmental management systems were a good proxy for environmental performance (and that reporting was merely the icing on the cake). Many companies still argue that 'regulatory relief' should be given to firms with environmental management systems certified to an Environmental Management and Auditing System (EMAS) or International Organization for Standardization (ISO) standard. But a project sponsored by the European Union (EU) has seriously undermined that idea (www.environmental-performance.org). The study compared the economic and environmental performance of 280 companies and 430 production sites in 6 industrial sectors across 6 European countries. It found that, in general, those companies with an environmental management system did not perform significantly better than those without. Indeed, in some cases they appeared to perform worse! The authors of the report suggest that policy-makers' attention should be focused on encouraging and rewarding reporting. The mere presence of management systems is not sufficient to drive the desired improvements in environmental performance (or business performance, for that matter). This conclusion was recently borne out by another study, commissioned by the UK's

Environment Agency, which found that industrial sites with certified environmental management systems are no more likely to comply with legal requirements than sites without them.

Since its genesis during the late 1980s, environmental reporting has increasingly established itself across the world as a mainstream business development tool for larger companies, with over 1000 having produced reports. Sectors that have led the way are utilities, chemicals, petrochemicals, forestry/paper products, transport and information technology. There has been much less enthusiasm among entertainment, leisure, hotels, restaurants, real estate, distributors and wholesalers. Up-to-date reporting information is available at CorporateRegister.com, an excellent free online database of several thousand social and environmental reports. From country to country there are significant variations in environmental disclosure, with the UK credited as having the world's highest incidence of environmental reporting. In the UK, around 70 per cent of FTSE100 companies voluntarily publish formal environmental reports. However, if one includes EMAS statements (as per European Council Regulation No 1836/93), then Germany demonstrates a level of environmental disclosure at least matching that of the UK. Many expect Japan to quickly become a world leader in this field in the near future.

Currently, social reporting is not as prevalent as environmental reporting, although it is rapidly growing. In the UK, the number of companies publishing specific reports on social policies rose from just 3 in 1996 to 28 in 1999. A 2001 survey conducted by the CSR network found that 54 per cent of Fortune 100 companies had begun reporting on their corporate social responsibility programmes. It can be anticipated that all companies engaged in voluntary environmental reporting will extend their disclosure to social issues over the next two or three years.

It is interesting to note how quickly aspects of sustainability reporting can grow in a given sector. As recently as 1999, a paper appeared in *Greener Management International* from KPMG Finland that noted that both environmental reporting and assurance were 'rare' in the financial services sector. Just 15 per cent of the Fortune 250 largest financial institutions produced an environmental report and just 18 per cent of all reports studied had any form of independent verification. Just three years later, an article in *Environmental Finance* (Scott and John, 2002) noted the 'explosion' in environmental reporting in the sector (there were now more than 150 different reporters) and the fact that half of these had some form of independent verification (which compared well with the average 38 per cent of current verified reports for all sectors combined).

Legislative and other drivers

It is often stated that a company promoting issues of ecological sustainability and social responsibility can realize a sustainable competitive advantage. This is possible, as is proven by the Co-operative Bank. However, it is probable that ethical and ecological business practice will never become the business norm until companies are mandated to develop appropriate indicators and report accordingly. Thankfully, this is now beginning to happen. The option of not disclosing environmental information (and, in some cases, social information) is increasingly being removed. In Norway, Denmark, The Netherlands, Australia and Sweden there exists some form of mandatory environmental disclosure requirement. France has called for mandatory social and environmental reporting, extending its already innovative Bilan Sociale, and heated debate exists in the UK, where there are proposals to increase the rudimentary social disclosure requirements that are already in place. In 2000, UK Prime Minister Tony Blair stated his belief that all of the UK's top 350 companies should be engaged in environmental reporting, and threatened legislation should action not be taken voluntarily. However, the current voluntary approach to social and environmental reporting is proving ineffective. The government's own data shows that, in 2002, just 99 of the FTSE350 were publicly reporting on their environmental performance and including at least some data on their key impacts.

The financial services sector is another increasingly important driver for social and environmental reporting, particularly in the US and UK, which are two of the world's three leading financial centres. Cerulli Associates have calculated that, worldwide, socially screened portfolios hold US$1.5 trillion of assets, most of which is held in US institutions. If one includes portfolios that support shareholder advocacy, then the figure rises further. Research undertaken by the Social Investment Forum has found that US$1 out of every US$8 under professional management in the US is part of a socially responsible portfolio, or US$2.2 trillion.[3] A recent survey in the City of London conducted by Business in the Community found that 33 per cent of analysts and 40 per cent of investors thought that environmental issues were important factors in decision-making.[4] This represents a significant increase on 1994, when a similar survey revealed that just 20 per cent of analysts considered environmental issues important. The figures for social issues have increased by an even wider margin, from 12 to 34 per cent of analysts. In the UK, pension fund trustees must now disclose the extent to which social, environmental or ethical considerations are taken into account in the selection, retention and realization of investments, and the policy directing the exercise of the rights attached to investments. Both Germany and Australia have announced plans to introduce similar disclosure requirements. In response to such drivers, one of the UK's largest insurance and pension fund managers, Morley Fund Management, which has UK£100 billion under management, has announced that it will vote against the annual accounts of any top 100 firm that doesn't produce an environmental report, and will abstain from voting on the accounts of any top 250 UK firm that doesn't produce a report. In 2002, leading UK institutional investor Co-operative Insurance Society (CIS) launched a UK first for the investment industry by putting its entire UK investment voting record on its website (www.cis.co.uk). The UK Association of British Insurers (ABI) has published guidelines that set out what social and environmental information institutional investors expect to see in the annual reports of companies in which they invest. The ABI plans to monitor the degree to which companies provide the information once the guidelines are in place. The recently launched FTSE4Good ethical investment index is expected to act as a further driver to reporting. Companies are assessed on the information that they publish about their policies, management and reporting on the environment, human rights and social issues. Nearly two-thirds of companies listed on the UK FTSE's main European share index have been excluded.

But a lot of what is published is a waste of paper

With some exceptions, the surge in environmental and social reporting has not delivered an improvement in the public's perception of business. This is principally because the quality of much of the reporting that has taken place is highly questionable. This is a view shared by the European Commission, which, in the introduction to its recommendation on environmental reporting, noted that 'environmental information disclosed by companies is often inadequate and unreliable'.[5]

Many firms that produce environmental reports bemoan the fact that the investment community does not take them seriously. However, this is hardly surprising considering the general poor quality of output. A Business in the Environment survey in the UK found that, while 90 per cent of analysts and 82 per cent of investors say that they use environmental and social information from companies, only about one third find the information of good quality, and independent third-party sources are considered more useful.[6]

The absence of *robust* independent third-party verification of data and commentary is another major factor undermining ethical and environmental reporting, although matters are improving. Research undertaken in 2002 by KPMG has found that 117 (27 per cent) of the 440 companies from the top 100 in 19 countries included a third-party verification statement, compared with 18 per cent in 1999.[7] Verification rates are by no means uniform across the world: in the UK 53 per cent of reports surveyed were verified, while in the US and Germany just 3 per cent and 6 per cent were verified, respectively.

Moreover, where independent audit and verification is undertaken, the work is all too often of questionable quality. A particularly problematic area is that of 'balance'; many reports devote pages of commentary to the highlights of their performance, while making little or no comment on less favourable areas (and these omissions often pass without comment in verification statements). *The Ecologist* journal has observed that:

> BP [British Petroleum] and Shell are among the most ambitious companies in the world in their targets for increasing their rate of extraction of oil and gas, Shell by 5 per cent a year, and BP by between 5.5 and 7 per cent. The cuts BP and Shell have promised are in greenhouse gas emissions from their own business operations – from gas flaring, from pipeline leakages, from energy usage (such as in powering refineries) – not in those from their core products.

True sustainability reporting
(and that means 'warts and all')

The key steps in producing a social report are described below. The aim is to improve and maintain stakeholder trust, and, ultimately, to improve business and social/environmental performance. A host of standards and guidelines is emerging in these fields, and one of the most difficult tasks for practitioners is picking their way through this morass. The standards identified here reflect the analysis and experience of the Co-operative Bank, which is described in more detail at www.co-operativebank.co.uk/partnership2000/standards_frameset. html.

Lack of resources is not usually a problem, just an excuse

It is the Co-operative Bank's experience that the resources required for sustainability reporting are small. There is, therefore, no practicable reason why listed companies and large unlisted companies (turnover in excess of UK£500 million) should not report on their social and environmental impacts. The bank's *Partnership Report* has received numerous commendations over the past three years, including best sustainability report in the UK (2002 and 2003), best environmental report in the UK (2001) and best social report in the UK (2000 and 2001). Most recently, the United Nations Environment Programme (UNEP) declared it to be the world's best sustainability report. This world-leading report is put together by a team of four over a period of four months, and external assurance and commentary comes to less than UK£50,000. The cost of the reporting exercise itself comes to less than UK£200,000, and includes the production of not just a 100-page paper report, but a summary that is distributed to more than 2 million customers and a range of internet materials that strive to be accessible with regard to disability and language. UK£250,000 may sound like a lot of money; but this needs to be considered against the cost of providing the usual 'glossy' warts-free accompaniment to the financial statements – something most major companies engage in – and the fact the largest 500 companies in the world now control an astonishing two-thirds of world trade. How can resources be a problem for them? The UK government commissioned research in 2001 that found that annual environmental reporting costs ranged widely from UK£6500 to UK£535,000, with an average cost of UK£92,716.[8] When the costs associated with strategy formulation and establishment of information systems were excluded, the range of reporting costs was UK£4500 to UK£259,500, with an average cost of UK£66,903.

Usually, the biggest block to social and environmental reporting is the prevalent internal corporate culture, not a lack of financial resources or technical expertise. Companies are traditionally geared to 'hype' the good news and 'kill' the bad news. To many, it is counter-intuitive to propose that a company should proactively communicate good and bad in a balanced way. Therefore, when the business case is put together for reporting, it is essential to tackle such inertia up front. A key message is to emphasize that partners live in the real world and do not expect perfect performance. They also have access to plenty of independent analysis of performance, typically via the media or pressure groups. However, it is the Co-operative Bank's experience that communicating poor performance makes any good performance all the more believable. Furthermore, by and large, media coverage tends to be fair, if not slightly sympathetic. In total, during April 1998, the bank's first *Partnership Report* was featured in more than 15 million newspapers and reached more than 9 million TV viewers and almost 3 million radio listeners. This was subsequently calculated to be worth more than UK£900,000 of equivalent advertising value.

The Co-operative Bank has now been producing independently verified triple bottom line sustainability reports for five years. However, it is still the only retail bank in the UK to do so. The bank has shown that there is a business case; ethical and ecological financial value analysis shows that the bank's ethical and ecological positioning made a sizeable direct contribution to profitability in 2001 of UK£21.5 million. This was arrived at by determining profitability for each product and the degree to which an ethical/ecological brand positioning motivated customer attraction and retention. It is the bank's experience that reporting drives improvements in performance. Improvements in performance, in turn, have a positive effect on staff recruitment and retention, customer recruitment and company reputation (see Box 14.1)

Box 14.1 Sustainability reporting drives performance

Staff recruitment and retention

The Co-operative Bank's staff turnover is well below that of the financial services average. The bank had an overall staff turnover of 14 per cent during 2001. By comparison, the Chartered Institute of Personnel and Development reports 24.7 per cent turnover in 2000 for the finance, insurance and real estate sector (www.cipd.co.uk).

Customer recruitment and retention

Since launching the Co-op's partnership approach in 1997, the number of customer accounts has increased by over 30 per cent and the bank's profitability has doubled. In addition, since launching its ethical policy in 1992, the bank's profitability has increased from UK£17.8 million (1993 figures) to UK£107.5 million in 2001 – a sixfold increase. Recent personal customer research shows that for 31 per cent of personal current account customers, ethical and ecological reasons are the most important influence in their decision to open and maintain an account with the bank (by far the most frequently specified reason).

Company reputation

An international survey by Echo Research has found that the Co-operative Bank is one of the five most trusted companies worldwide.[9] The independent researchers analysed over 1000 media items across six countries, interviewed more than 200 senior decision-makers and conducted an internet survey among leading public relation practitioners before coming up with the world's top corporate social responsibility (CSR) brands.

Report what stakeholders say is *material,* not what managers consider *convenient*

Sustainable development objectives can be extremely broad, and in order to deliver them, organizations need to focus on specific issues. One way of doing this is through indicators that quantify and illustrate the important issues. Return on equity, profit before taxation and cost/income ratios are widely recognized as key financial indicators of business performance. They are broad-brush, highly aggregated statistics that summarize the overall picture. Organizations use indicators to determine business strategy and stakeholders use them to judge how well a business is performing. According to conventional business wisdom, indicators should ideally meet a number of criteria referred to as SMART: specific, measurable, achievable, realistic and timely.

Identification of issues and, ultimately, indicators, can proceed via a bottom-up and/or top-down approach. 'Bottom up' means stakeholder-derived indicators, which flow from a dialogue process (for example, the bank's staff routinely cite 'salary and benefits' as a matter of high importance). 'Top down' means the recommendations of expert national/international panels (for example, the UK government suggests that all companies should report on the issues of climate change, water and waste in a very specific manner; see www.defra.gov.uk/environment/envrp/index.htm). The Co-operative Bank has, to date, opted to take a dual approach, giving stakeholders primacy in the development of economic and social indicators, but deferring to expert counsel on ecological matters. In addition, as recommended by the Centre for Tomorrow's Company, the bank reports on certain additional matters that are considered integral to its business success model (for example, staff understanding of mission and values). With regard to stakeholders such as 'local communities', the bank seeks the opinions of charities and campaigning groups as trusted proxy representatives. For example, community involvement accounting and reporting continues to evolve in line with Business in the Community's (www.bitc.org.uk) understanding of best practice.

With reference to stakeholder-derived indicators, rigorous guidance is available in the form of the AccountAbility's AA1000 framework (www.accountability.org.uk). Originally launched in late 1999, AA1000 focuses on improving the quality of social accounting, auditing and reporting. It comprises a basic planning model – underpinned by the core concept of *inclusivity* – that guides the process of defining stakeholders and then engages with them in identifying performance metrics. Other frameworks, such as total quality management (TQM)/ EFQM (on quality), SA8000 (on labour standards) or the Global Reporting Initiative (GRI) (on sustainability reporting) all mention stakeholders. But only the AA1000 series puts stakeholders at the heart of its understanding of quality, accountability and the driver of change. Throughout 2003, AccountAbility will extend and deepen its framework (henceforth known as the AA1000 series) with the release of a series of specific modules, one of which will concentrate on stakeholder engagement. *Accountability Quarterly*, the institute's journal, presents early thinking as to what constitutes quality in stakeholder engagement. Rightly, it notes that definitions of excellence will transcend aspects of *procedure* (how was the engagement undertaken?) and concentrate more and more on *responsiveness* (was there evidence of organizational learning through the engagement, and of putting such learning into practice in policies and decisions?) and *outcomes* (were there tangible outcomes in terms of changed performance that benefited stakeholders?). The great strength of AA1000 is that it helps to tackle the key challenge of *materiality*. There are a million and one things that a company could account for and report on; but what are the issues that most concern stakeholders (and this includes investors)?

The most widely accepted sustainability reporting template is the GRI, which sets out a comprehensive set of guidelines that cover the whole triple bottom line of social, environmental and economic reporting (www.globalreporting.org/). Under development since 1997, and published in August 2002, these guidelines have been referred to, or followed, by over 140 corporations around the world, including BASF, British Telecom, Bristol-Myers Squibb, Canon, the Co-operative Bank, Danone, Electrolux, Ford, General Motors, KLM, NEC, Nike, Novo Group, Nokia, SAB Miller and Shell. GRI's great strength is that it strives to focus on impact, and not merely engagement. The indicators are usually, but not always, quantitative (for example, water consumption per unit of product, adherence to a specific international standard on child labour, and net monetary contributions per year to host communities). Reporters are encouraged to normalize information (as well as to provide absolute values) where such ratios will make the information easier to interpret and understand. The Co-operative Bank's preferred ratio unit is 'per customer account'.

Of course, all social performance management is underpinned by engagement; but, ultimately, it is outputs and impacts that need to be reported and managed. Focusing on process does not only short-change stakeholders, but also management. As observed earlier in this chapter, the time and effort invested by many companies in the pursuit of certified environmental management systems could be misplaced. Similarly, the Co-operative Bank, in its pre-*Partnership Report* days, won many awards for its ethnic minority recruitment policies and processes; but the bank's actual work force was, and still is, far from being representative of the local population norm. However, it is still the case, much to the disappointment of stakeholders, that companies tend to report more on processes than performance.

The importance of independent assurance

Independent third-party verification statements are becoming increasingly important when corporate social responsibility claims are made. Verification is being demanded by society in everything from organic farming (Soil Association label in the UK), sustainable timber (Forestry Stewardship Council and a host of other 'trade' labels), greenhouse gas emissions and carbon dioxide sequestration in woodland management.

In June 2002, AccountAbility launched a consultation document on an assurance standard linked to the AA1000 series. It has been designed specifically to complement reporting standards such as the GRI and quality management systems such as the sustainability integrated guidelines for management (SIGMA), as well as serving as a stand-alone assurance standard. Following extensive consultation, the assurance standard was launched in March 2003. However, even in the absence of the assurance standard, AA1000 has been the basis for the independent verification statements accompanying a whole host of social and sustainability reports. Assurance providers such as Bureau Veritas have developed what it calls, VeriSEAAR, an assurance process based on the AA1000 framework that assesses the quality of stakeholder engagement. Similarly KPMG utilized AA1000, which it states as best practice, as the basis of its assessment of the 2001 CIS social report (winner of the 2000 UK Social Reporting Awards). Each of the Co-operative Bank's five partnership reports have also been assessed against the principles of AA1000 by ethics, etc.

The 'credibility' of the auditor/verifier to stakeholders should not be underestimated. Research undertaken by MORI (Evans, 2001) in the UK has found that just 37 per cent of those polled believed that 'Accountants can be trusted to ensure that companies report their financial figures honestly.' Imagine how low the levels of trust might be if the question had asked about social and environmental figures! Stakeholders are looking for individuals and organizations who not only have the technical expertise required to undertake an audit, but also have the ethical knowledge base and integrity to say what needs to be said in verification statements. Stakeholders expect verification commentary to contain a degree of criticism, as well as praise. If criticism is absent, and the organization under scrutiny is far from perfect, then the integrity and credibility of verifiers will be questioned. That in itself undermines the whole social reporting process and its objective of building trust with partners.

Previously, the NGO movement and media have taken a relaxed view of the quality of audit and verification, principally in order to encourage first-time reporters. However, as ethical and environmental reporting has grown, so has the willingness of influencers to comment on shortfalls. For example, Friends of the Earth has alleged that Indonesian multinational Asia Pulp and Paper (APP) is 'one of the world's biggest and most destructive paper companies', despite the fact that APP's forestry and mill operations hold 16 ISO14001 certificates that are re-audited every six months by consultancies including SGS and DNV (www.foe.org.uk).

The Co-operative Bank's auditor, Richard Evans, recently set out his approach, which is driven by the letter *and spirit* of AA1000:

> *Assurance or verification should not be seen as a quality refinement for only the most advanced reporters. Neither should it be reduced to no more than an independent assessment of a company's accountability, risk management and governance systems. Verification looks for truth in the way an organization's performance has been reported. It is interested, above all, in the balanced, complete and accurate portrayal of all outcomes that may affect stakeholders in the areas that stakeholders have identified as critical.*

Notes

1   *The Guardian*, 31 December 2002
2   MORI interviewed a representative quota sample of 2001 adults aged 15 and over in Great Britain between 6 July to 19 August 2002.
3   An article based on Social Investment Forum research and reporting: 'Schemes Failing To Put Money on Their Morals', *Financial Times*, 5 November 2001
4   'Investing in the Future: City Attitudes to Environmental and Social Issues', *Business in the Environment*, May 2001
5   See www.europa.eu.int.
6   See www.business-in-environment.org.uk.
7   KPMG (2002) *International Survey of Corporate Sustainability Reporting 2002*
8   Environ (2001) *Report on a Survey of Environmental Reporting Costs and Benefits*. Environ, prepared for DEFRA
9   See www.echoresearch.com/reports/csr2.htm.

Chapter 15

Addressing the Economic Bottom Line

Vernon Jennings

Introduction

This chapter looks at how Novo Nordisk, the Danish healthcare company and a world leader in diabetes care, has approached the economic bottom line and is using socio-economics to help improve diabetes care.

During the early 1990s, Novo Nordisk recognized that sustainable development would be high on the new agenda for business. The company began by addressing the most familiar and immediately challenging part of the agenda – environmental responsibility and eco-efficiency – and adopted a proactive environmental strategy based on stakeholder engagement that went beyond regulatory compliance.

Dialogue with environmental and consumer non-governmental organizations (NGOs) and others identified the new issues that would need to be addressed, and – as a biotechnology and pharmaceutical company – the ethical implications of genetic engineering and animal experimentation emerged as important topics to include in the learning process. However, it was realized early on that sustainable development is not just about the environment, it is also about people and how they interact.

Moreover, outside the walls of the company, its activities and performance have far-reaching impacts and consequences. As global corporate citizens, international companies not only need to behave responsibly, but also need to be accountable to society, as well as to their employees, customers, shareholders and other stakeholders. Progressive companies now recognize that they must engage with a variety of stakeholders across national and international borders

Figure 15.1 *The capital model and the triple bottom line*

to help create policies and practices that will shape the future sustainable development agenda.

Today, Novo Nordisk, like a number of other companies, measures business performance against the triple bottom line (TBL) concept of sustainable development, which attempts to integrate not only the environmental and social aspects, but also the economic aspects. This is a complex equation and many companies are only just beginning to explore the real implications. The triple bottom line brings together three critical elements: environmental responsibility, social equity and economic performance. By adopting this formulation, companies hope to be able to take a more systematic and sustainable approach to managing business risks, staying attuned to the concerns of society and to spotting opportunities, as well as potential problems.

In reality, the three bottom lines are closely inter-linked; but the concept of the triple bottom line is a convenient reflection of the different types of capital that any company or other organization uses in providing goods and services to society, as illustrated in Figure 15.1. The challenge for business – and societies worldwide – is to operate in ways that maximize *all* of the scarce forms of capital involved in producing goods and services, recognizing that there are three main types of capital, rather than one: environmental (or natural), social (or human) and human-made (or economic).

Defining the economic bottom line

Publicly listed companies are required by law to make freely available certain information about their business, to file particular information for public inspection and to circulate accounts to their shareholders. Corporate annual reports primarily address the immediate needs of shareholders and financial analysts; but they do not directly account for what is important to stakeholders in economic, as opposed to purely financial, terms. For example, investments made by a company in training and educating employees make an economic contribution beyond the company's boundaries by building national productive capacity in society at large. Yet, such information is not provided in a traditional financial report. To illustrate the point further, financial reports do not detail the wider economic impacts of a company's activities at the local community level through the provision of employment, the income that employees earn and use and the taxes that they pay, as well as the impact on local suppliers and service providers.

So, while the economic component of the triple bottom line is often assumed to be synonymous with financial performance, in fact, there are significant differences between the two. In its simplest form, finance is about the provision of money when and where required for consumption or for investment in commerce. As such, it concerns the market valuation of transactions that pass through a company's books. Economics, on the other hand, is the means by which society uses human and natural resources in the pursuit of human welfare. As a result, economics extends beyond the boundaries of a single organization and is inextricably linked to both the environmental and social elements of sustainable development.

However, economic growth on its own is an inadequate indicator of progress towards sustainable development. From both an environmental and social perspective, the growth in human-made capital may imply either improvement or deterioration. Although damage is rarely deliberate, the long-term consequences can be irreversible. Yet, efforts to remedy environmental damages or to alleviate social inequity require financial resources, generated through economic prosperity.

Economic growth, therefore, is not a goal in itself. Rather, we need to look at how the benefits are achieved, who benefits and how we can offset any harm done. Companies today are primarily rewarded for their financial performance – even if what they are delivering to society may be socially or environmentally damaging.

A company's economic impact may be seen as either positive or negative, but neither is measured in today's traditional financial accounts. A company's investment in a community can serve as an engine of growth in the economy through employment, boosting local supply chains and developing a new skills base. The goods and services that companies produce can also contribute to a higher quality of life.

Yet, growth in economic activity and wealth does not necessarily reduce poverty, provide a cleaner environment, or achieve greater equality or better quality of life. In fact, there is widespread disagreement about the type of economic growth that supports sustainable development. It is only by attempting to understand, manage and communicate economic impacts that the areas in which corporate activities have positive environmental and social outcomes can be identified, as well as the areas where there is room for improvement.

Obtaining information about our economic impact requires that we measure in concrete quantitative terms the operational outcome of corporate decision-making. By reporting on various economic indicators, companies can gain a picture of the status of their operations and can use this knowledge to measure whether they conduct their business in a way that supports their vision.

However, company responsibility cannot replace societal responsibility. The government is important in its role of ensuring proper regulation, introducing the right incentives and creating laws that enhance our understanding of the type of economic and social behaviour that is to be rewarded by society.

In addition, current price structures do not reflect the real costs of, for example, clean air and freshwater. Creating an environment in which companies and consumers are rewarded for alleviating social and environmental problems, and penalized for negative impacts, poses a major challenge for governments and businesses alike.

One way in which to create this environment is to begin assessing not only the financial, but the wider economic impact of a company. For example, what is the impact of a company's operation on the community seen from a social, environmental and economic point of view? This is a difficult task and, currently, no single method can be applied; but early pioneers have included British Telecom (BT) and South African Breweries (SAB), both of which have attempted to address these issues to some degree in their annual environmental and social reports.

An explicit relationship should also be established between the financial and the economic bottom line, otherwise the economic bottom line will not materialize and management will not be able to argue effectively that the economic bottom line is essential for business, as well as for society. Especially in hard times, pressure will be put on all issues that are regarded as non-essential for survival regardless of the true relationships.

Pilot studies on socio-economic impact

In 1999, Novo Nordisk began to explore more systematically the wider socio-economic aspects of its business with case studies at the local level. A pilot study was undertaken at the company's largest production site at Kalundborg in Denmark in its first attempt to map out the issues at the local level. The aim was to use the experience gained from this study to begin to develop models and measures to record the socio-economic, social and environmental impact of the company's other sites. A stakeholder approach was adopted and the major local stakeholder representatives were asked to define the issues and dilemmas that they thought were most important. In addition, an analysis of the economic impact of the operations on the local community was performed, as shown in Figures 15.2 and 15.3.

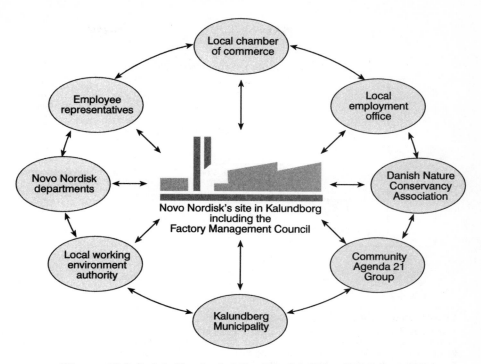

Figure 15.2 *Stakeholders in the Novo Nordisk Kalundborg pilot study*

The results are detailed in Novo Nordisk's 1999 social and environmental report (www.novonordisk.com). The presence of a big employer such as Novo Nordisk is of great importance to a small community like Kalundborg. For example, it influences the employment structure as 60 per cent of the factory's 1657 employees reside there. In fact, Novo Nordisk employs one in ten of the working population of the municipality of Kalundborg and is, therefore, the community's largest private employer. Obviously, this dominant position implies a strong contribution to the local economy. The total gross salaries paid to the households by Novo Nordisk amount to 10 per cent of the total income in the community. The municipality's budget also benefits from the tax revenues generated by the activities at Novo Nordisk. For 1999, the estimated company tax to be paid by Novo Nordisk to the municipality amounted to 26 million Danish kroner (DKK). In addition, the contribution of income tax from Novo Nordisk employees to the municipality was valued at DKK 58 million, which amounted to 6 per cent of the municipality's total tax revenues. On the other hand, Novo Nordisk received around DKK 3.5 million in 1999 as reimbursements for wage costs to employees on maternity leave and during periods of sickness.

Building on the work undertaken at Kalundborg, in 2000 a case study was undertaken analysing the general economic impact of the Novo Nordisk insulin

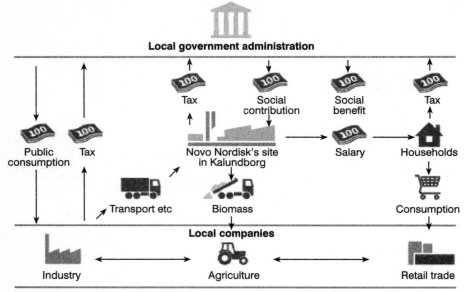

Circulation of money in the local community

This figure illustrates how activities at Novo Nordisk influence the circulation of money in Kalundborg. The company pays its employees (households) and it pays taxes. The households, in turn, spend money on consumption and taxes, and the local authorities spend money on social contributions and other public spending.

Figure 15.3 *Circulation of money in the local community in Kalundborg*

plant in Clayton, North Carolina, US. The results were presented in the company's 2000 environmental and social report (www.novonordisk.com), and a summary in which the various contributions were quantified is shown in Figure 15.4.

The Clayton analysis demonstrated that the local plant has numerous impacts on the local community, employees and suppliers, and is a stimulus to local trade and industry. Furthermore, employee salaries and wages and income to suppliers spent locally multiply through the local economy as employees become consumers.

Measuring economic footprints

Understanding the economic impacts at the local level can be helpful in building up a picture of the economic footprint of a company. However, as yet, there is no systematic approach to accounting and reporting on a company's overall economic performance and the area is still evolving. Novo Nordisk has used the Global Reporting Initiative (GRI) as a framework for analysing the company's impact on the creation of economic wealth and on the economic stakeholders

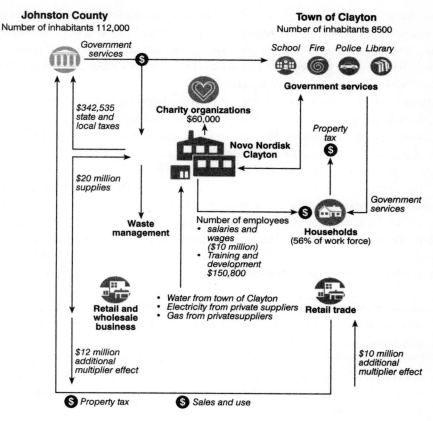

Figure 15.4 *Circulation of money and services at Clayton, North Carolina*

that benefit from its activities. In the GRI's 2002 *Sustainability Reporting Guidelines* (GRI, 2002) the focus is on how the economic status of the stakeholder changes as a result of the organization's activities, rather than on the financial condition of the organization itself.

According to the GRI, each company has to determine what constitutes its own specific communities. A company that operates in multiple sites, in multiple countries, has a diverse supply chain, or has an unusual set of stakeholder groups may need to perform specific analyses that address these communities. A unified approach to the different sites may not always be appropriate. Taking inspiration from the GRI, Novo Nordisk began to create a systematic approach that started with an analysis of the company's direct economic impacts. As a company, the most direct contribution to wealth creation is through employing people's skills in creating goods and services and investing in new plants and equipment. Indirect impacts, in turn, refer to when a company's operations multiply through society and affect the economic activities and performance of others, both individuals and organizations. The direct impacts are equivalent to the impacts on the economic stakeholders who directly profit from the company's activities, while the indirect impacts describe how income earned in society is used to create new income. Indirect impacts are also sometimes external to the market in the sense that current price structures do not reflect the real costs of the company's activities to society and, therefore, have an indirect impact not reflected in the monetary flows of social and national accounts.

The kind of data and indicators available today make accounting for the direct impact a manageable task; but getting a better grasp of the indirect impacts presents a challenge.

The direct effects of Novo Nordisk's activities impact upon certain groups of economic stakeholders, as defined by GRI, who have a direct financial interest in the company. These include suppliers, employees, shareholders, the public sector and a company's management, who control what is retained in the company for future growth and investment. The GRI framework will help companies to achieve the following goals:

- Measure and report economic performance in terms of the financial wealth created by the company, defined by where products are manufactured and where income is earned.
- Examine the direct and indirect impacts of company wealth on selected stakeholders in different regions and countries to obtain information about those who benefit from the company's activities and where these stakeholders are located.
- Address the economic impacts of the consumption of the company's products from a general economic perspective and, for Novo Nordisk, from a health economics perspective.

In the case of Novo Nordisk, the consumption of pharmaceutical products has both direct and indirect impacts on people and affects quality of life. Indeed, the impact of pharmaceuticals, such as insulin for the treatment of diabetes, on human health is perhaps the greatest economic impact as a pharmaceutical company. Nevertheless, the full value of the products is achieved only through interaction with the healthcare infrastructure provided by the society. Novo Nordisk has been addressing health economic issues for many years now and, more recently, has begun to examine these impacts in greater depth. While the indirect economic impact is difficult to quantify, the company has formed new partnerships to further develop its knowledge in this area. The direct impact of the products relates to the health and survival of the patient in question, while the indirect impact is measured through the consequences that better health has on quality of life and productivity of the patient, as well as on the patient's family.

However, trying to extend the positive economic impact of a company's products presents a dilemma. How a product, such as Novo Nordisk's insulin, is used is a function of the product itself, its price and its distribution and availability within the particular healthcare infrastructure. Not all of these are within a company's control. For example, it is not always possible to control wastage or damage to a product due to improper storage, or to control the optimal use of the product due to lack of awareness and knowledge about the disease. But, as a profit-maximizing company, Novo Nordisk can exercise influence over the price of the product.

Herein lies the dilemma. It is Novo Nordisk's vision to have a positive impact on human health through the use of the company's products, particularly in the developing world. Therefore, how the company impacts upon human health through its pricing cannot be disregarded. An affordable product price level needs to be found that allows the company to remain profitable and to deliver a healthy return to investors. Novo Nordisk attempts to begin resolving this dilemma through the application of a new pricing strategy for the least developed countries where insulin is offered at 20 per cent of the average price in Europe, North America and Japan.

In its 2001 triple bottom line report (www.novonordisk.com), Novo Nordisk set out data on the distribution of created wealth by the company using the approach described by the GRI and earlier adopted by South African Breweries. This showed how the company's cash received was distributed across different stakeholders. For example, suppliers received 47 per cent and the remaining 53 per cent was attributed to various economic stakeholder groups profiting from company value added. The impact of the company wealth on selected stakeholders in different regions provided information about where those economic stakeholders are located.

The local studies of community impact presented above show that it may be difficult to take an overall and generic approach to TBL with regard to quantification.

In the eyes of society, our licence to operate as a company is justified by our ability to contribute to social welfare and quality of life. In the same way, the various policies and initiatives taken internally in the company must be justified by its ability to contribute to the financial health of the company. The triple bottom line means that the company focuses on creating value not just for shareholders, but for a broader group of stakeholders, some of whom are internal while others are external. An additional dimension has thus been added to the financial bottom line by supplementing financial profitability with positive socio-economic contributions as company objectives.

The Novo Nordisk economic stakeholder model attempts to summarize the socio-economic impact of the company based on the consumption and production activities. The model illustrates the interaction between the company

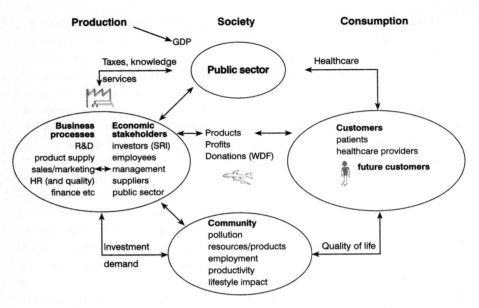

Figure 15.5 *The Novo Nordisk economic stakeholder model*

and the stakeholders in society, including suppliers, patients and healthcare providers, local communities, global communities and the public sector.

The company's added value is created through a range of internal business processes within which the commitment to TBL is integrated. In each of these business processes the added value is generated through interaction with various stakeholders. This kind of model prompts a new kind of decision-making in which we achieve a better understanding of the company's socio-economic impact.

The Novo Nordisk economic stakeholder model is shown in Figure 15.5.

Socio-economic impact of diabetes care

Understanding the economic bottom line can also help a company like Novo Nordisk to understand its wider socio-economic impacts and where it adds – and can add – value, depending upon the available healthcare infrastructure. But as a healthcare and pharmaceutical company, Novo Nordisk faces particular dilemmas relating to access to health and health economics. The economic prosperity of a nation and the health of its work force are largely dependent upon the investment made in the health of its people. Diabetes, which is Novo Nordisk's main treatment area, has been shown by the World Health Organization (WHO) to be one of the four major killers in the world and is often called the 'silent killer' as it kills through the late complications caused by inefficient care. Over the next 25 years the number of people with diabetes is set to more than double to 300 million, and 80 per cent of those individuals will be living in developing countries.

Those seeking to head off this pandemic face a dilemma. It is known how to optimize care; but, in practice, this happens too infrequently for a variety of reasons, such as lack of information, education, infrastructure, funding and medicine. In addition, poor decisions are occasionally made due to lack of knowledge about the options for addressing disease in the most economical way. Health economics, which present the costs and consequences of diabetes, is one way of showing how investments in healthcare can improve the overall level of care. Economic data that underline the costs associated with diabetes and the economic value of diabetes intervention are widely used to underscore the importance of the disease and its impact on the healthcare system. Health economics illuminates the choices to be made regarding limited healthcare resources, the effectiveness of healthcare treatments, the pricing of products and many other factors. Novo Nordisk has long used health economics as a decision-making tool that focuses the company's efforts, as well as a basis for informing decision-makers about the economic consequences of their choices.

Most people would agree that access to healthcare is a pre-condition for societal prosperity. The benefits of access to healthcare outweigh the costs for two reasons. Firstly, survival and improved health have an intrinsic positive value and, secondly, health improves the productive national capacity by realizing a human and national potential that otherwise would be wasted through sickness and death.

But what are the advantages for a society in ensuring access to insulin and improved diabetes care? To answer that question Novo Nordisk has been developing a model that helps to examine the socio-economic cost and benefits of diabetes and diabetes care, and takes into account quality-of-life factors.

WHO estimates that 9 per cent of all global deaths are caused by diabetes, primarily among people in their most productive years. In countries where access to healthcare is available, the care of people with diabetes also entails significant costs to the health system. Hospitalization and treatment of late complications (for example, blindness, amputations and heart-related problems) due to poorly treated diabetes are the main cost drivers. It is estimated that the costs of diabetes and its complications already account for between 5 and 10 per cent of total healthcare spending in most countries and up to 25 per cent in some.

In contrast, treatment with insulin has positive impacts upon human health and, consequently, people with diabetes can live an almost normal life and reduce the risk of disabilities and premature death. For people with diabetes, access to insulin positively impacts upon their financial situation through improved quality of life and productivity. Their intellectual and emotional capacity, and that of their families, is no longer primarily focused upon worries about health, but rather upon more positive, forward-looking and productive activities.

Conclusions

Much progress has been achieved in understanding the triple bottom line of sustainable development since the early 1990s. Understanding the economic bottom line, as opposed to the purely financial, is an essential pre-condition to achieving sustainability. However, understanding and measuring the interactions between the economic and the social and between the economic and the environmental bottom lines remain the key challenges.

References

ACCA (2001) *Advances in Environmental Accounting*. London, ACCA/Environment Agency Seminar, Certified Accountants Educational Trust.

ACCA (2002) *ACCA and Sustainability*. London, Association of Certified Chartered Accountants.

AccountAbility (1999) *AccountAbility 1000 (AA1000) Framework Standard, Guidelines and Professional Qualification*. London, AccountAbility.

AccountAbility (2002) *AA1000 Assurance Standard: Guiding Principles*. London, AccountAbility.

Adams, C A (1999) *The Nature and Processes of Corporate Reporting on Ethical Issues*. London, CIMA.

Adams, C A (2002a) 'Internal Organisational Factors Influencing Corporate Social and Ethical Reporting: Beyond Current Theorising', *Accounting, Auditing and Accountability Journal* 15(2): 223–250.

Adams, C A (2002b) 'Factors Influencing Corporate Social and Ethical Reporting: Moving On from Extant Theories', *Accounting, Auditing and Accountability Journal* (forthcoming).

Adams, C A (forthcoming) *A Critique of Reporting on Ethical, Social and Environmental Issues: The Case of ICI*. Resubmitted to Abacus.

Adams, C A and N Kuasirikun (2000) 'A Comparative Analysis of Corporate Reporting on Ethical Issues by UK and German Chemical and Pharmaceutical Companies', *European Accounting Review* 9(1): 53–80.

The Age (2002) 'Car Makers Off the Hook in Pollution Suit', *The Age*. Melbourne.

AICPA (1977) *The Measurement of Corporate Social Performance: Determining the Impact of Business Actions on Areas of Social Concern*. New York, American Institute of Certified Public Accountants.

Anderson, S and J Cavanagh (1996) *The Top 200: The Rise of Corporate Global Power*. Washington, DC, Institute of Policy Studies.

ASSC (1975) Accounting Standards Committee (formerly Accounting Standards Steering Committee) *The Corporate Report*. London, ICAEW.

Atkinson, A and M Epstein (2000) 'Measure for Measure', *CMA Management* 74: 22–28.

Atkinson, G, T Hett et al (1999) *Measuring 'Corporate Sustainability'*. London, Centre for Social and Economic Research on the Global Environment, University College London, University of East Anglia.

AWG (2001) *Transforming Our World: Sustainable Development Report 2001*, Huntingdon, UK.

Ayres, R U (1998) *Turning Point: The End of the Growth Paradigm*. London, Earthscan.

Ball, A, D Owen et al (2000) 'External Transparency or Internal Capture? The Role of Third Party Statements in Adding Value to Corporate Environmental Reports', *Business Strategy and the Environment* 9(1): 1–23.

Baxter, T, J Bebbington et al (2002) 'The Sustainability Assessment Model (SAM)', SPE International Conference on Health, Safety and Environment in Oil and Gas Exploration and Production, Malaysia.

Bebbington, J (2001) *Sustainability Assessment Modelling at BP: Advances in Environmental Accounting*. London, ACCA, pp55–66.

Bebbington, J and R Gray (2001) 'An Account of Sustainability: Failure, Success and a Reconception', *Critical Perspectives on Accounting* 12(5): 557–587.

Bebbington, J, R Gray et al (2001) *Full Cost Accounting: An Agenda for Action*. London, Association of Chartered Certified Accountants.

Beder, S (1997) *Global Spin: The Corporate Assault on Environmentalism*. London, Green Books.

Bennett, M and P James (1998) *The Green Bottom Line: Environmental Accounting for Management; Current Practice and Future Trends*. Sheffield, Greenleaf Publishing Limited.

Bernal, P (2002) 'Statement by the Executive Secretary of the Inter-governmental Oceanographic Commission (UNEXCO-IOC)', International Panel of the US Commission on Ocean Policy, Washington, DC.

Bierma, T, F Waterstraat et al (1998) 'Shared Savings and Environmental Management Accounting: Innovative Chemical Supply Strategies' in M Bennett and P James (eds) *The Green Bottom Line: Environmental Accounting for Management; Current Practice and Future Trends*. Sheffield, Greenleaf Publishing Limited, pp258–273.

Bradbury, H and B Lichtenstein (2000) 'Relationality in Organizational Research: Exploring the Space Between', *Organization Science* 11(5): 551–564.

British Petroleum (2001) *BP Environment and Social Report*.

Brown, L et al (1997) *State of the World*. London, World Watch Institute, Norton.

Brown, L et al (1999) *State of the World*. London, World Watch Institute, Norton.

Burritt, R (1998) 'Cost Allocation: An Active Tool for Environmental Management Accounting?' in M Bennett and P James (eds) *The Green Bottom Line: Environmental Accounting for Management; Current Practice and Future Trends*. Sheffield, Greenleaf Publishing Limited, pp152–161.

Cairncross, F (1991) *Costing the Earth*. Harvard, Harvard Business School Press.

Cash, R M, A M Cantu et al (2001) *A Review of Government Reporting*. McLean, Logistics Management Institute.

CERES and Innovest (2002) *Value at Risk: Climate Change and the Future of Governance*. Boston and New York, www.ceres.org/newsroom/press/climate.htm.

Cerin, P (2002a) 'Communication in Corporate Environmental Reports', *Corporate Social Responsibility and Environmental Management* 9: 46–66.

Cerin, P (2002b) 'Characteristics of Environmental Reporters on the OM Stockholm Exchange', *Business Strategy and the Environment* 11: 298–311.

CGG (1995) *Our Global Neighbourhood:The Report of the UN Commission on Global Governance*.

Chayes, A and A H Chayes (1993) 'On Compliance', *International Organization* 47(2): 175–205.

Chayes, A and A H Chayes (1995) *The New Sovereignty: Compliance with International Regulatory Agreements.* Cambridge, Mass, Harvard University Press.

CIA (2002) 'Responsible Care', www.cia.org.uk/industry/care.htm, Chemical Industries Association.

Cohen, D and L Prusak (2001) *In Good Company: How Social Capital Makes Organizations Work.* Boston, Harvard Business School Press.

Co-operative Bank and the New Economics Foundation (2002) *Ethical Purchasing Index 2002.* Manchester and London.

Corporate Watch (2001) 'Unilever's Mercury Fever', www.corpwatch.org.

Cowe, R (2001) 'In the Black, Red or Green?' *Green Futures* 27(March/April): 60.

Cowe, R and J Porritt (2002) *Government's Business: Enabling Corporate Sustainability.* London, Forum for the Future.

Cramer, J (2002) 'From Financial to Sustainable Profit', *Corporate Social Responsibility and Environmental Management* 9: 99–106.

Crooks, E (2002) 'Nestle Claiming $6 Million Compensation against Ethiopia', *Financial Times*, 19 December 2002.

CSD (2002) *Report of the UN Commission for Social Development.* New York.

Dahl, A (1995) *Towards Indicators of Sustainability.* Wuppertal, SCOPE Scientific Workshop on Indicators for Sustainable Development.

Daly, H E (1992) 'Allocation, Distribution and Scale: Towards an Economics that is Efficient, Just and Sustainable', *Ecological Economics* 6: 185–194.

Daryl, D (1995) *Green Ledgers: Case Studies in Corporate Environmental Accounting.* New York, World Resources Institute.

Davis, A and H Aldrich (2000) *Organizational Advantage? Social Capital, Gender and Small Business Owners Access to Resources.* Washington, DC, American Sociological Association Meeting.

Deegan, C (1999) 'Implementing Triple Bottom Line Performance and Reporting Mechanisms', *Charter* 70: 40–42.

DEFRA (1999) *Achieving a Better Quality of Life.* London, Department for Environment, Food and Rural Affairs.

Denisov, N and L Christoffersen (2000) *Impact of Environmental Information on Decision-Making Processes and the Environment.* UNEP GRID–Arendal.

Design Council (2001) *Design in Britain.* London, Design Council.

Design Council (2002) *Design in Britain.* London, Design Council.

Ditz, D, Ranganathan, R and Banks, D (eds) (1995) *Green Ledgers: Case Studies in Environmental Accounting.* Washington, DC, World Resources Institute.

Dixon, J A, L F Scura et al (1996) *Economic Analysis of Environmental Impacts.* London, Earthscan.

DJSI (2002a) *Corporate Sustainability Assessment, Dow Jones Sustainability Indexes,* see www.indexes.dowjones.com.

DJSI (2002b) *Corporate Sustainability Assessment Criteria and Their Weightings, Dow Jones Sustainability Indexes,* see www.indexes.dowjones.com.

DJSI (2002c) *Corporate Sustainability, Dow Jones Sustainability Indexes,* see www.indexes.dowjones.com.

DTI (2001) *Creating Value from Your Intangible Assets*. London, Department of Trade and Industry Future and Innovation Unit.

Eccleston, C H (2001) *Effective Environmental Assessments: How to Manage and Prepare NEPA EAs*. Boca Raton, Florida, and London, Lewis Publishers.

Ekins, P (1999) 'Business and the Environment: The Economics of Clean Business' in W E Halal and K B Taylor (eds) *Twenty-First Century Economics: Perspectives of Socioeconomics for a Changing World*. Macmillan.

Elkington, D (1999) 'Diversity don'ts', *Food Management* 34(October): 22.

Elkington, J (1994) 'Towards the Sustainable Corporation: Win–Win–Win Business Strategies for Sustainable Development', *California Management Review* 36(2).

Elkington, J (1997) *Cannibals with Forks: The Triple Bottom Line of 21st Century Business*. Oxford, Capstone.

Elkington, J (1998) 'The Sustainability Agenda: Not for the Short Sighted', *Accounting and Business*

Elkington, J (1999a) 'The Triple Bottom Line: Implications for the Oil Industry', *Oil and Gas Journal* 97(13 December): 139–141.

Elkington, J (1999b) 'Triple Bottom Line Revolution – Reporting for the Third Millennium', *Australian CPA* (November).

Elkington, J (1999c) 'Triple Bottom Line Reporting: Looking for Balance', *Australian CPA* 69: 18–21.

Elkington, J (2000) 'Sustainable Profits', *Charter* 71(April): 36–37.

Elkington, J (2001) *The Chrysalis Economy: How Citizens, CEOs and Corporations can Fuse Values and Value Creation*. London, Capstone.

Elkington, J and J Hailes (1988) *The Green Consumer Guide: From Shampoo to Champagne; High Street Shopping for a Better Environment*. London, Victor Golancz.

Environ (2001) *Report on a Survey of Environmental Reporting Costs and Benefits*. Environ, prepared for DEFRA.

Environment Agency (2002) *Environment Management Systems and Operator Performance at Sites Regulated under Integrated Pollution Control*. Technical Report P6-017/2/TR, Environment Agency.

Epstein, M and M-J Roy (1998) 'Integrating Environmental Impacts into Capital Investment Decisions' in M Bennett and P James (eds) *The Green Bottom Line: Environmental Accounting for Management; Current Practice and Future Trends*. Sheffield, Greenleaf Publishing Limited, pp100–114.

EU (1992) *Fifth Action Programme Commission*. Brussels, European Union.

Evans, R (2001) *Accountability Quarterly* 17.

Fineman, S (1994) *Going Green – Corporate Angst, Action and Inaction*. Birmingham, Aston University.

Fineman, S (1996) 'Emotional Subtexts in Corporate Greening', *Organisation Studies* 17(3): 479–500.

Fineman, S (1997) 'Constructing the Green Manager', *British Journal of Management* 8: 31–38.

Frederick, W C (1986) 'Towards CSR3: Why Ethical Analysis is Indispensable and Unavoidable in Corporate Affairs', *California Management Review* 28(2): 126–274.

Fritz, J-S (1997) *Earthwatch 25 Years On: Between Science and International Environmental Governance*. Laxenburg, International Institute for Applied Systems Analysis.

Frost, G R (2000) *Environmental Reporting: An Analysis of Company Annual Reports of the Australian Extractive Industries*. Armidale, University of New England.

Ghoshal, S and C Bartlett (1997) *The Individualised Corporation: A Fundamentally New Approach to Management*. New York, Harper Business.

Gilmour, G and A Caplan (2001) 'Social Reporting: Sustainability Business – Who Cares?' *Accountancy* 1 September.

Gladwin, T N, W E Newbury et al (1997) 'Why Is the Northern Elite Mind Biased Against Community, the Environment and a Sustainable Future?' in M H Bazerman, D Messick, A Tenbrunsel and K A Wade-Benzoni (eds) *Environment, Ethics and Behaviour: The Psychology of Environmental Valuation and Degradation*. San Francisco, New Lexington, pp234–274.

Golding, T (2003) *The City: Inside the Great Expectation Machine*. London, Prentice Hall.

Goldsmith, E (1998) *The Way: An Ecological World-View*. Athens, Ga, University of Georgia Press.

Gonella, C, A Pilling et al (1998) *Making Values Count: Contemporary Experience in Social and Ethical Accounting, Auditing and Reporting*. London, Chartered Accountants Educational Trust.

Gray, R and J Bebbington (2000) 'Environmental Accounting, Managerialism and Sustainability', *Advances in Environmental Accounting and Management* 1: 1–44.

Gray, R and J Bebbington (2001) *Accounting for the Environment*. London, Sage.

Gray, R et al (1993) *Accounting for the Environment*. London, Paul Chapman Publishing.

Gray, R, C Dey et al (1997) 'Struggling with the Praxis of Social Accounting: Stakeholders, Accountability, Audits and Procedures', *Accounting, Auditing and Accountability Journal* 10(3): 325–364.

Gray, R, R Kouhy et al (1995) 'Corporate Social and Environmental Accounting: A Review of the Literature and a Longitudinal Study of UK Disclosure', *Accounting, Auditing and Accountability Journal* 8(2): 47–77.

Gray, R and M J Milne (2002) 'Sustainability Reporting: Who's Kidding Whom?' *Chartered Accountants Journal of New Zealand* 81(6): 66–70.

Gray, R, D Owen et al (1987) *Corporate Social Reporting: Accounting and Accountability*. Englewood Cliffs and London, Prentice-Hall International.

Gray, R, D Owen et al (1996) *Accounting and Accountability: Changes and Challenges in Corporate Social and Environmental Reporting*. London, Prentice Hall.

Green Futures (2001) 'In the Black, Red or Green', *Green Futures* 27 (March–April), pp60–61.

GRI (2002) *Sustainability Reporting Guidelines*. Boston and Amsterdam, Global Reporting Initiative.

The Guardian (2002) 'Earth – Special Supplement', *The Guardian*, London, August 2002.

Hackston, D and M J Milne (1996) 'Some Determinants of Social and Environmental Disclosures in New Zealand', *Accounting, Auditing and Accountability Journal* 9(1): 77–108.

Hamilton, K (1996) *Pollution and Pollution Abatement in the National Accounts. Marginal Damages or Maintenance Costs?* Stockholm, London Group on National Accounts and the Environment.

Hanson, D J (2002) *Incorporating Sustainability into US Investment*.

Harbord, J (1999) 'Company Reports: A Lean Vision of an Inclusive Annual Report', *Management Accounting* 77: 36.

Harman, W (1996) 'The Shortcomings of Western Science', *Qualitative Enquiry* 2(1): 30–38.

Hart, S J (1997) 'Beyond Greening: Strategies for a Sustainable World', *Harvard Business Review* January–February.

Hartman, C and E Stafford (1996) 'Market-Based Environmentalism: Developing Green Marketing Strategies and Relationships', American Marketing Association Winter Educators' Conference.

Hawken, P (2002) 'McDonald's and Corporate Social Responsibility', Press Release from Food First and Institute for Food and Development Policy.

Hawken, P, A B Lovins et al (1999) *Natural Capitalism: The Next Industrial Revolution.* London, Earthscan.

Hayward, C (2002) 'How to be Good', *Financial Management* October: 14–16.

Hemmati, M (2002) *Multi-stakeholder Processes for Governance and Sustainability.* London, Earthscan.

Henderson, J (2002) *2002 Global Reporting Initiative.* London, SustainAbility.

Henriques, A (2001) *Sustainability, A Manager's Guide.* London, British Standards Institution.

Hewson, M and T J Sinclair (eds) (1999) *Approaches to Global Governance Theory.* Albany, State University of New York Press.

Hicks, J (1946) *Value and Capital.* Oxford, Oxford University Press.

Howes, R (2000) *Corporate Environmental Accounting: Accounting for Environmentally Sustainable Profits.* Volume in the International Library of Ecological Economics J Proops and S Simon (eds). Cheltenham, Edward Elgar Publishers.

Howes, R (2001) *Taking Nature into Account and the Evolution of a Sustainability Accounting Framework: Advances in Environmental Accounting and Management.* London, ACCA, pp28–38.

Howes, R (2002a) *Environmental Cost Accounting: An Introduction and Practical Guide.* London, Chartered Institute of Management Accountants (CIMA).

Howes, R (2002b) *Accounting for Environmentally Sustainable Profits.* London, CIMA, Research Update, pp2–4.

Howes, R, J Skea et al (1997) *Clean and Competitive: Motivating Environmental Performance in Industry.* London, Earthscan.

Hüppi, R and P Seeman (2000) *Social Capital.* London, Financial Times and Prentice Hall.

ICAEW (1975) *The Corporate Report.* Accounting Standards (formerly Steering) Committee. London, ICAEW.

IISD and BFSD (1999) *Beyond Delusion: A Science and Policy Dialogue on Designing Effective Indicators for Sustainable Development, Costa Rica.*

INSEAD (2001) *Harmonisation of the GRI Sustainability Guidelines with Key Multilateral Environmental Agreements.* Paris, UNEP and GRI.

Jacobs, M (1991) *The Green Economy: Environment, Sustainable Development and the Politics of the Future.* London, Pluto Press.

John, P (2002) 'Cable and Wireless to Exit FTSE 100 Index, *Financial Times*, 10 December 2002.

Jones, R (2000) *The Big Idea.* London, HarperCollins.

Kamp-Roelands, N (1999) *Audits of Environmental Reports: Are We Witnessing the Emergence of Another Expectation Gap?* The Netherlands, Koninklijik Nederlands Instituut van Registeraccountants.

Knoepfel, I (2002) *DJSI Corporate Sustainability Assessment Methodology and Review 2001.*

Koehler, D A (2001) 'Developments in Health and Safety Accounting at Baxter International', *Eco-Management and Auditing* 8: 229–239.

KPMG (2002) *KPMG International Survey of Corporate Reporting 2002.* Amsterdam, KPMG Global Sustainability Services.

Kuhn, T S (1996) *The Structure of Scientific Revolutions.* Chicago, Chicago University Press.

Larsen, L B (2000) 'Strategic Implication of Environmental Reporting', *Corporate Environmental Strategy* 7: 276–287.

Leadbeater, C (2000) *Living on Thin Air: The New Economy.* London, Penguin Books.

Leduc, L (2001) 'Measuring Social Responsibility', *CA Magazine* 143: 33–34.

Leenders, R and S Gabbay (1999) *Corporate Social Capital and Liability.* Dordrecht, Kluwer Academic Publications.

Long, F J and M B Arnold (1995) *The Power of Environmental Partnerships.* Dryden.

MacGillivray, A (2002) *What's Trust Worth?* London, New Economics Foundation.

MacGillivray, A and D Doane (2001) *The Business of Staying in Business: The Economics of Sustainability.* London, Sigma Project.

MacGillivray, A, A Potts et al (2002). *Secrets of Their Success: Fast Growth.* London, Inner City 100/New Economics Foundations/Royal Bank of Scotland.

MacGillivray, A and P Walker (2000). 'Local Social Capital: Making It Work on the Ground' in Baron, Field and Schuller (eds) *Social Capital: Critical Perspectives.* London, Oxford University Press.

Madden, C (1991) *When Humans Roamed the Earth.* London, Earthscan.

Mason, J and S Jones (2002) 'Food Shoppers Appear to Shun Ethical Goods', *Financial Times,* 21 November 2002.

Mayhew, N (1997) 'Fading to Grey: The Use and Abuse of Corporate Executives' Representational Power' in R Welford (ed) *Hijacking Environmentalism: Corporate Response to Sustainable Development.* London, Earthscan, pp63–95.

McAfee, K (1999) 'Selling Nature to Save It? Biodiversity and Green Developmentalism', *Environment and Planning D: Society and Space* 17: 133–154.

McGee, J (1998). 'Commentary on Corporate Strategies and Environmental Regulations: An Organizing Framework', *Strategic Management Journal* 19: 377–387.

Miall, H (1994) 'Wider Europe, Fortress Europe, Fragmented Europe?' in H Miall (ed) *Redefining Europe: New Patterns of Conflict and Co-operation.* London, Pinter.

Milne, M J, D Owen et al (2001) 'Corporate Environmental Reporting: Are New Zealand Companies Being Left Behind?' *University of Auckland Business Review* 3(2): 24–36.

Milward, A S (1992) *The European Rescue of the Nation State.* London, Routledge.

Moodie, D (1999) 'The Greening of the Boards', *Charter* 70: 32–34.

MORI (2002) *Annual Corporate Social Responsibility Study.* MORI.

Murphy, D (1996) 'In the Company of Partners. Businesses, NGOs and Sustainable Development: Towards a Global Perspective', Cambridge Environmental Initiative Professional Seminar Series, Environmentalist and Business Partnerships: A Sustainable Model 9.

Murphy, D and J Bendell (1997) *In the Company of Partners*. Bristol, Polity Press.

Newson, M (2001) *New 'Ethical' Disclosure Requirements*. Institute of Chartered Accountants in Australia.

Nieto, C and P Durbin (1995) 'Sustainable Development and Philosophies for Technology', *Society for Philosophy and Technology* 1 (1&2).

Nordika (2001) *Intellectual Capital: Managing and Reporting*. Oslo, Nordic Industrial Fund.

O'Dwyer, B (2001a) 'Business, Accountancy and Sustainable Development', *Accountancy Ireland* 33: 20–23.

O'Dwyer, B (2001b) 'Corporate Environmental Reporting', *Accountancy Ireland* 33(2): 18–19.

OECD (1995) *The Economic Appraisal of Environmental Projects and Policies: A Practical Guide*. Paris, OECD.

OECD (1999) *Voluntary Approaches for Environmental Policy: An Assessment*. Paris, OECD.

OECD (2000) *Codes of Corporate Conduct – An Expanded Review of Their Contents*. Paris, OECD, Working Party of the Trade Committee.

OECD (2001) 'Private Incentives for Corporate Responsibility: An Analysis', Working Papers on International Investment 1.

Orr, D (1992) *Ecological Literacy: Education for a Postmodern World*. Albany, State University of New York Press.

Owen, D, R Gray et al (1997) 'Green Accounting: Cosmetic Irrelevance or Radical Agenda for Change?' *Asia Pacific Journal of Accounting* 4(2): 175–198.

Owen, D, T Swift et al (2000) 'The New Social Audits: Accountability, Managerial Capture or the Agenda of Social Champions?' *The European Accounting Review* 9(1): 81–98.

Owen, D, T Swift et al (2001) 'Questioning the Role of Stakeholder Engagement in Social and Ethical Accounting, Auditing and Reporting', *Accounting Forum* 25(3): 264–282.

Papmehl, A (2002) 'Beyond the GAAP: Triple-Bottom-Line Reporting Changes How Businesses and Shareholders View Corporate Imperatives', *CMA Management* 21–25.

Parker, L (1999) *Environmental Costing: An Exploratory Examination*. Melbourne, Australian Society of Certified Practising Accountants.

Payne, N (2002) 'The Big Sustainability Picture', *Accountancy SA*: 31.

Pearce, B (2002) *Sustainability Pays*, Co-operative Insurance Society and Forum for the Future.

Pearce, D W, K Hamilton et al (1996) 'Measuring Sustainable Development: Progress on Indicators', *Environment and Development Economics* 1(1).

Peters, T J and R H Waterman (1982) *In Search of Excellence: Lessons from America's Best-run Companies*. New York, Harper and Row.

Peterson, M J (1998) 'Organizing for Effective Environmental Co-operation', *Global Governance* 4: 415–438.

Pezzey, J (1992) 'Sustainability: An Interdisciplinary Guide', *Environmental Values* 1: 321–352.

Phillips, M (2002) ''03 Forks', *Mountain Bike* 18(November): 38–43.

Porritt, J (2000) *Playing Safe: Science and the Environment*. London, Thames and Hudson.

Prahalad, C K and S Hart (2001) 'The Fortune and the Bottom of the Pyramid', *Strategy and Business* 26.

Purser, R E (1994) 'Guest Editorial: "Shallow" versus "Deep" Organizational Development and Environmental Sustainability', *Journal of Organizational Change Management* 7(4): 8–18.

Putnam, R (2001) *Bowling Alone: The Collapse and Revival of American Community*. New York, Touchstone.

Raynard, Sillanpää and Gonella (2001) 'From Little Things Big Things Grow', *Tomorrow* April: 26–28.

Rees, S and G Rodley (1995) *The Human Costs of Managerialism: Advocating the Recovery of Humanity*. Leichhardt, New South Wales, Pluto Press.

Rees, S and S Wright (2000) *Human Rights, Corporate Responsibility: A Dialogue*. Sydney, Pluto Press.

Reid, M L (2002) *$30 Billion Venture Fund Forming for Alternative Energy*. Gene Rineer.

Renzulli, L, H Aldrich et al (2000) 'Family Matters: Gender, Networks and Entrepreneurial Outcomes', *Social Forces* 79(2): 523–546.

Rhode, B (1992) 'The Principle of Spatial Responsibility: Understanding the Background of Co-operative Environmental Policies in Europe' in M Jachtenfuchs and M Strubel (eds) *Environmental Policy in Europe*. Baden-Baden, Nomos Verlagsgesellschaft.

Rosenau, J N (1990) *Turbulence in World Politics*. Princeton, Princeton University Press.

Rosenau, J N and E-O Czempiel (eds) (1992) *Governance and Government: Order and Change in World Politics*. Cambridge, Cambridge University Press.

Rosenberg, D (2002) *Cloning Silicon Valley: The Next Generation of High-tech Hotspots*. Reuters/Pearson Education.

Rosinski, N (2002) 'Sustainability Challenges in the Automotive Industry', *DJSI Newsletter* 2/2002.

Roth, G and A Kleiner (1995) *Learning about Organizational Learning – Creating a Learning History*. Cambridge, Mass, MIT Centre for Organizational Learning.

Roth, G and A Kleiner (1998) 'Developing Organizational Memory through Learning Histories', *Organizational Dynamics* 272: 43–61.

Sagoff, M (1988) *The Economy of the Earth*. Cambridge, Cambridge University Press.

Said, E (1978) *Orientalism*. London, Routledge and Kegan Paul.

Sawyer, G C (1979) *Business and Society: Managing Corporate Social Impact*. Boston, Houghton Mifflin Co.

Saxenian, A (1996) *Regional Advantage: Culture and Competition in Silicon Valley and Route 128*. Cambridge, Harvard University Press.

Schaltegger, S (2000) *Contemporary Environmental Accounting – Issues, Concepts and Practice*. Sheffield, Greenleaf Publishing.

Schaltegger, S and K Müller (1998) 'Calculating the True Profitability of Pollution Prevention' in M Bennett and P James (eds) *The Green Bottom Line: Environmental Accounting for Management; Current Practice and Future Trends*. Sheffield, Greenleaf Publishing Limited, pp86–99.

Schmidheiny, S (1992) *Changing Course: A Global Perspective on Development and the Environment*. Cambridge, MA, MIT Press.

Schwartz, P and B Gibb (1999) *When Good Companies Do Bad Things: Responsibility and Risk in an Age of Globalization*. New York, John Wiley.

Scott, P and S John (2002) 'Banks Look to Indirect Impacts', *Environmental Finance*, November 2002.

Sen, A K (2001) *Development as Freedom*. Oxford, Oxford University Press.

Serck-Hanssen, L (2002) *Moving Towards a Sustainable Food Industry*.

Shah, R A (2000) 'The Relationship between Living Earth and Shell: Emergence of a Progressive Partnership?' in S Heap (ed) *NGOs Engaging with Business: A World of Difference and a Difference to the World*, Volume 11. Oxford, INTRAC.

Shah, R A (2001) *Relational Praxis in Transition towards Sustainability: Business–NGO Collaboration and Participatory Action Research*. Bath, University of Bath.

Shields, D, B Beloff et al (1998) 'Environmental Cost Accounting for Chemical and Oil Companies: A Benchmarking Study' in M Bennett and P James (eds) *The Green Bottom Line: Environmental Accounting for Management; Current Practice and Future Trends*. Sheffield, Greenleaf Publishing Limited, pp188–211.

Shiva, V (1989) *Staying Alive: Women, Ecology and Development*. London, Zed Books.

Shrivastava, P (1995) 'Ecocentric Management for a Risk Society', Academy of Management Review 20(1): 118–137.

SIGMA (2001) *The SIGMA Guidelines* (Pilot Draft). London, SIGMA.

Smith, D (2002) *Demonstrating Corporate Values: Which Standard for Your Company?* London, Institute of Business Ethics.

South African Breweries plc (2002) *SABMiller plc Corporate Accountability Report 2002*, see www.sab.co.za.

SPDC (1997) *People and the Environment Annual Report*. Lagos, SPDC.

Standards Association of Australia (1997) *Environmental and Other Management Standards*. Strathfield, New South Wales, Standards Association of Australia.

Stec, S and S Casey-Lefkowitz (2000) *The Arhaus Convention: An Implementation Guide*. Geneva, UNECE.

Stewart, T (1998) *Intellectual Capital: The New Wealth of Nations*. London, Nicholas Brealey Publishing.

Stiglitz, J E (2002) *Globalization and Its Discontents*. London, Allen Lane.

Sullivan, R and H Wyndham (2001) *Effective Environmental Management : Principles and Case Studies*. Crows Nest, New South Wales, Allen and Unwin.

SustainAbility (2002) *Trust Us: The Global Reporters 2002 Survey of Corporate Sustainability Reporting*. London, SustainAbility Ltd.

SustainAbility and UNEP (1996) *Engaging Stakeholders 1996; The Social Reporting Report*. UNEP–Engaging Stakeholders Series. London, SustainAbility Ltd.

SustainAbility and UNEP (1999) *Engaging Stakeholders 1999; The Social Reporting Report*. UNEP–Engaging Stakeholders Series. London, SustainAbility Ltd.

SustainAbility and UNEP (2002a) *Trust Us: The Global Reporters 2002 Survey of Corporate Sustainability Reporting*. London, SustainAbility Ltd.

SustainAbility and UNEP (2002b) *Good News and Bad: The Media, Corporate Responsibility and Sustainable Development*. London, SustainAbility Ltd.

Synnestvedt, T (2001) 'Debates over Environmental Information to Stakeholders as a Policy Instrument', *Eco-Management and Auditing* 8: 165–178.

Tarnas, R (1991) *The Passion of the Western Mind: Understanding Ideas that Have Shaped Our World View*. New York, Ballantine Books.

Thielemann, U (2000) 'A Brief Theory of the Market – Ethically Focused', *International Journal of Social Economics* 27(1): 6–31.

This Day (2003) 'Warri: NNPC, Oil Chiefs Hold Emergency Meeting', *This Day*, Lagos, 25 March 2003.

Thomson, K (1998) *Emotional Capital: Maximising the Intangible Assets at the Heart of Brand and Business Success.* Oxford, Capstone.

Tippet, J and P Leung (2001) 'Defining Ethical Investment and Its Demography in Australia', *Australian Accounting Review* 11(3): 44–55.

UNCTAD (1996) *Incentives and Disincentives for the Adoption of Sustainable Development by Transnational Corporations. United Nations Conference on Trade and Development 1995.* Geneva, United Nations.

UNEP (2001) *International Environmental Governance: Multilateral Environmental Agreements (MEAs).* Paris, UNEP.

UNEP (2002). *Industry as a Partner for Sustainable Development: The Overview Report.* Paris, UNEP, Division of Technology, Industry and Economics.

UNEP and GRID–Arendal (2000) *Cities Environment Reports on the Internet: Understanding the CEROI Template.* Geneva, UNRISD.

UNNGLS and UNRISD (2002) *Voluntary Approaches to Corporate Responsibility: Reading and a Resource Guide.* Geneva, United Nations Non-Governmental Liaison Service.

UNWCED (1987) *Our Common Future* (The Brundtland Report). Oxford, Oxford University Press.

Utting, P (2000) *Business Responsibility for Sustainable Development*, UNRISD Occasional Paper 2. Geneva, United Nations Research Institute for Social Development.

van der Lugt, C (2000) Baden-Baden, Nomos.

Visser, W and C Sunter (2002) 'Beyond Reasonable Greed', *Accountancy SA*: 3.

Vitousek, P M and P R Ehrlich (1986) 'Human Appropriation of the Products of Photosynthesis', *BioScience* 36: 368–373.

Wackernagel, M and W Rees (1996) *Our Ecological Footprint: Reducing Human Impact on the Earth.* Gabriola Island, New Society Publishers.

Waddock, S A and S B Graves (1997) 'The Corporate Social Performance – Financial Performance Link', *Strategic Management Journal* 18(4): 303–319.

Walley and Whitehead (1994) 'It's not Easy Being Green', *Harvard Business Review:* 46–52.

Wapner, P (1998) 'Reorienting State Sovereignty: Rights and Responsibilities in the Environmental Age' in K T Litfin (ed) *The Greening of Sovereignty in World Politics.* Cambridge, MIT Press.

Wartick, S L and D J Wood (1998) *International Business and Society.* Malden, Mass, Blackwell Business.

WBCSD (1997) *Environmental Performance and Shareholder Value.* Geneva, WBCSD.

WBCSD (2001) *The Business Case for Sustainable Development.* Geneva, WBCSD.

WBCSD (2002) 'Striking the Balance: a Fresh Slant on Sustainable Development Reporting', *Sustain Quarterly Newsletter* 20: 6–8.

Wheeler, D and J Elkington (2001) 'The End of the Corporate Environmental Report?' *Business Strategy and the Environment* 10(1): 1–14.

Wheeler, D and M Sillanpää (1997) *The Stakeholder Corporation; A Blueprint for Maximising Stakeholder Value.* London, Pitman.

Zadek, S (2001) *The Civil Corporation.* London, Earthscan.
Zadek, S and C Tuppen (2000) *Adding Values: The Economics of Sustainable Business.*

Index